KAPLAN

TEST PREP AND ADMISSIONS

MCAT*

Lesson Book

*MCAT is a registered trademark of the Association of American Medical Colleges.

Special thanks to the team that worked tirelessly on this program:

Ben Baron, Gabe Bunda, Terrence Carter, Ryan Clay, Chris Combs, Brandon Conley, Rachel Dada, Kunal Domakonda, Wade de Gottardi, David Elson, Marilyn Engle, Matt Fidler, Jeannie Ho, Jeffrey Koetje, Paul Labay, Dianne Lake, Michael Lanfranchi, Keith Lubeley, Glenn Maciag, Marcel Muscat, Petros Minasi, Amjed Mustafa, Joanna Myllo, Maria Nicholas, Walt Niedner, Alana Ohana, Jeff Olson, Michael Palmer, Christine Resuma, Marc San Luis, Gajan Sivananthan, Scott Solow, Pierce Stewart, Martha P. Torres, Bob Verini, Luke White

Materials in the Verbal Reasoning chapters were adapted from the following sources:
Daniel C. Dennett, *Elbow Room: The Varieties of Free Will Worth Wanting*, ©1984 by The MIT Press
John Horgan, "The Solar Inconstant," ©1988 *Scientific American*
Irving Howe, *Politics and the Novel*, ©1957
Milan Kundera, *The Book of Laughter and Forgetting*, ©1980 Alfred A. Knopf, Inc.
Alice M. Rivlin, "Economics and the Political Process," ©1987 *American Economic Review*
Miriam Silverberg, "The Modern Girl as Militant," *Recreating Japanese Women, 1600–1945*
Gail Lee Bernstein, ed. ©1991 by The Regents of the University of California

TABLE OF CONTENTS

Unit 1: Critical Reading

Unit 2: Questions and Answers

Unit 3: Integrated Practice

Appendix

USER'S GUIDE

Registering for the MCAT

The MCAT will be administered 22 times a year spread across the months of January, April, May, June, July, August, and September. Information about registering for the MCAT can be found at **www.aamc.org/MCAT**.

Registration is available only online at **www.aamc.org/MCAT**. A registration booklet called *MCAT Essentials* is also available as a PDF. This booklet contains important information about MCAT fees, score reporting, and how to complete the registration process.

Additional information can be obtained by contacting the MCAT Program Office:

MCAT Program Office

Association of American Medical Colleges

Section for Applicant Assessment Services

2450 N St., NW

Washington, DC 20037

www.aamc.org/MCAT

mcat@aamc.org

(202) 828–0690

The Structure of the MCAT

Format

The MCAT underwent its biggest change in a decade with its conversion to a new computer-based format in 2007. Some elements of the computer-based exam are outlined on the following page:

The New MCAT	
Format	All administrations on computer
Content	144 multiple-choice questions: 52 Physical Sciences, 40 Verbal Reasoning, 52 Biological Sciences
	Two essays
Breaks	Optional breaks
	No lunch hour given
Length of Test Day	5.5 hours; both A.M. and P.M. options
Test Date	24 test administrations spread throughout the year
Delivery of Results	Students receive scores in 30 days
	Electronic and paper scores available
Check-in Security Requirements	Government-issued photo ID
	Electronic thumbprint
	Electronic signature verification
Testing Centers	Small computer testing sites

Content

The MCAT is nearly six hours long and consists of four scored sections: Physical Sciences, Verbal Reasoning, Writing Sample, and Biological Sciences.

The MCAT is both a science exam and a critical-thinking exam. 100% of the Verbal Reasoning questions, as well as 75% of the Physical Sciences and Biological Sciences questions, are passage-based. The Physical Sciences and Biological Sciences questions involve interpretation of science passages, not mere regurgitation of science facts. The MCAT requires use of basic science knowledge, as well as information presented in the passage, to solve higher-order problems.

Verbal Reasoning may seem familiar to you from the SAT and other standardized tests as "reading comprehension," but don't be fooled—Verbal Reasoning is much more complicated and difficult than reading comprehension. The Verbal Reasoning section of the MCAT consists of seven passages, with 5–7 multiple-choice questions per passage. You are given 60 minutes to answer a total of 40 questions. The passage subjects are drawn from the social sciences, the humanities, and from those areas of the natural sciences not tested on the two science sections of the MCAT. No outside knowledge is tested. While this section of the MCAT may appear less challenging than the others, the scoring is tougher. When preparing for the MCAT, Verbal Reasoning should not be underestimated. Medical schools want reassurance that you possess critical reading skills and that you can draw reliable conclusions from what you read.

Physical Sciences and Biological Sciences each consist of 7 science passages with 4–8 multiple-choice questions per passage. These questions test not only your conceptual understanding of the passage and your analytical reasoning skills, but also your grasp of basic science knowledge in biology, organic chemistry, general chemistry, and physics. Medical schools need reassurance that you can apply basic science knowledge to solve complex science problems. In addition, there are 13 independent (not passage-based) multiple-choice questions. Each section consists of a total of 52 questions to be answered in 70 minutes. About half of the questions and passages in the Physical Sciences section are physics, and the other half is general chemistry. About 65–75% percent of the passages and questions in the Biological Sciences section are biology; the remaining 25–35% percent are organic chemistry.

The Writing Sample presents you with two essay topics for which you must develop two coherent essays. You are given 30 minutes per essay. Medical schools want an assessment of your written communication skills, since this is a reflection of your ability to effectively convey information to patients, healthcare colleagues, and the public.

Scoring

Your score report will contain five separate scores—one for each section of the test, and a composite score. On the three multiple-choice sections—Physical Sciences, Verbal Reasoning, and Biological Sciences—the number of correct answers are counted (your raw score) and converted to a score on a 1–15 scale. For the Writing Sample, each of your two essays is read and scored independently by two readers. The four essay scores are then added and converted into an alphabetical scale ranging from J to T.

Section	Number of Questions	Time (Minutes)	Scoring Scale
Physical Sciences	52	70	1–15
Verbal Reasoning	40	60	1–15
Writing Sample	2	60	J–T
Biological Sciences	52	70	1–15
Composite			3–45, J–T

In addition to your scaled scores, your score report will contain scaled score means, standard deviations, percentages of students receiving each scaled score for each section, and percentile rankings. These values vary slightly with each administration.

What Your Kaplan Course Includes

Diagnostic Testing

Your Kaplan MCAT Training begins with a comprehensive work-up that includes a Personal Profile and two Diagnostic Tests. The Personal Profile contains questions about your academic background, study habits, perceived academic strengths and weaknesses, MCAT goals, etc. One of the diagnostic tests, the Science Assessment Exam, consists of 120 discrete science questions covering biology, general chemistry, organic chemistry, and physics. This test is specifically designed to assess your basic knowledge in the science areas covered on the MCAT. The other diagnostic, the MCAT Diagnostic Test, is a simulated MCAT (without Writing Sample). This test measures your critical thinking and problem solving abilities by evaluating how well you handle MCAT-style questions and passages.

Our computers will analyze your responses to the Personal Profile questions and compare them to your performance on the Diagnostic Tests. We will provide you with comprehensive computerized feedback that not only will identify your actual academic strengths and weaknesses, but will also prescribe a personalized "MCAT training program"—a study regimen tailored to build up your knowledge in weak subject areas, reinforce your knowledge in stronger areas, and emphasize the higher order analytical thinking and problem solving skills the MCAT tests. With this feedback, you'll start down the road to success on Test Day.

Review Notes and Flashcards

Kaplan's MCAT Review Notes—totaling over 1,300 pages—is a multi-volume set of the most complete and concise MCAT prep materials available! The Biological Sciences and Physical Sciences volumes review the official topics listed in the AAMC Website, chapter by chapter.

Each chapter contains helpful notes, strategies, summaries, and pointers to help you maximize your study efforts. In addition, the page margins provide you with ample space to add your own notes. Each chapter concludes with a battery of questions—some multiple choice, some short answer—to help you evaluate your understanding of the material. For your convenience, each science volume is indexed and includes a glossary for quick reference.

The Verbal Reasoning Strategy and Practice book contains Verbal Reasoning chapters, in addition to eleven full-length Verbal Reasoning tests, the Kaplan 5-Step Method for the Writing Sample, essay-construction exercises, a grammar review, and a number of practice essay topics.

Kaplan's MCAT Flashcards offer a convenient way of improving your retention of the most high-yield MCAT concepts.

MCAT QuickSheets

For additional reference and study on the go, use the MCAT QuickSheets. These laminated reference guides contain all of the highest-yield subject matter in a convenient, portable format. Do not just memorize the equations and figures, make sure you understand the concepts and relationships these equations and figures represent.

Lesson Book

Kaplan's MCAT Lesson Book is your guide through the classroom or online lecture experience. The Lesson Book maps out the structure and content of the Kaplan MCAT Training Program. Each Lesson is divided into a Preview, Lesson, and Review. The Reviews and Previews are located on Homework pages between Lessons and are critical for success on the test. The Preview sections will set the tone for each upcoming class and provide you with the pre-class assignments. Each Review section lists homework materials that reinforce each Lesson. The Lesson sections are your maps during class; the Lessons outline the concepts your instructor will reinforce and the passages your instructor will demystify during class. These Lessons are organized into Units, which will address Content, Critical Thinking, and Computer-Based strategies. Remember to bring your Lesson Book to class!

Foundation Review Series

The Foundation Review Series (Organic Chemistry, Physics, Biology, Math, General Chemistry, and Verbal Reasoning) is designed to get you up to speed in the respective topics before you attend the Lessons. Each Foundation Review Unit covers the basics using simple, straightforward definitions and explanations. If it's been a while since you had organic chemistry, or if you never understood magnetism the first time around, the Foundation Review Series will provide you with a solid foundation before we flesh out the details in the Lessons. If you're starting your preparation early, the Foundation Review Series, in conjunction with the Review Notes and the Subject Tests (see below), is a great place to begin. To access the Foundation Review series please see the Foundation Review Companion Booklet to each MCAT science and the MCAT verbal, all available in your Kaptest.com online study center.

Lessons

The classroom experience is the foundation of Kaplan's MCAT program. Our classes will train you to master the MCAT. Your instructor not only will review relevant MCAT content in detail, but will also guide you through MCAT-style passages and questions on the topics just covered. In Unit 1, your instructor will deconstruct the MCAT passage and teach you the critical thinking skills necessary to read and analyze MCAT passages and ace MCAT questions. In Unit 2, your instructor will teach you how to recognize the common wrong answers choices on the MCAT. Unit 3 provides integrated practice so that the techniques you learn become an integral part of your Test Day performance.

If you skip class, you're skipping an important part of your MCAT preparation. If you must miss one of your scheduled classes, you can attend an alternate section at any Kaplan Center—or watch the Lessons-on-Demand that are available in your online syllabus.

The MCAT Strategy and Critical Thinking Lessons

Your classroom instruction begins with the MCAT Strategy and Critical Thinking Lesson. In this class, we'll introduce you to the critical thinking skills that are key to scoring high on the computer-based version of the MCAT. These skills will be further developed and reinforced in conjunction with content review in the subsequent Lessons. In class, we'll teach you just what the MCAT is specifically designed to test.

In MSCT 2, you will learn Kaplan's Pacing Strategy and Crisis Prevention techniques. In MSCT 3, you will walk through Test Day and image the experience to insure the best possible results for the day. We will also workshop your Writing Samples and review some of your full-length passages in these Lessons.

The Science Lessons

All the science you need to know to score high on the MCAT is reviewed in class. We encourage you to participate and ask questions. In these Lessons, we will not only review science, but demonstrate how it is likely to appear on the MCAT. Furthermore, we will show you how to handle the test writers' favorite passage type: basic principles disguised as unfamiliar and intimidating topics (e.g. hereditary spherocytosis or the magnetic susceptibility of quaternary chalcogenides). The Critical Thinking Units are done in the context of these Lessons.

The Verbal Reasoning and Writing Sample Lessons

There is no content component to the Verbal Reasoning and Writing Sample sections— it's all reading, reasoning, and writing. Some people say Verbal Reasoning can't be taught. We believe otherwise, and the number of students we have helped into medical school attest to our belief. Our Lessons emphasize the critical thinking skills and strategies to help you master this section of the test. We'll teach you how "mapping" the passage is the best way to handle both Verbal and Science MCAT passages.

We'll also teach you The Kaplan Method for the Writing Sample. Our method provides you the framework to produce a solid, unified essay on any topic you're given on Test Day.

Kaplan Study Center

Kaplan's exclusive Student Study Center is an arsenal of practice materials to train you for the MCAT. First, you'll take practice tests designed to consolidate your basic science knowledge. Then you'll proceed to our focused, MCAT-style topical tests to test your critical-thinking skills, as well as your ability, to apply your science knowledge. Next, you'll transition to longer MCAT-style exams, ultimately leading to our full-length practice MCATs. Below is a summary of the various Kaplan practice tests and how they are structured to accomplish this task. Please refer to the MCAT Menu at the back of this Lesson Book for a complete listing of all our practice materials.

The online Student Study Center was created for your convenience. When you can't make it into a center to find the synergy with other students, do your practice materials in the comfort of your own home. Every Kaplan-produced item is available online in the new computer-based format of the MCAT for realistic practice.

The Subject Tests (five Biology, five Organic Chemistry, five General Chemistry, and five Physics) are designed to help you reinforce your science foundation. They are NOT designed to mimic the MCAT; rather they provide practice in your content area. These tests consist of multiple-choice questions that focus on fundamental science concepts. You may find them to be a good "warm up" before you tackle the Topical Tests.

The MCAT Topical Tests are short, focused tests that cover specific MCAT science topics. They are assigned to you as homework after each class. These tests assess your understanding of specific science concepts in MCAT-style passages. They correspond to specific chapters in your Review Notes, as well as specific class sessions.

The Biological Sciences and Physical Sciences Section Tests are structured in full-length duration to allow you to improve your accuracy while also increasing your timing and endurance. Kaplan's Verbal Reasoning Section Tests are structured similarly. They focus on specific aspects of the Verbal Reasoning section that often give students trouble.

Don't forget to view Kaplan's MCAT Smart Reports. These vital tools aggregate every test question and identify your personal strengths and weaknesses. You'll find this tool in your online syllabus.

Also, you can practice your writing skills for the MCAT essay with Kaplan's Writing Sample Practice Tests, which include sample topics on which you can write essays. Kaplan has identified 10 categories of prompts for the Writing Sample of the MCAT. Each of your Full-Length Exams covers two of these categories, to give you practice with each.

Don't forget: every Kaplan Study Center item comes with comprehensive explanations. It is as important to know why the wrong answers are incorrect as it is to realize why the correct answer is correct.

Online Resources

Please see "How to Access Your Online Resources" towards the end of this section for instructions on logging into your MCAT course homepage.

Online Workshops

Kaplan's Online Workshops help you prepare for the MCAT at your leisure. Each Workshop is designed to take from 30 to 45 minutes, and most are followed by a quiz. You can return to them whenever you like. Check your course syllabus for specific assignments for each Workshop.

These Workshops are an important and mandatory part of your course. The instruction you receive in each classroom Lesson assumes that you have been through each of the Online Workshops specified in that Lesson's Preview.

The first Workshop is an online orientation to your course and an overview of the trends that Kaplan has noticed in recent MCAT administrations.

Six of the Workshops cover the Verbal Reasoning section of the test. Three of them tackle Critical Reading—they take you through the most efficient techniques for reading the passages. Two Workshops cover argument dissection—the type of critical thinking tested by most of the Verbal Reasoning questions. The sixth Workshop covers Diagnosing Questions— how to recognize what the question is truly asking, and what to do once you know.

Three additional Workshops discuss how to handle the Writing Sample section of the MCAT. Two Writing Sample Skills Workshops (Grammar and Usage, and Writing) take you through the basics—what you need to know to write an effective essay. The third Workshop, Writing Sample: Advanced, includes additional strategies beyond those presented in the Skills Workshops, for those looking for an additional leg up on Test Day.

There are sixteen science content Workshops. Each covers a related series of science concepts that appear on the MCAT, including all of the MCAT sciences: Physics, General Chemistry, Biology, and Organic Chemistry. After you have spent enough time with a Workshop, you can take a quiz to test your understanding.

Finally, there is a Stress Management Workshop that was created to help you deal with the many pressures you face preparing for the MCAT, applying to and choosing a medical school, and coping with college courses.

The Kaplan Online Study Center

The Online Study Center, available on your My Kaplan homepage, allows you to take all Kaplan produced tests on your own computer. The Kaplan Online Study Center provides a list of all your scored tests, along with access links to your feedback and to the test questions and explanations (if applicable). If you have scored a test online, it should appear in your test history shortly after your submission. Tests scored in-center may take up to 3 days to appear in your test history.

Full-Length Tests

You will take a minimum of five full-length administered MCATs during your Kaplan MCAT Training. Computer-analyzed feedback and scores are provided for all exams.

There's a psychological and physical challenge to taking the MCAT that has nothing to do with the questions themselves. MCAT Test Day is one of the longest in standardized testing—over 5.5 hours by the time IDs are checked and testing procedures are explained. If you've never had a similar experience, it can be quite disconcerting and exhausting.

To prepare you for these stresses and to eliminate all surprises, Kaplan provides you with 11 practice MCATs. They are the ultimate MCAT test runs—simulated full-length MCATs.

About half of the way through the course, we will administer the first full-length MCAT to monitor your progress. At this point, you will have had plenty of experience with MCAT materials; now it's time to see how your stamina and pacing hold up under the pressure of a full-length MCAT. Make no mistake about it: it's a grueling experience and a long day. Even though you will not have had all the science content review, the feedback you will receive will help you identify your weak areas. Invest more time on those subjects, and revisit the relevant Topical Tests if necessary.

Four more full-length tests are to be taken several weeks before the actual exam. This is the Simulation portion of your Kaplan MCAT Program, designed to develop your endurance. These will give you an opportunity to see how everything is coming together: your science knowledge base, critical thinking skills, timing, test-taking strategies, etc. Each time, you will follow modified MCAT security and testing procedures (everything except the thumbprint!), and then take a full-length MCAT.

Kaplan now has 11 full-length tests to help you prepare for Test Day, and the equivalent of nearly 40 in other practice material. Between your last Lesson and Test Day, use these extra tests to refine your skills and boost your confidence.

By taking these exams, you'll discover how your own body and mind react to the stresses of an MCAT. Your computer-analyzed feedback will tell you which areas to focus on during your final days of studying. On Test Day, you'll have more confidence—a key to scoring well on standardized tests—because you'll know what to expect, both from yourself and from the test.

By the end of MCAT training, you will have built your skills and endurance and maximized your timing and confidence.

Set aside a whole day for each exam; testing time is approximately five hours, and you'll want to take breaks as recommended. Simulate the Test Day experience as much as you can. Use the online assets available to you so that you are prepared for a computer-based test.

Of course, complete explanations for all tests are available in the Online Study Center.

Additionally, Kaplan students have access to all AAMC exams. Those tests are available in your online syllabus and should be taken in addition to your Kaplan full-lengths.

The Pre-Med Edge

In addition to being a resource for the online components of your course, the Kaplan Website (**www.kaptest.com**) offers important and timely information for pre-meds. Also, Kaplan's free monthly newsletter, the *Pre-Med Edge*, provides medical school admissions advice, verbal strategies, science quizzes, and more. Sign up for it at **www.kaptest.com/edge**.

Medical School Admissions

From time to time, Kaplan is able to offer expert admissions advice from Kaplan admissions experts, med school advisors, former medical school deans of admissions, and former chairs of the Committee on Admissions for the AAMC. Check with your local Kaplan Center to see whether any of these presentations are available in your area.

Academic Help

Fill out the Academic Help Form found on your member homepage at kaptest.com. Once we receive your question, we will forward your inquiry to our expert staff. These pros will give you an answer within 72 hours.

How Your Kaplan Lessons Are Structured

Your Kaplan course concentrates on the specific skill sets and test strategies that will bring success on Test Day.

Previews

To get the most out of each Lesson, you need to be familiar with the topics that will be covered in class before the class meets. This will allow your instructor to focus on specific test-taking strategies during class, rather than spending time reviewing the basics in detail. In particular, it is important to spend time with the assigned Online Workshops—they contain material that won't be covered in class.

Class Sessions

The most important part of your course is the classroom component, delivered by Kaplan's expert teachers. Each class session is three hours in duration. In these classes, you will review much of the science content you will need on Test Day, and have repeated practice with MCAT-style passages and questions. Your instructors will use the Lessons as an opportunity to teach you how to read passages, how to answer questions, and how to write effective essays for the Writing Sample section.

If you miss a class, don't worry. You can make up the class by attending another session, or by viewing the missed lesson online. These online lessons are called Lessons-on-Demand and can be found on your online syllabus.

Reviews (After-Class Homework)

Kaplan's MCAT course provides after-class materials to help enforce what you learned in class. You will find Review assignments at the end of each Lesson. They will direct you to the appropriate training library and online items.

How to Access Your Online Resources

You'll access all your online resources via a personalized homepage we've created for you at **http://www.kaptest.com**.

To access your homepage:

1. Look up your personal USERNAME and PASSWORD.

We automatically generate a USERNAME and PASSWORD and activate your online resources within 4 calendar days of processing your paid-in-full enrollment request. If you haven't received an e-mail containing your USERNAME and PASSWORD within 4 calendar days, please do the following:

Log on to **http://www.kaptest.com** and click on the "Sign In" link at the top of the page. Click on the link next to the *"Don't know your username or password?"* option. You can either provide your e-mail address or answer a few simple questions to receive your USERNAME and PASSWORD.

2. Log onto kaptest.com.

Enter your USERNAME and PASSWORD in the spaces provided after clicking on the "Sign In" link at the top of the page. If this is your first time logging in, you will need to complete your Membership Profile (be sure to select "Pre-Med" as your Area of Interest to ensure the components of your homepage are specific to your course of study). Next, click on the "Start" button under *My Courses and Services*. When you make this selection, you'll be asked to review Kaplan's Enrollment Agreement, as well as to make an important selection pertaining to your Higher Score Guarantee eligibility. Be sure to review all of the online documents in the "Read This First (includes technical requirements)" link on your homepage.

The online resources on your member homepage will stay active for the duration of your Kaplan course.

3. If you want to change your password:

After you have logged on, you can change your password by clicking on the "Edit My Profile" link in your homepage.

Having problems logging on?

You may not have provided an e-mail address when you enrolled.

We must have an e-mail address on file for you in order to activate your online resources. If you did not have an e-mail address when you enrolled, but now have one, please let us know so we can activate your online resources. Call us at 1–800–KAPTEST or visit www.kaptest.com/contactus. Within 48 hours, we'll activate your resources, and you'll be able to look up your USERNAME and PASSWORD, as described in Step 1, above.

We may not have processed your order.

If you enrolled via **http://www.kaptest.com**, your order was processed—and online access activated—immediately. If you enrolled via telephone or at your local Kaplan Center, it can take up to 4 days for us to process your credit card payment and activate your online resources. In this case, please wait and then try looking up your USERNAME again.

Need additional help?

If you have your USERNAME and PASSWORD and experience difficulties accessing your member homepage, or if it has been over 4 days since you paid in full for your course and you still can't look up your USERNAME and PASSWORD, please call us at 1–800–KAPTEST.

Want to make the most of your Kaplan resources?

Please do not share your member password with anyone. Some of your online resources—in particular some of the tests that are housed in the Online Study Center—can only be taken once. You'll want to save them for use at the appropriate points in your studies (for specific guidance on which resources to use when, consult your syllabus online. If you are using a public computer (in a computer lab, library, etc) click on "Logout" and close your browser so that when your session is finished, your online resources will not be available to the next user.

How You Can Achieve Your Best Score

Test Awareness

To do your best on the MCAT, you must always keep in mind that the test is like no other test you've taken, both in terms of content and in terms of the scoring system. If you took a test in high school or college and got a number of the questions wrong, you wouldn't receive a perfect grade. But on the MCAT, you can get a handful of questions wrong and still get a "perfect" score.

What does this mean for you? Well, just as you shouldn't let a bad passage ruin an entire section, you shouldn't let what you consider to be a sub-par performance on one section ruin your performance on the entire test. If you allow that sub-par performance to rattle you, it can have a cumulative negative effect, setting in motion a downward spiral. It's that kind of thing that could potentially do serious damage to your score. Losing a few extra points won't do you in, but losing your cool will!

Remember, if you feel you've done poorly on a section, don't sweat it. Chances are it's just a difficult section, and that factor will already be figured into the scoring curve. Remain calm and collected. Simply do your best on each section, and once a section is over, forget about it and move on!

Stamina

You must work on your test-taking stamina. Overall, the MCAT is a grueling experience and some test takers simply run out of gas on the last section. To avoid this, you must prepare by taking full-length practice tests in the weeks before the test, so that on Test Day, three sections plus a writing sample will seem like a breeze—or at least not a hurricane. Make sure to take advantage of the full-length practice tests included in you Kaplan course.

Confidence

Confidence feeds on itself, and unfortunately, so does its opposite—self-doubt. Confidence in your ability leads to quick, sure answers and a sense of well-being that translates into more points. If you lack confidence, you end up reading the sentences and answer choices two, three, or four times, until you confuse yourself and get off track. This leads to timing difficulties, which only perpetuate the downward spiral, causing anxiety and a tendency to rush in order to finish sections.

If you subscribe to the MCAT mindset we've described, however, you'll gear all of your practice toward the major goal of taking control of the test. When you've achieved that goal, you'll be ready to face the MCAT with supreme confidence. And that's the one sure way to score your best on Test Day.

The Right Attitude

Those who approach the MCAT as an obstacle usually don't fare as well as those who see the MCAT as an opportunity to show off the knowledge and reasoning skills that medical schools are looking for. Don't waste time making value judgments about the MCAT. Those who look forward to doing battle with the MCAT—or, at least, who enjoy the opportunity to distinguish themselves from the rest of the applicant pack—tend to score better than do those who resent or dread it.

It may sound a little dubious, but take our word for it: attitude adjustment is a proven test-taking technique. Here are a few steps you can take to make sure you develop the right MCAT attitude:

- Look at the MCAT as a challenge, but try not to obsess over it; you certainly don't want to psyche yourself out of the game.
- Remember that, yes, the MCAT is obviously important, but, contrary to what some premeds think, this one test will not single-handedly determine the outcome of your life.
- Try to have fun with the test. Learning how to match your wits against the test makers can be a very satisfying experience, and the reading and thinking skills you'll acquire will benefit you in medical school, as well as in your future medical career.
- Remember that you're more prepared than most people. You've trained with Kaplan. You have the tools you need, plus the know-how to use those tools.

HIGHER SCORE GUARANTEE ORIENTATION

Part One: Guaranteeing My Success

What guarantee does Kaplan offer me?

✔ If I feel that I'm **not ready** to take the test, I may **study again**.

✔ If, after taking the test, I feel that I'm **not satisfied with my test score**, I may **study again**.

✔ If my **score does not improve** over my baseline score, I may **study again, or** receive a **full refund of my tuition**.

How much can I expect my score to go up?

Part Two: Following the Program

What do I have to do to qualify for the Guarantee?

- Go to Class

- Do All the Required Work

- Meet Eligibility Requirements

Part Three: Tracking My Progress Online

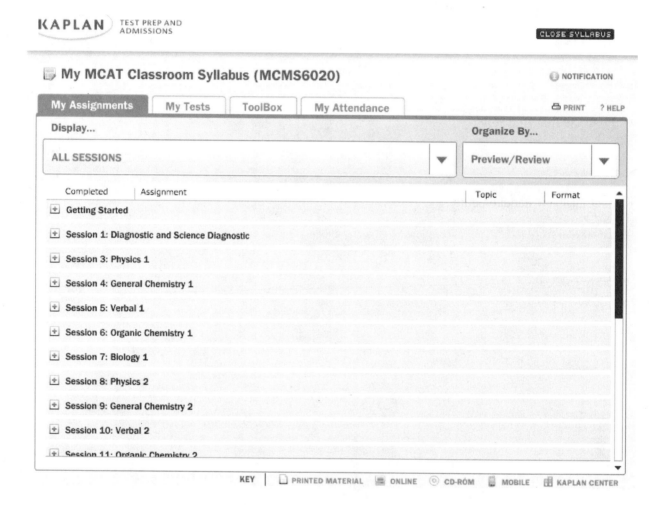

HOMEWORK

Preview for MSCT 1

Online Workshops	❏ MCAT Orientation
Lesson Book	❏ User's Guide on pages *ix–xxiv*

Review for MSCT 1

Flashcards	❏ Tear apart and organize

Preview for Physics 1

Physics Review Notes	❏ *Chapters 1–3
Foundation Review	❏ Unit 1 (Optional, MM3259A)
Math Foundation Review	❏ (Optional, MM3259A)
Online Workshops	❏ *Units and Kinematics

Review for Physics 1

Topical Tests	❏ Translational Motion Test 1 ❏ Force, Motion, Gravitation and Equilibrium Test 1 ❏ Work, Energy and Momentum Test 1
Subject Tests	❏ Test 1 (Optional, DF3015) ❏ Test 2 (Optional, DF3016) ❏ Test 3 (Optional, DF3017)

Preview for General Chemistry 1

General Chemistry Review Notes	❑	*Chapters 1–3 and 7
Foundation Review	❑	Unit 1 (Optional, MM3258)
Online Workshops	❑	*Quantum Numbers and Electron Configuration

Review for General Chemistry 1

Topical Tests	❑ ❑	Electronic Structure and the Periodic Table Test 1 Bonding Test 1
Subject Tests	❑ ❑	Test 1 (Optional, DD3074) Test 2 (Optional, DD3075)

Preview for Verbal Reasoning & Writing Sample 1

Verbal Reasoning Strategy and Practice	❑	*Chapters 1–3
Writing Sample section in Verbal Reasoning Strategy and Practice	❑	*Chapters 1 and 2
Foundation Review	❑	Unit 1 (Optional, MM3261A)
Online Workshops	❑	*Critical Reading Skills

Review for Verbal Reasoning & Writing Sample 1

Verbal Reasoning Strategy and Practice	❑ *Test 1
Writing Sample section in Verbal Reasoning Strategy and Practice	❑ *Chapter 3
Section Tests	❑ Verbal Reasoning Test 1
Online Workshops	❑ *Critical Reading Basics ❑ *Writing Sample Skills: Grammar and Usage ❑ *Writing Sample Skills: Writing ❑ *Diagnosing Questions Workshop ❑ *Arguments Dissection Basics Workshop

Preview for Organic Chemistry 1

Organic Chemistry Review Notes	❑ *Chapters 1–5
Foundation Review	❑ Unit 1 (Optional, MM3257A)
Online Workshops	❑ *Nomenclature and Functional Groups

Review for Organic Chemistry 1

Topical Tests	❑ Hydrocarbons Test 1 ❑ Molecular Structure of Organic Compounds Test 1
Subject Tests	❑ Test 1 (Optional, DD3080) ❑ Test 2 (Optional, DD3081) ❑ Test 3 (Optional, DD3082)

Preview for Biology 1

Biology Review Notes	❑ *Chapters 1–5 and 13
Foundation Review	❑ Unit 1 (Optional, MM3260A)
Online Workshops	❑ *Generalized Eukaryotic Cell ❑ *Microbiology

Review for Biology 1

Topical Tests	❑ Generalized Eukaryotic Cell Test 1 ❑ Reproductive System and Development Test 1 ❑ Microbiology Test 1
Subject Tests	❑ Test 1 (Optional, MM3211) ❑ Test 2 (Optional, MM3212) ❑ Test 3 (Optional, MM3213)

Preview for Physics 2

Physics Review Notes	❑ *Chapters 4, 6–9
Foundation Review	❑ Unit 2 (Optional, MM3259A)
Online Workshops	❑ *DC and AC Circuits ❑ *Thermodynamics ❑ *Magnetism

Review for Physics 2

Topical Tests	❑ Wave Characteristics and Periodic Motion Test 1 ❑ Electric Circuits Test 1 ❑ Sound Test 1 ❑ Electrostatics and Electromagnetism Test 1
Subject Tests	❑ Test 4 (Optional, DF3018) ❑ Test 5 (Optional, DF3019)

Preview for General Chemistry 2

General Chemistry Review Notes	❑ *Chapters 4–6, 8 and 9
Foundation Review	❑ Unit 2 (Optional, MM3258A)
Online Workshops	❑ *Reaction Types ❑ *Chemical Kinetics

Review for General Chemistry 2

Topical Tests	❏ Kinetics and Equilibrium Test 1 ❏ Thermodynamics and Thermochemistry Test 1 ❏ Stoichiometry Test 1
Subject Tests	❏ Test 3 (Optional, DD3076) ❏ Test 4 (Optional, DD3077) ❏ Test 5 (Optional, DD3078)

Preview for Verbal Reasoning & Writing Sample 2

Verbal Reasoning Strategy and Practice	❏ *Chapter 4
Writing Sample section in Verbal Reasoning Strategy and Practice	❏ *Chapters 2 and 4
Foundation Review	❏ Unit 2 (Optional, MM3261A)

Review for Verbal Reasoning & Writing Sample 2

Verbal Reasoning Strategy and Practice	❏ *Test 2
Writing Sample section in Verbal Reasoning Strategy and Practice	❏ *Chapter 5, Part 1
Section Tests	❏ Test 2 ❏ Test 3 ❏ Test 4
Online Workshops	❏ *Argument Dissection Basics ❏ *Writing Sample: Advanced

Preview for Organic Chemistry 2

Organic Chemistry Review Notes	❏ *Chapters 6–10, 13
Foundation Review	❏ Unit 2 (Optional, MM3257A)
Online Workshops	❏ *Addition and Elimination Reactions ❏ *Spectroscopy

Review for Organic Chemistry 2

Topical Tests	❑ Molecular Spectroscopy Test 1
	❑ Oxygen-Containing Compounds Test 1
Subject Tests	❑ Test 4 (Optional, DD3083)
	❑ Test 5 (Optional, DD3084)

Preview for Biology 2

Biology Review Notes	❑ *Chapters 6, 7, 9 and 12
Foundation Review	❑ Unit 2 (Optional, MM3260A)
Online Workshops	❑ *The Skeletal System and the Immune System

Review for Biology 2

Topical Tests	❑ Circulatory and Lymphatic Systems Test 1
Subject Tests	❑ Test 4 (Optional, MM3214)
	❑ Test 5 (Optional, MM3215)

Preview for MSCT 2

| Section Tests | ❑ Physical Sciences Test 1 |
| | ❑ Bring to class scratch paper used during Full-Length 1 |

Review for MSCT 2

| Online Workshops | ❑ Stress Management Workshop |

Preview for Physics 3

Physics Review Notes	❏ *Chapters 5, 10–12
Section Tests	❏ Physical Sciences Test 2
	❏ Physical Sciences Test 3
Foundation Review	❏ Unit 3 (Optional, (MM3259A)
Online Workshops	❏ *Atomic and Nuclear Phenomena

Review for Physics 3

Topical Tests	❏ Light and Geometrical Optics Test 1
	❏ Atomic and Nuclear Structure Test 1
	❏ Fluids and Solids Test 1
	❏ Physics Discretes Test 1
	❏ Physics Discretes Test 2
	❏ Physics Strategic Supplemental (MM3230)
Section Tests	❏ Physical Sciences Test 4
	❏ Physical Sciences Test 5

Preview for General Chemistry 3

General Chemistry Review Notes	❏ *Chapters 8–11
Foundation Review	❏ Unit 3 (Optional, (MM3258A)
Online Workshops	❏ *Properties of Solutions

Review for General Chemistry 3

Topical Tests	❏ Acids and Bases Test 1
	❏ Electrochemistry Test 1
	❏ General Chemistry Discretes Test 1
	❏ General Chemistry Discretes Test 2
	❏ General Chemistry Strategic Supplemental
Section Tests	❏ Physical Sciences Test 6
	❏ Physical Sciences Test 7

Preview for Verbal Reasoning & Writing Sample 3

Verbal Reasoning Strategy and Practice	❑ Tests 4 and 5
Writing Sample section in Verbal Reasoning Strategy and Practice	❑ *Chapter 5, Part 2
Foundation Review	❑ Unit 3 (Optional, MM3261A)
Online Workshops	❑ *Critical Reading Challenge ❑ *Argument Dissection Challenge
Section Test	❑ Test 5

Review for Verbal Reasoning & Writing Sample 3

Verbal Reasoning Strategy and Practice	❑ *Test 3 ❑ Tests 6–11
Writing Sample section in Verbal Reasoning Strategy and Practice	❑ *Chapter 5, Parts 3 and 4

Preview for Organic Chemistry 3

Review Notes	❑ *Chapters 11, 12, 14, 15
Foundation Review	❑ Unit 3 (Optional, MM3257A)

Review for Organic Chemistry 3

Topical Tests	❑ Separations and Purifications Test 1 ❑ Biological Molecules Test 1 ❑ Organic Chemistry Discretes Test 1 ❑ Organic Chemistry Discretes Test 2 ❑ Organic Chemistry Strategic Supplemental (MM3229) ❑ Amines Test 1
Section Tests	❑ Biological Sciences Test 3 ❑ Biological Sciences Test 4

Preview for Biology 3

Biology Review Notes	❏ *Chapters 8, 10, 11, 14 and 15
Foundation Review	❏ Unit 3 (Optional, MM3260A)
Online Workshops	❏ *The Lymphatic System and the Respiratory System ❏ *Molecular Genetics

Review for Biology 3

Topical Tests	❏ Digestive and Excretory Systems Test 1 ❏ Endocrine System Test 1 ❏ Molecular Biology Test 1 ❏ Molecular Genetics Test 1 ❏ Respiratory and Skin Systems Test 1 ❏ Biology Discretes Test 1 ❏ Biology Discretes Test 2 ❏ Biology Strategic Supplemental (MM3228)
Section Tests	❏ Biological Sciences Test 1 ❏ Biological Sciences Test 2 ❏ Biological Sciences Test 5

Preview for MSCT 3

	❏ Bring to class your essays and scratch paper from Full-Length 2

Review for MSCT 3

Section Tests	❏ Biological Sciences Test 6 ❏ Biological Sciences Test 7

* Required for Higher Score Guarantee.

MCAT Strategy & Critical Thinking 1

- The MCAT
- The Kaplan Strategy
- CBT Tutorial
- MCAT Scoring

WHAT THE MCAT WILL TEST

Learning with the Three C's

	The Three C's
1	Content
2	Critical Thinking (synthesis & application)
3	Crisis Prevention

Identify the "C"

4. Once in a geosynchronous orbit, which of the following statements about the acceleration of the satellite is true?

_____Content_____

62. Based on the passage, what can be inferred about the significance of the Devil's laughter?

_____Critical thinking_____

103. G-protein-coupled receptors are transmembrane protein molecules that participate in a number of different signaling pathways. During synthesis, G-protein-coupled receptors would primarily be found in association with which of the following intracellular compartments?

_____Crisis prevention (content and critical thinking)_____

Unit 1

TEST DAY: PHYSICAL SCIENCES

Time: 70 minutes

Passages: 7

Questions: 52 total

    39 passage-based

    13 discrete

Questions per passage:

Minutes per passage: 8

Passage I

Type: _Information_

Geosynch

Explicit: orbits/satellite **Implicit:** gravity, Newton's
                                       Laws

Another consideration for satellites in orbit around the Earth is gravitational potential energy. For objects close to the Earth's surface, where the acceleration due to gravity is constant, the gravitational potential energy is given by the equation U = mgh. However, when dealing with greater distances of separation such as the distance between a satellite in orbit and the Earth, a different expression for gravitational potential is needed. This is because the acceleration due to gravity decreases as you move away from the Earth's surface, which results in a decrease in the gravitational force. A satellite orbiting around the Earth has gravitational potential energy given by the equation:

$$U = \frac{-GMm}{r}$$

where G is the universal gravitational constant, M is the mass of the Earth, m is the mass of the satellite, and r is the distance between the center of the Earth and the satellite…

Passage II

Type: _Experimental_

Explicit: digestion chem. **Implicit:** acids & bases
                                            (balancing)

When food is ingested, it is stored in the stomach, where it is mixed with acid, mucus, and pepsin (a digestive enzyme). In its resting state, the human stomach contains approximately 0.15 N HCl. In people with sensitive stomachs, this concentration of acid can cause indigestion and general discomfort, and aggravate ulcers (regions of the stomach lining lacking the protective mucous membrane). Various drugs may be used to combat stomach acidity; they generally consist of an active ingredient which can neutralize the acid, along with inert filler material. Carbonate compounds are very effective, but can cause physiological problems with prolonged use. Aluminum and magnesium salts, whose buffer activity raises stomach pH to approximately 4, are preferred.

The neutralization of acid by aluminum hydroxide is shown in the following reaction:

$$Al(OH)_3 + 3\ HCl \rightarrow AlCl_3 + 3\ H_2O$$

Passage III

Type: _Persuassive arguement_

Bohr vs.

Explicit: quantum **Implicit:** orbitals &
                                       electrons

Theory 1

In the Bohr Model the neutrons and protons occupy a dense central region called the nucleus, and the electrons orbit the nucleus much like planets orbiting the Sun (but the orbits are not confined to a plane as is approximately true in the Solar System). The similarity is that the attractive gravitational…

Theory 2

In the quantum theory model one says that the energy is _quantized_. This means that only certain orbits with certain radii are allowed; orbits in between simply don't exist. These levels are labeled by an integer _n_ that is called a _quantum number_. The lowest energy state is generally termed the…

TEST DAY: VERBAL REASONING

Passage I Natural Science

awareness of

Explicit: Pollution **Implicit:** indoor pollution

Outdoor air pollution has been studied almost since the beginning of the Industrial Revolution. Until recently, however, scientists virtually ignored the dangers of indoor air pollution. Research into this relatively new field has already yielded some startling results. In fact, researchers have found that the interior atmospheres of many homes and office buildings are more polluted than the outside air, with many of the pollutants originating from within the buildings themselves.

The sheer variety of pollutants and risks they pose in homes and offices is bewildering. Radon gas seeps into buildings from the ground beneath. …

Passage II Humanities

Explicit: Authors **Implicit:** Refute claims

of critics

W.H. Auden's reputation, already declining by the 1950s, reached its nadir with the publication of his posthumous collection *Thank you Fog* (1974). Critics almost unanimously found his last work trite and garrulous. Indeed, the assessment has served as a retrospective judgment on the poet's final three decades.

Auden's early popularity stemmed in part from his ability to articulate political and psychological dilemmas felt by many young Englishmen in the uneasy calm between the two world wars. While remarkable for its novel use of lyric and ballad forms and its overall musicality, Auden's early poetry nevertheless responded to social concerns and conveyed truths, inspired by Marxist and Freudian precepts, which his contemporaries felt older, more conservative poets ignored. …

Passage III Social Science

Explicit: law suits **Implicit:** needless lawsuits

The number of new cases heard by every branch of the U.S. judiciary has risen radically in the last 20 years. The Supreme Court caseload alone has increased fourfold, with lower courts in yet more dire straits. Former Chief Justice Burger perceived an "irrational focus—virtually a mania—on litigation as the way to solve all problems." We have, in short, become a nation of litigants.

Many of these cases deserve to be heard. Our world grows more complex daily, and important social and technical advances raise questions that properly fall within the jurisdiction of the courts. But the litigation process is prey to abuse. …

Field	Includes:
Humanities	Literature, art, music, religion, philosophy, popular culture
Social Science	History, economics, sociology, psychology, anthropology, business
Natural Science	Sciences not included in other sections, like astronomy, geology, ecology, paleontology

Time: 60 minutes

Passages: 7

Questions: 40

Questions per passage: 5–7

Minutes per passage:

8

Unit 1

TEST DAY: WRITING SAMPLE

Consider this statement:

Freedom of speech is essential to the preservation of any democracy.

Write a unified essay in which you perform the following tasks. Explain what you think the above statement means. Describe a specific situation in which the loss of free speech would not destroy a democracy. Discuss what you think determines whether or not freedom of speech is essential to preserving a democracy.

Prompt Categories:

Advertising/Media

Business

Education

Government

History

International Politics

Law

National Politics

Science/Technology

Sociology

Time: 60 minutes

Essays: 2, separately timed
   30 minutes each

Scored: J–T

TEST DAY: BIOLOGICAL SCIENCES

Time: 70 minutes

Passages: 7

Questions: 52

>   39 passage-based

>   13 discrete

Questions per passage:

Minutes per passage:

Passage I

Type: _Information_

Explicit: _Pedigree_ **Implicit:** _Hardy Wienberg_

The frequency of the albino gene in the general population is 0.001, and is higher in many isolated populations, including the Amish and many Native American tribes. The pedigree in Figure 1 illustrates the pattern of inheritance for one form of human albinism.

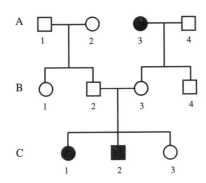

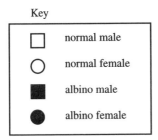

Key

□ normal male

○ normal female

■ albino male

● albino female

Figure 1

Passage II

Type: _Experimental_

Explicit: _bacteria/micro_ **Implicit:** _Scientific method_

The plates were incubated at 37°C for 48 hours. Only bacteria that regain the ability to synthesize histidine through *back-mutation* will be able to survive on these plates. The results of the experiments are shown in Figure 1.

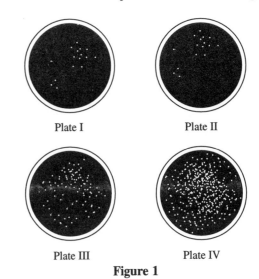

Plate I   Plate II

Plate III   Plate IV

Figure 1

Passage III

Type: _Persuassive arguement_

Explicit: _hypothesis_ (Cell diferentiating) **Implicit:** _Morphogen hyp._

The vertebrate limb provides a good model for studying pattern formation. The experiment that established the role of ZPA in anterior-posterior patterning of the limb involved grafting a portion of ZPA from the limb bud in the chick.

Two hypotheses were proposed to account for the results of this experiment.

Morphogen Hypothesis

The morphogen hypothesis proposes that positional information is based on gradients of morphogens in developing limb.

Unit 1

KAPLAN MCAT STRATEGIES

THE COURSE
THE SECTION
THE PASSAGE
THE QUESTION

THE ANSWER CHOICE

CRITICAL MASS

KAPLAN SECTION STRATEGY

Triage

Definition - catogerizing based on difficulty

Why We Triage

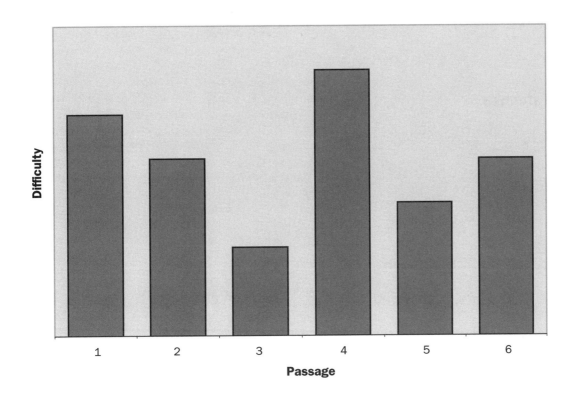

KAPLAN PASSAGE MAPPING STRATEGY (SCIENCES)

Unit 1

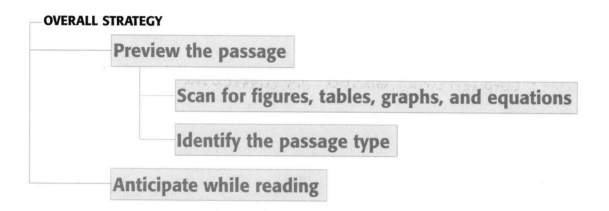

OVERALL STRATEGY

Preview the passage

Scan for figures, tables, graphs, and equations

Identify the passage type

Anticipate while reading

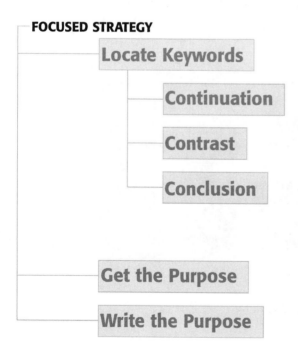

FOCUSED STRATEGY

Locate Keywords

Continuation

Contrast

Conclusion

Get the Purpose

Write the Purpose

APPLYING THE KAPLAN SCIENCES PASSAGE STRATEGY

Diagnostic Physical Sciences Passage IV

The mass spectrometer is a device that utilizes electric and magnetic fields to determine the masses of the elements, or compounds, that exist within a certain sample. The operation of the mass spectrometer relies on the fact that the path of a moving charge is affected by the presence of electric and magnetic fields.

To analyze a sample, it must first be ionized. This may be accomplished by heating the sample, or more commonly, by bombarding it with a stream of electrons. The ionized particles are then accelerated through a potential difference of several thousand volts that is set up between two slits S_1 and S_2 (see figure below). For the mass spectrometer to give useful results, all the particles entering the chamber below S_3 must be traveling at the same velocity. This is assured by passing the particles through a *velocity selector*, a region of a crossed magnetic field, B, and an electric field, E, located between S_2 and S_3. This electric field is produced by two charged parallel plates, P_1 and P_2. Only particles that are traveling at a velocity such that the force due to the electric field (qE) and that due to the magnetic field (qvB) cancel one another will remain undeflected and pass through the slit in S_3.

The stream of charged particles then passes through another magnetic field, B′, but this time, there is no electric field. The second magnetic field is perpendicular to the page, and deflects the particles in a circular path, towards the detector. Based on the radius of curvature of the path of the particle, its mass can be determined from the formula:

$$\frac{q}{m} = \frac{E}{rBB'}$$

where q is the charge of the particle, m is the mass of the particle, E is the electric field, and r is the radius of the circular path of the particle. In the mass spectrometer below, $E = 8 \times 10^4$ V/m, B = 0.4 T, and B′ = 0.5 T.

(Note: The fundamental unit of charge is 1.6×10^{-19} C.)

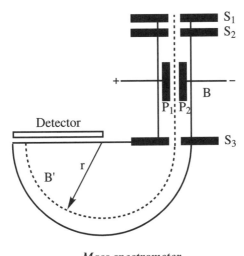

Mass spectrometer

THE KAPLAN QUESTION STRATEGY (SCIENCES)

STOP

Characterize the answer choices

THINK

What is the question really asking

What topic is being tested

What relevant information do you need

PREDICT

Formulate a framework or prediction for your answer

MATCH

Which answer truly meets the requirements of the prediction

APPLYING THE KAPLAN SCIENCES QUESTION STRATEGY

21. What is the velocity of the particles entering the mass spectrometer?

   A. q/m
   B. E/B'
   C. B'/E
   D. E/B

Stop

_____

Think

_____

Predict

_____

Match

_____

KAPLAN'S PASSAGE MAPPING STRATEGY (VERBAL)

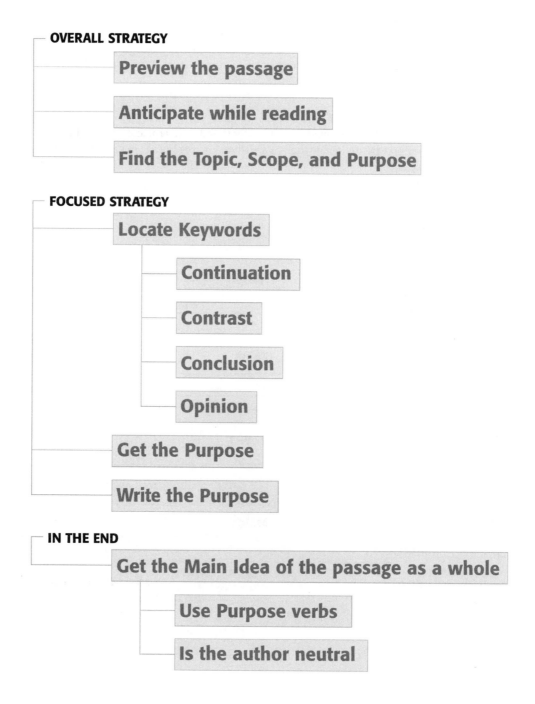

OVERALL STRATEGY

Preview the passage

Anticipate while reading

Find the Topic, Scope, and Purpose

FOCUSED STRATEGY

Locate Keywords

Continuation

Contrast

Conclusion

Opinion

Get the Purpose

Write the Purpose

IN THE END

Get the Main Idea of the passage as a whole

Use Purpose verbs

Is the author neutral

APPLYING THE KAPLAN VERBAL PASSAGE STRATEGY

Diagnostic Verbal Reasoning Passage I

W.H. Auden's reputation, already declining by the 1950s, reached its nadir with the publication of his posthumous collection *Thank You, Fog* (1974). Critics almost unanimously found his last work trite and garrulous. Indeed, the assessment has served as a retrospective judgment on the poet's final three decades.

Auden's early popularity stemmed in part from his ability to articulate political and psychological dilemmas felt by many young Englishmen in the uneasy calm between the two world wars. While remarkable for its novel use of lyric and ballad forms and its overall musicality, Auden's early poetry nevertheless responded to social concerns and conveyed truths, inspired by Marxist and Freudian precepts, which his contemporaries felt older, more conservative poets ignored.

After the outbreak of World War II and his emigration to the United States, Auden, while not entirely rejecting the theme of political insecurity, manifested decidedly different concerns. Although he maintained his interest in technique by experimenting with meter and form, he increasingly felt that the lyricism that came so naturally to him gave rise to dishonest sentiment and didacticism. Gradually Auden developed a middle manner—less grand, more discursive—that could accommodate his new thematic interests.

Often called dry and prosaic, Auden's mature style should be seen as an appropriate vehicle for his later concerns. Thematically, the shift can be viewed as one from society to the self, though this would not take into account Auden's growing absorption in the Anglican Church. Unwilling to come to terms with the change in Auden's intellectual concerns and misinterpreting his rejection of lyric excitement, critics wrongly dismissed the later works as productions of a worn-out talent. "Auden is using extraordinary skill in managing a sorely reduced income," intoned Randall Jarrell in judging *The Shield of Achilles* (1955).

Less defensible than his changing poetic concerns was Auden's reshaping of his earlier poetry. Lines were rewritten, stanzas revoked, whole poems whisked from the canon. Auden refused, for instance, to reprint "September 1, 1939"—his response to the Nazi invasion of Poland—because it contained what he came to consider spurious ideas. Gone was one of Auden's famous lines—a catchphrase for a whole generation—"We must love one another or die," because it expressed an optimism to which Auden could no longer subscribe.

If Auden's altering and deleting early works is questionable on artistic grounds, nevertheless his motives for doing so are consistent with his abiding belief that poetry must mirror reality. Implicit in much of the criticism of his tampering is the wrong-headed idea that an artist must not disappoint an audience prepared to accept one point of view by evolving as a thinker.

Unit 1

KAPLAN QUESTION STRATEGY (VERBAL)

STOP

Characterize the question type

THINK

What is the question really asking

How does the passage map help answer the question

What is the relevant information in the passage

PREDICT

Formulate a framework or prediction for your answer

MATCH

Which answer truly meets the requirements of the prediction

APPLYING THE KAPLAN VERBAL QUESTION STRATEGY

1. According to the passage, Auden's later poetry failed to win acceptance primarily because:

   A. critics objected to the politically-conservative ideas expressed in it.

   B. the content was unnecessarily obscured by a discursive mode of presentation.

   C. its style was less pleasing than that of his earlier work.

   D. its predominantly religious themes were not appreciated by most readers.

Stop

_____

Think

_____

Predict

_____

Match

_____

CBT TUTORIAL

What functionalities are available on the computer-based test interface?

Practice Test Interface vs. Test Day Interface

Can I highlight keywords located in the passage or in the question stem?

highlight passages (only 1 at time)

Can I strike out wrong answer choices using the mouse?

yes (left mouse on text)

Can I access a Periodic Table when needed using an icon on the screen?

yes (takes up whole screen

Can I type notes on my screen as I work though passages?

Not on real test

Will I be able to adjust the screen layout?

Not on real test

Is a test timer provided? If so, where will it be located?

yes, bottom (count down)

Will I be able to right click when using the mouse?

not on real test

Can I mark questions that I would like to go back and review if time has not expired?

yes (mark as guess)

THE KAPLAN INTERFACE

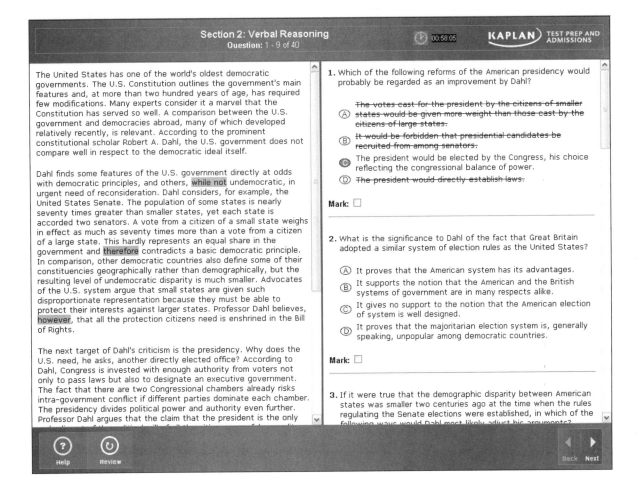

KAPLAN ANALYSIS

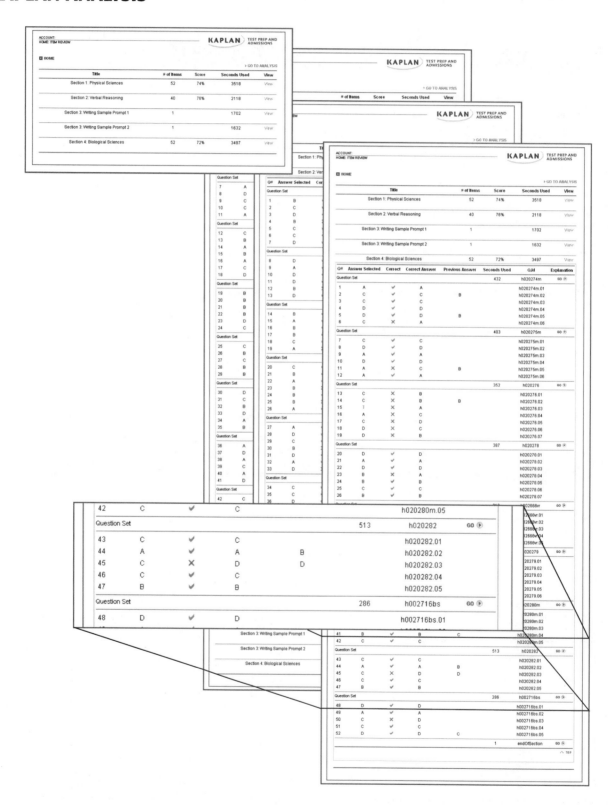

KAPLAN ANALYSIS: DIAGNOSTIC FEEDBACK

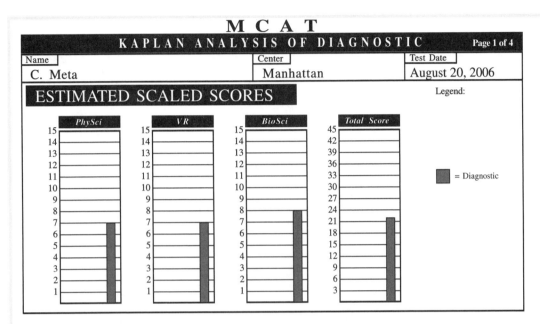

M C A T
KAPLAN ANALYSIS OF DIAGNOSTIC

Page 1 of 4

Name	Center	Test Date
C. Meta	Manhattan	August 20, 2006

ESTIMATED SCALED SCORES

Legend: = Diagnostic

KAPLAN DIAGNOSTIC MCAT
SCORE CONVERSION CHART

PHYSICAL SCIENCES		VERBAL REASONING		BIOLOGICAL SCIENCES	
Raw Score	Estimated Scaled Score	Raw Score	Estimated Scaled Score	Raw Score	Estimated Scaled Score
0	1	0-2	1	0-1	1
1-2	2	3-7	2	2-3	2
3	3	8-14	3	4-8	3
4-8	4	15-17	4	9-13	4
9-11	5	18-21	5	14-16	5
12-15	6	22	6	17-19	6
16-18	7	23-24	7	20-22	7
19-20	8	25	8	23-26	8
21-23	9	26	9	27-29	9
24-25	10	27	10	30-32	10
26-27	11	28	11	33-34	11
28-30	12	29	12	35-36	12
31-33	13	30	13	37	13
34-36	14	31	14	38	14
37+	15	32	15	39	15

KAPLAN SAMPLE MCAT
SCORE CONVERSION CHART

PHYSICAL SCIENCES		VERBAL REASONING		BIOLOGICAL SCIENCES	
Raw Score	Estimated Scaled Score	Raw Score	Estimated Scaled Score	Raw Score	Estimated Scaled Score
0-5	1	0-5	1	0-10	1
6-7	2	6-9	2	11-13	2
8-11	3	10-13	3	14-16	3
12-14	4	14-18	4	17-19	4
15-16	5	19-21	5	20-21	5
17-19	6	22-23	6	22-24	6
20-22	7	24-25	7	25-26	7
23-25	8	26-27	8	27-29	8
26-27	9	28-29	9	30-32	9
28-30	10	30-31	10	33-35	10
31-33	11	32-33	11	36-38	11
34-36	12	34-35	12	39-40	12
37-40	13	36-37	13	41-43	13
41-46	14	38-39	14	44-50	14
47-52	15	40	15	51-52	15

KAPLAN SAMPLE MCAT
SCORE CONVERSION CHART

PHYSICAL SCIENCES		VERBAL REASONING		BIOLOGICAL SCIENCES	
Raw Score	Estimated Scaled Score	Raw Score	Estimated Scaled Score	Raw Score	Estimated Scaled Score
0-5	1	0-2	1	0-7	1
6-7	2	3-6	2	8-12	2
8-11	3	7-9	3	13-15	3
12-15	4	10-11	4	16-18	4
16-19	5	12-13	5	19-21	5
20-23	6	14-15	6	22-24	6
24-27	7	16-17	7	25-27	7
28-31	8	18-20	8	28-30	8
32-34	9	21-23	9	31-34	9
35-37	10	24-26	10	35-37	10
38-40	11	27-29	11	38-40	11
41-42	12	30-31	12	41-43	12
43-45	13	32-34	13	44-46	13
46-49	14	35	14	47-49	14
50-52	15	36-40	15	50-52	15

KAPLAN ANALYSIS: DIAGNOSTIC FEEDBACK

M C A T

KAPLAN ANALYSIS OF DIAGNOSTIC

Page 2 of 4

Name	Center	Test Date
C. Meta	Manhattan	August 20, 2006

PHYSICAL SCIENCES

THIS TEST (Diagnostic):

CORRECT	18
INCORRECT	18
OMITTED	3
% CORRECT	46%
EST. SCALED SCORE [†]	7

Percentage Correct

Question Types		0	20	40	60	80	100
Discrete	n* = 8						
Passage-based	n= 31						

Content Areas

Physics	n= 19						
General Chemistry	n= 20						

Physics Topics

Translational Motion (Ch. 1)	n= 1
Force/Motion/Grav./Equilib. (Ch. 2)	n= 2
Momentum/Work/Energy (Ch. 3,4)	n= 1
Wave Chars./Periodic Motion (Ch. 9)	n= 1
Sound (Ch. 9)	n= 0 — n/a
Fluids/Solids (Ch. 5)	n= 2
Electrostatics/Electromag. (Ch. 6,7)	n= 5
Electric Circuits (Ch. 8)	n= 0 — n/a
Light/Geometrical Optics (Ch. 10)	n= 4
Atomic/Nuclear Structure (Ch. 11,12)	n= 3

General Chemistry Topics

Stoichiometry (Ch. 4)	n= 2
Electronic Struc./Per. Table (Ch. 1,2)	n= 2
Bonding (Ch. 3)	n= 1
Phases/Phase Equilibria (Ch. 7,8)	n= 4
Solution Chemistry (Ch. 9)	n= 1
Acids/Bases (Ch. 10)	n= 2
Thermodynam./Thermochem. (Ch. 6)	n= 4
Rate Proc./Kinetics/Equilib. (Ch. 5)	n= 2
Electrochemistry (Ch. 11)	n= 2

*n = the total number of questions in that category.

Focus your studies on those areas in which you performed poorly as indicated by the graphical analysis above.

Work with the appropriate material in the Physical Sciences Review Notes, as well as with the Topical Tests that correspond to the categories of Physics topics and General Chemistry topics listed in the graphical analysis above. For more detailed instructions on how to work with our MCAT practice material see the Syllabus in your MCAT Lesson Book.

KAPLAN

[†]See score conversion chart on the last page of this report.

4.76

KAPLAN ANALYSIS: DIAGNOSTIC FEEDBACK

M C A T
KAPLAN ANALYSIS OF DIAGNOSTIC

Name	Center	Test Date
C. Meta	Manhattan	August 20, 2006

VERBAL REASONING

THIS TEST (Diagnostic):

CORRECT	23
INCORRECT	6
OMITTED	3
% CORRECT	72%
EST. SCALED SCORE [†]	7

Percentage Correct

Passage Types		0	20	40	60	80	100
Humanities	n* = 8						
Social Sciences	n= 15						
Natural Sciences	n= 9						

Question Types							
Global	n= 3						
Detail	n= 7						
Deduction	n= 5						
Evaluation	n= 11						
Application	n= 5						
Incorporation	n= 1						

*n = the total number of questions in that category.

Focus your studies on those areas in which you performed poorly as indicated by the graphical analysis above.

Work with the appropriate material in the Verbal Reasoning Review Notes, as well as with the Verbal Reasoning Section Tests.

For more detailed instructions on how to work with our MCAT practice material see the Syllabus in your MCAT Lesson Book.

KAPLAN

[†]See score conversion chart on the last page of this report.

4.76

KAPLAN ANALYSIS: DIAGNOSTIC FEEDBACK

M C A T
KAPLAN ANALYSIS OF DIAGNOSTIC

Page 4 of 4

Name	Center	Test Date
C. Meta	Manhattan	August 20, 2006

BIOLOGICAL SCIENCES

THIS TEST (Diagnostic):

CORRECT	23
INCORRECT	16
OMITTED	0
% CORRECT	59%
EST. SCALED SCORE †	8

Percentage Correct

Question Types (0 20 40 60 80 100)

| Discrete | n* = 8 |
| Passage-based | n= 31 |

Content Areas

| Biology | n= 24 |
| Organic Chemistry | n= 15 |

Biology Topics

Molecular Biology (Ch. 2,3,14)	n= 1
Microbiology (Ch. 1,14)	n= 3
Generalized Eukaryotic Cell (Ch. 1)	n= 1
Nervous/Endocrine Sys. (Ch. 11,12)	n= 6
Circ./Lymph./Immune Sys. (Ch. 9)	n= 6
Digestive/Excretory Sys. (Ch. 7)	n= 1
Muscle/Skeletal Sys. (Ch. 6)	n= 0	n/a
Respiratory/Skin Sys. (Ch. 8,10)	n= 0	n/a
Reproductive Sys./Develop. (Ch. 4,5,11)	n= 1
Genetics/Evolution (Ch. 13,15)	n= 5

Organic Chemistry Topics

Biological Molecules (Ch. 14,15)	n= 5
Oxygen-containing Cmpd. (Ch. 7,8,9,10)	n= 3
Amines (Ch. 11)	n= 1
Hydrocarbons (Ch. 4,5,6)	n= 1
Molec. Struc. of Org. Cmpd. (Ch. 1,2,3)	n= 3
Separations/Purifications (Ch. 12)	n= 1
Spectroscopy (Ch. 13)	n= 1

*n = the total number of questions in that category.

Focus your studies on those areas in which you performed poorly as indicated by the graphical analysis above. Work with the appropriate material in the Biological Sciences Review Notes, as well as with the Topical Tests that correspond to the categories of Biology topics and Organic Chemistry topics listed in the graphical analysis above.

For more detailed instructions on how to work with our MCAT practice material see the Syllabus in your MCAT Lesson Book.

KAPLAN

†See score conversion chart on the last page of this report.

4.76

KAPLAN ANALYSIS: SCIENCE ASSESSMENT EXAM FEEDBACK

M C A T
KAPLAN ANALYSIS OF SCIENCE ASSESSMENT EXAM   Page 1 of 2

Name	Center	Test Date
C. Meta	Manhattan	August 20, 2006

PHYSICS

CORRECT	16
INCORRECT	14
OMITTED	0
% CORRECT	53%

GENERAL CHEMISTRY

CORRECT	14
INCORRECT	16
OMITTED	0
% CORRECT	47%

Percentage Correct

Content Areas		0 20 40 60 80 100
Physics	$n^* = 30$	
General Chemistry	$n = 30$	

Physics Topics		
Translational Motion (Ch. 1)	$n = 2$	
Force/Motion/Grav./Equilib. (Ch. 2)	$n = 5$	
Momentum/Work/Energy (Ch. 3,4)	$n = 8$	
Wave Chars./Periodic Motion (Ch. 9)	$n = 0$	n/a
Sound (Ch. 9)	$n = 3$	
Fluids/Solids (Ch. 5)	$n = 3$	
Electrostatics/Electromag. (Ch. 6,7)	$n = 2$	
Electric Circuits (Ch. 8)	$n = 2$	
Light/Geometrical Optics (Ch. 10)	$n = 3$	
Atomic/Nuclear Structure (Ch. 11,12)	$n = 2$	

General Chemistry Topics		
Stoichiometry (Ch. 4)	$n = 3$	
Electronic Struc./Per. Table (Ch. 1,2)	$n = 7$	
Bonding (Ch. 3)	$n = 2$	
Phases/Phase Equilibria (Ch. 7,8)	$n = 6$	
Solution Chemistry (Ch. 9)	$n = 1$	
Acids/Bases (Ch. 10)	$n = 3$	
Thermodynam./Thermochem. (Ch. 6)	$n = 2$	
Rate Proc./Kinetics/Equilib. (Ch. 5)	$n = 3$	
Electrochemistry (Ch. 11)	$n = 3$	

*n = the total number of questions in that category.

KAPLAN

KAPLAN ANALYSIS: SCIENCE ASSESSMENT EXAM FEEDBACK

MCAT

KAPLAN ANALYSIS OF SCIENCE ASSESSMENT EXAM		Page 2 of 2
Name C. Meta	Center Manhattan	Test Date August 20, 2006

BIOLOGY

CORRECT	23
INCORRECT	7
OMITTED	0
% CORRECT	77%

ORGANIC CHEMISTRY

CORRECT	4
INCORRECT	26
OMITTED	0
% CORRECT	13%

Percentage Correct

Content Areas		0	20	40	60	80	100
Biology	n*= 30						
Organic Chemistry	n= 30						

Biology Topics

Molecular Biology (Ch. 2,3,14)	n= 2	
Microbiology (Ch. 1,14)	n= 9	
Generalized Eukaryotic Cell (Ch. 1)	n= 0	n/a
Nervous/Endocrine Sys. (Ch. 11,12)	n= 2	
Circ./Lymph./Immune Sys. (Ch. 9)	n= 3	
Digestive/Excretory Sys. (Ch. 7)	n= 2	
Muscle/Skeletal Sys. (Ch. 6)	n= 1	
Respiratory/Skin Sys. (Ch. 8,10)	n= 2	
Reproductive Sys./Develop. (Ch. 4,5,11)	n= 5	
Genetics/Evolution (Ch. 13,15)	n= 4	

Organic Chemistry Topics

Biological Molecules (Ch. 14,15)	n= 4	
Oxygen-containing Cmpd. (Ch. 7,8,9,10)	n= 8	
Amines (Ch. 11)	n= 2	
Hydrocarbons (Ch. 4,5,6)	n= 6	
Molec. Struc. of Org. Cmpd. (Ch. 1,2,3)	n= 6	
Separations/Purifications (Ch. 12)	n= 2	
Spectroscopy (Ch. 13)	n= 2	

*n = the total number of questions in that category.

KAPLAN

THE MCAT SCORE

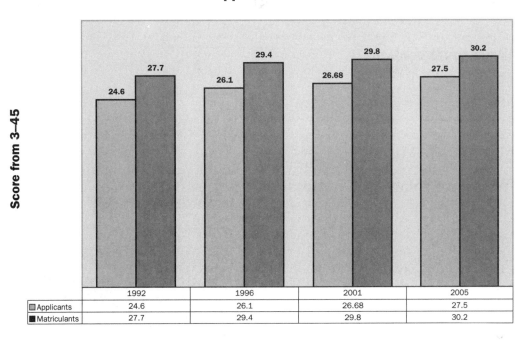

Applicants vs Matriculants

	1992	1996	2001	2005
Applicants	24.6	26.1	26.68	27.5
Matriculants	27.7	29.4	29.8	30.2

Staying Competitive

Average MCAT Score:

Average Applicant:

Average Matriculant:

Target Score:

- Shows MCAT Score report
- Average scores for test takers, applicants, matriculants
- Individual sections vs. overall score (high scores on *all* sections important)

THE KAPLAN MCAT PROGRAM

Will we cover content?

What are we going to do in class?

How can I expect my scores to increase? By how much?

How should I study?

AN OUTLINE OF TEST DAY

Sections	Breakdown
Jumpstart with FLASHCARDS until you check in	
Tutorial:	5 min, optional
Physical Sciences:	50% Physics and 50% G-Chem 70 min, 52 questions, 7 passages, 13 discretes, scored 1–15
10-min Break (optional): Go to bathroom, eat your snack, drink Gatorade	
Verbal Reasoning:	60 min, 40 questions, 7 passages, Scored 1–15
10-min Break (optional): Go to bathroom, eat your snack, drink Gatorade	
Writing Sample:	2 Essays, 30 min each, Scored J–T
10-min Break (optional): Go to bathroom, eat your snack, drink Gatorade	
Biological Sciences:	75% Bio and 25% Orgo 70 min, 52 questions, 7 passages, 13 discretes, scored 1–15
5-min Survey, then **relax**, enjoy, and tell us how you did	

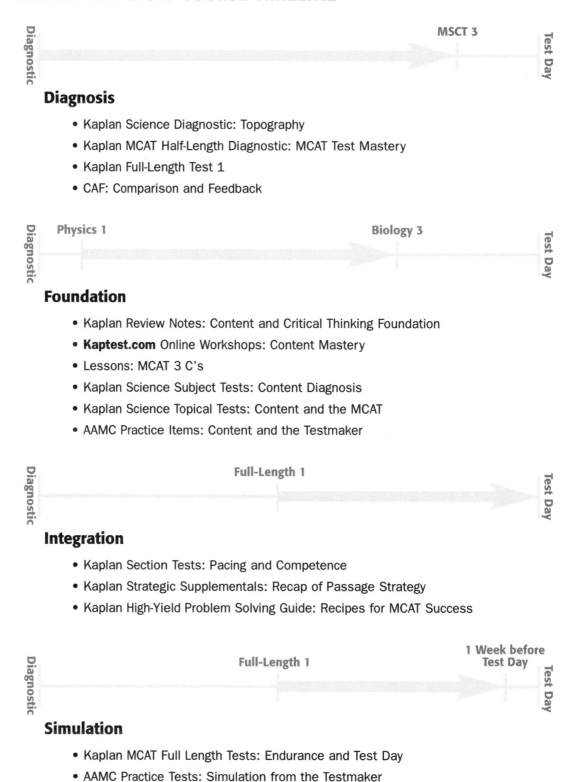

THE KAPLAN MCAT COURSE TIMELINE

Unit 1

Diagnostic ———————————————————→ MSCT 3 | **Test Day**

Diagnosis

- Kaplan Science Diagnostic: Topography
- Kaplan MCAT Half-Length Diagnostic: MCAT Test Mastery
- Kaplan Full-Length Test 1
- CAF: Comparison and Feedback

Diagnostic | Physics 1 ———————————→ Biology 3 | **Test Day**

Foundation

- Kaplan Review Notes: Content and Critical Thinking Foundation
- **Kaptest.com** Online Workshops: Content Mastery
- Lessons: MCAT 3 C's
- Kaplan Science Subject Tests: Content Diagnosis
- Kaplan Science Topical Tests: Content and the MCAT
- AAMC Practice Items: Content and the Testmaker

Diagnostic | Full-Length 1 ———————————→ | **Test Day**

Integration

- Kaplan Section Tests: Pacing and Competence
- Kaplan Strategic Supplementals: Recap of Passage Strategy
- Kaplan High-Yield Problem Solving Guide: Recipes for MCAT Success

Diagnostic | Full-Length 1 ———————→ 1 Week before Test Day | **Test Day**

Simulation

- Kaplan MCAT Full Length Tests: Endurance and Test Day
- AAMC Practice Tests: Simulation from the Testmaker

The Lesson Continues
on the Next Page

HOMEWORK

Review for MSCT 1

Flashcards	☑ Tear apart and organize.

Preview for Physics 1

Physics Review Notes	☑ *Chapters 1–3
Foundation Review	☐ Unit 1 (Optional, MM3259A)
Math Foundation Review	☐ (Optional, MM3259A)
Online Workshops	☑ *Units and Kinematics

CRITICAL READING

Physics 1

CRITICAL READING: FOUNDATION

- Newtonian Mechanics
- Rotational Equilibrium
- Work, Energy, and Momentum

THE KAPLAN MCAT TRAINING PROGRAM

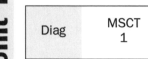

Diag	MSCT 1

* **Unit 1: Critical Reading**

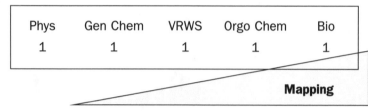

Phys	Gen Chem	VRWS	Orgo Chem	Bio
1	1	1	1	1

Mapping

Unit 2: Attacking Questions

Phys	Gen Chem	VRWS	Orgo Chem	Bio
2	2	2	2	2

Scoring Points

FL#1	MSCT 2

Unit 3: Integrated Practice

Phys	Gen Chem	VRWS	Orgo Chem	Bio
3	3	3	3	3

Pacing & Focus

Unit 4: Test Day Simulation

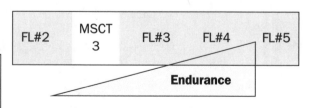

FL#2	MSCT 3	FL#3	FL#4	FL#5

Endurance

* **YOU ARE HERE**

KAPLAN PASSAGE STRATEGY

OVERALL STRATEGY

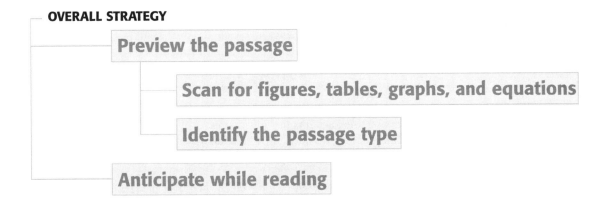

Preview the passage

Scan for figures, tables, graphs, and equations

Identify the passage type

Anticipate while reading

FOCUSED STRATEGY

Locate Keywords

Continuation

Contrast

Conclusion

Get the Purpose

Write the Purpose

Passage I (Questions 1–3)

When evaluating the causes and effects of automobile accidents, there are three major factors to consider: reaction time, braking distance, and passive safety restraints.

A driver's reaction time, t, is the time elapsed between observing a dangerous situation and acting on it. If the car is moving at speed v, it will travel a distance vt before the driver can react. If the car is too close to the hazard, there won't be enough time to avoid a collision. For a car traveling at speed v, the minimum safe distance, d, between the car and the hazard is:

$$d = vt_{reaction} + \frac{v^2}{2a},$$

where $t_{reaction}$ is the reaction time, and a is the maximum rate of deceleration of the car. The second term in the equation is the stopping distance, the minimum distance over which a car can come to rest once the brakes have been applied.

Driving or riding in an automobile has become much safer over the last few decades, due to innovations in passenger safety. The seatbelt wraps around the waist and over the shoulder, restraining the wearer against sharp forward motion and distributing the force of impact over the rider's chest and pelvis. Riders wearing a seatbelt have a good chance of surviving a collision, as long as their deceleration doesn't exceed $30g$. Airbags, installed in the center of the steering wheel, inflate quickly after impact, forming a cushion for the driver. The bag takes about 45 milliseconds to inflate, and the driver strikes it 15 milliseconds later. For the next 40 milliseconds, the airbag deflates as it cushions and decelerates the driver's head and chest. The timing is important; if the driver hits the airbag while it inflates, the force of impact can be fatal. Crumple zones in the front and rear of a car are designed to absorb the impact from a head-on collision. A large fraction of the energy of a crash can be absorbed by designing the front portion of the car to collapse without damaging the passenger compartment. When a head-on, inelastic collision occurs, most of the energy of the collision will be absorbed, instead of transferred to the passengers.

Scratch Paper
Paragraph 1
Paragraph 2
Equation
Paragraph 3

Scratch Paper

Stop:

What information from the passage can be used here?

Think:

In what direction is the acceleration of the car?

Can we eliminate any answer choices?

Which equation do we need to calculate the acceleration?

Predict:

Match

Stop:

Think:

Do we have enough information to calculate the time needed for the car to come to a stop? If not, how do we proceed?

Predict:

Match

Stop:

Are any calculations required to answer this question correctly?

Think:

Does the equation from the passage apply to this situation?

Predict:

Match

1. Decelerating uniformly, a car traveling north at 25 m/s takes ten seconds to come to a complete stop. What is the magnitude and direction of the car's acceleration as it slows down?

   A. North, at 2.5 m/s^2
   B. South, at 2.5 m/s^2
   C. North, at 9.8 m/s^2
   D. South, at 25 m/s^2

2. In a head-on collision, a car moving at 10 m/s is uniformly brought to a halt over a distance of 0.5 m, the size of the car's crumple zone. How much time does it take for the car to come to a complete stop?

   A. 0.05 s
   B. 0.1 s
   C. 0.2 s
   D. 0.5 s

3. If a car moving at 15 m/s suffers a collision, causing it to decelerate uniformly at 1 m/s^2, approximately how far does the car travel while the airbag inflates?

   A. $\left((15)(45 \times 10^{-3}) + \frac{1}{2}(45 \times 10^{-3})^2 \right)$ m

   B. $\left((15)(15 \times 10^{-3}) - \frac{1}{2}(15 \times 10^{-3})^2 \right)$ m

   C. $\left((15)(45 \times 10^{-3}) + \frac{(15)^2}{2} \right)$ m

   D. $\left((15)(45 \times 10^{-3}) - \frac{1}{2}(45 \times 10^{-3})^2 \right)$ m

Directed Practice

- *Physical Sciences Review Notes*: Physics Ch. 1

NEWTONIAN MECHANICS

Newton's First Law

An object in motion at a constant velocity or at rest will stay that way, unless acted upon by an external force.

Newton's Second Law

$$\vec{F}_{net} = m\vec{a}$$

Critical Thinking Exercise

An object in free fall first accelerates at $9.8 \frac{m}{s^2}$ and after a few seconds has an acceleration of 0. Why?

Newton's Third Law

$$\vec{F}_{AB} = -\vec{F}_{BA}$$

Every action has an equal and opposite reaction.

Forces, Statics, and Dynamics

Kinetic Friction

$$f_k = \mu_k F_n$$

Static Friction

$$f_s \leq \mu_s F_n$$

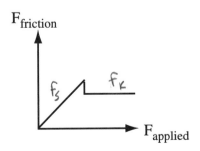

Gravitation

$$F = \frac{Gm_1m_2}{r^2}$$

Two masses will exert an attractive force on one another inversely proportional to the square of the distance between them.

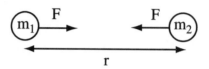

The Inclined Plane

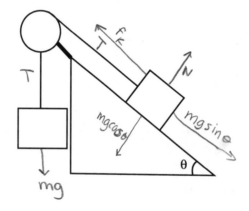

Centripetal Motion

The net force on an object moving at a constant speed on a circular path points toward the center of the circle.

Directed Practice

- *Physical Sciences Review Notes*: Physics Ch. 1
- *Topical Tests*: Force, Motion, Gravitation, and Equilibrium Test 1 (Passage II)

Rotational Motion

Torque

$\tau = rF \sin\theta$

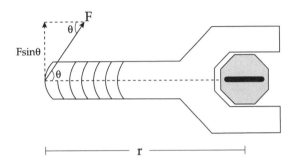

Rotational Equilibrium

An object is in rotational equilibrium when the sum of the torques acting on it is zero.

Critical Thinking Exercise

What has to be true for the seesaw below to be in rotational equilibrium?

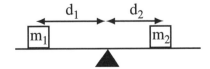

Passage II (Questions 4–7)

A physics class is attempting to measure the acceleration due to gravity g by throwing balls out of classroom windows. They performed the following two experiments:

Experiment 1

Two class members lean out of different windows at the same height, $h = 5.2$ m, above the ground and drop two different balls. One ball is made out of lead and has a mass of 5 kg. The other ball is made out of plastic and has a mass of 1 kg. The students measure the velocity of the lead ball just before impact with the ground and find it to be 10 m/s. They also find that when the plastic ball hits the ground it bounces, and its momentum changes by 18 kg · m/s.

Experiment 2

Instead of dropping the plastic ball, a student throws the ball out of a higher window and observes its projectile motion. The ball is thrown from a height of 10 m above the ground with a velocity of 4 m/s directed at an angle of 30° above the horizontal.

(Note: Assume that the air resistance is negligible unless otherwise stated.)

Scratch Paper

Paragraph 1

Experiment 1

Experiment 2

Scratch Paper

Stop:

Think:

What is g? What does its value depend on?

What equations for gravitational force do you already know?

Predict:

Match

Stop:

Think:

What is the expression for the momentum of an object?

Where is this change in momentum taking place?

Predict:

Match

4. Which of the following would change the measured value of g in Experiment 1?

    I.   Increasing the mass of the Earth

    II.   Using balls having a different mass but the same volume

    III.   Throwing the balls horizontally instead of dropping them vertically

  A.   I only

  B.   III only

  C.   I and II only

  D.   II and III only

5. In Experiment 1, the change in momentum that the plastic ball experiences when it bounces off the ground does NOT depend on: (Note: Assume that the collision is perfectly elastic.)

  A.   the velocity of the ball just before impact.

  B.   the mass of the ball.

  C.   the mass of the Earth.

  D.   the volume of the ball.

Scratch Paper

Stop:

Think:

What does the presence of air resistance mean for the motion of an object?

How do we determine the value of g from the motion of the object?

Predict:

Match

Stop:

Think:

What determines the maximum height of an object in projectile motion?

Predict:

Match

6. The students did not account for air resistance in their measurement of g in Experiment 1. How does the value of g they obtained compare to the actual value of g?

   A. The value of g obtained in Experiment 1 is greater than the actual value of g because air resistance increases the time it takes the balls to fall from the windows to the ground.

   B. The value of g obtained in Experiment 1 is greater than the actual value of g because air resistance decreases the kinetic energy of the balls just before impact.

   C. The value of g obtained in Experiment 1 is less than the actual value of g because air resistance decreases the velocity of the balls just before impact.

   D. The value of g obtained in Experiment 1 is less than the actual value of g because air resistance decreases the time it takes the balls to fall from the windows to the ground.

7. In Experiment 2, what was the maximum height above the window reached by the plastic ball? (Note: The acceleration due to gravity is $g = 9.8$ m/s^2, $\sin 30° = 0.50$, and $\cos 30° = 0.866$.)

   A. 10.2 cm
   B. 20.4 cm
   C. 30.6 cm
   D. 61.2 cm

Unit 1

WORK, ENERGY, AND MOMENTUM

Work

$W = Fd \cos \theta$

Energy

Kinetic energy

$KE = \dfrac{1}{2} mv^2$

Work-Energy Theorem

$W_{net} = \Delta KE$

Critical Thinking Exercise

How much work is done by the force of gravity on a satellite which moves in a circular orbit?

Critical Thinking Exercise

Scratch Paper

Stop:

Think:

What forces are acting on the box?

How does work relate to forces?

Does the box change in kinetic energy?

What does this tell us about the net work done on the box?

Predict:

Match

8. A box that is initially at rest is pushed by a person at an angle θ with a force F until it reaches a speed of v. (See diagram below.) The coefficient of kinetic friction between the box and the surface is μ. Which of the following relationships is necessarily true?

A. The work done by the person is equal in magnitude to the work done by the friction force.

B. The work done by the person is greater in magnitude than the work done by the friction force.

C. The magnitude of the work done by the person is equal to the change in the kinetic energy of the box.

D. The kinetic energy gained by the box is greater than the energy dissipated by friction.

Gravitational potential energy

$U = mgh$

Conservation of mechanical energy $(\Delta E = \Delta U + \Delta K)$

When no dissipative forces act on an object, its total mechanical energy is conserved.

PE=100
KE=0
50/50
PE=0
KE=100

Conservative vs non-conservative forces

	Conservative Forces	**Non-conservative Forces**
Mechanical Energy	conserved	not conserved
Path Independent	yes	NO
Examples	- gravity - electrostatic - spring	- friction - air resistance

Average power

$P = \dfrac{\Delta E}{\Delta t} = \dfrac{W}{t}$ (watts)

Directed Practice
- *Physical Sciences Review Notes*: Physics Ch. 3
- *Topical Tests*: Work, Energy, and Momentum Test 1 (Passage I)

Momentum

$$\vec{p} = m\vec{v} \qquad \left(\frac{kg \cdot m}{s} \right)$$

Conservation of linear momentum

The total momentum of a system of objects is conserved as long as no external forces act on that system.

(same velocity)

←○ ○→

(different v)

←○ ○→

○○→

Type of Collisions	Equations
elastic collisions	$P_b = P_a$ $KE_b = KE_a$
inelastic collisions	$P_b = P_a$ $KE_b > KE_a$
totally inelastic collisions	$P_b = P_a$ $KE_b > KE_a$

Critical Thinking Exercise

Two objects with equal masses are moving towards each other with the same speed. How do they move after the collision if the collision is (i) elastic (ii) totally inelastic?

Impulse

$$I = \Delta p = F_{av}\Delta t$$

A force applied to an object over time causes a change in the object's momentum called an impulse.

The Lesson Continues
on the Next Page ⟶

Passage III (Questions 9–13)

The model of the atom as a dense, positively-charged nucleus surrounded by a cloud of electron density was first established by an experiment conducted by Ernest Rutherford and his students in 1911, in which they observed the behavior of α-particles as they were scattered by a thin piece of gold foil. The modern technique of Rutherford backscattering spectrometry is based on the same general principle. The experimental setup for this technique is shown in Figure 1.

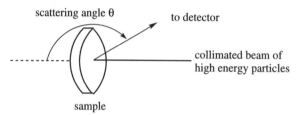

scattering angle θ

to detector

collimated beam of high energy particles

sample

Figure 1

In the experiment, a beam of particles (usually ^{4}He ions) with the same energy (a few MeV) is incident on the sample. The particles collide elastically with and transfer energy to the sample atoms which recoil under the impact. The incident particles are scattered backwards to a detector where their final energy is measured.

The kinematic factor, K, is defined as the ratio of the final energy to the initial energy of the incident particle. For a given scattering angle and a given type of incident particles, one can plot the kinematic factor as a function of the target mass m_2. Examples of such plots for two different incident masses m_1 are shown in Figure 2.

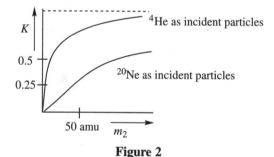

K

^{4}He as incident particles

0.5

^{20}Ne as incident particles

0.25

50 amu m_2

Figure 2

The value of the kinematic factor depends not only on the mass of the target atom but also on the depth into the target sample the incident particle reaches before it backscatters.

Scratch Paper

Paragraph 1

Figure 1

Paragraph 2

Paragraph 3

Figure 2

Scratch Paper

Stop:

Think:

Given the energy, how do we determine how rapidly a particle is moving?

Predict:

Match

Stop:

Think:

What reaches the detector?

How is it affected by the atoms of the sample?

Predict:

Match

Stop:

Think:

What does the value of the kinematic factor tell us about the loss or transfer of energy?

Predict:

Match

9. The source aperture from which a beam of 2-MeV helium ions emerge is at a distance of 15 cm from the sample. How long does it take for one of these incident particles (each with mass 4 amu) to reach the target? (1 amu $= 1.66 \times 10^{-27}$ kg; 1 eV $= 1.60 \times 10^{-19}$ J)

   A. 1.5×10^{-8} s
   B. 1.0×10^{-7} s
   C. 1.5×10^{-6} s
   D. 1.0×10^{-5} s

10. If the sample consists of more than one type of atom, what would be observed at the detector?

   A. particles of different masses but the same energy
   B. particles of the same mass but different energies
   C. particles of different masses and different energies
   D. particles of the same mass and the same energy

11. For which of the following sample atoms would an alpha particle backscatter from the surface with the lowest kinematic factor?

   A. Oxygen
   B. Nitrogen
   C. Carbon
   D. Hydrogen

Scratch Paper

Stop:

Think:

What concept does this problem demonstrate?

Draw a diagram to get an intuitive insight into the problem.

Predict:

Match

Stop:

Think:

Is this an elastic or inelastic collision?

How does the fact that the two pucks are of equal mass simplify the problem?

Predict:

Match

12. A massless plank with a length of 4 m has two weights placed upon it. One with a mass of 10 kg is on the left edge of the plank, while the other with a mass of 20 kg is placed 1.5 m inward from the opposite (right) edge. Where should the fulcrum be located if the plank with the weights on it were to remain horizontal?

   A. 0.7 m in from the right edge of the plank.
   B. 1.5 m in from the right edge of the plank.
   C. 0.7 m in from the left edge of the plank.
   D. 1.7 m in from the left edge of the plank.

13. Two hockey pucks of equal mass undergo a head-on collision. Initially, puck 1 is traveling north at 2 m/s, and puck 2 is traveling south at 4 m/s. After the collision, puck 1 is traveling south at 3 m/s. What is the velocity of puck 2 after the collision?

   A. 1 m/s, south
   B. 1 m/s, north
   C. 3 m/s, south
   D. 3 m/s, north

Directed Practice

   • *Topical Test*: Work, Energy, and Momentum Test 1 (Passage II)

The Lesson Continues
on the Next Page
⟶

HOMEWORK

Review for Physics 1

Topical Tests	☑ Translational Motion Test 1 ❑ Force, Motion, Gravitation and Equilibrium Test 1 ❑ Work, Energy and Momentum Test 1
Subject Tests	❑ Test 1 (Optional, DF3015) ❑ Test 2 (Optional, DF3016) ❑ Test 3 (Optional, DF3017)

Preview for General Chemistry 1

General Chemistry Review Notes	☑ *Chapters 1–3 and 7
Foundation Review	❑ Unit 1 (Optional, MM3258)
Online Workshops	☑ *Quantum Numbers and Electron Configuration

General Chemistry 1

CRITICAL READING: COMPREHENSION

- Atomic Structure
- Periodic and Group Trends
- Bonding
- Molecular Structure (VSEPR)
- Intermolecular Forces
- Properties of Gases

KAPLAN STRATEGY FOR WORKING WITH THE PASSAGE

OVERALL STRATEGY

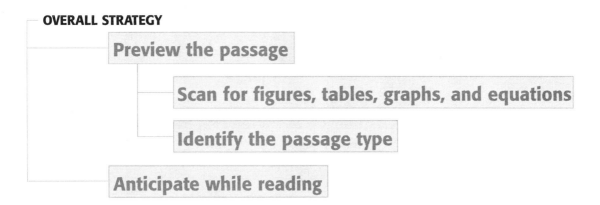

Preview the passage

Scan for figures, tables, graphs, and equations

Identify the passage type

Anticipate while reading

FOCUSED STRATEGY

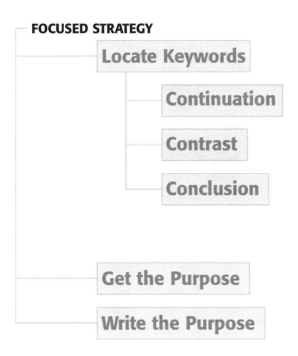

Locate Keywords

Continuation

Contrast

Conclusion

Get the Purpose

Write the Purpose

Passage I (Questions 1–3)

Niels Bohr proposed that the single electron in the hydrogen atom moves in a circular orbit around the nucleus, that only certain orbits were allowed, and that the energy of these orbits was defined as:

$$E = -h \times \frac{R}{n^2} \text{ with } n = 1, 2, 3, \ldots$$

Equation 1

where h is Planck's constant, 6.6×10^{-34} J·s, R is the Rydberg constant for hydrogen, and n is the principal quantum number. Bohr also extended his theory to model other one-electron systems, such as He^+ and Li^{2+}. According to Bohr's theory, the radius of a single electron orbiting a fixed nucleus is:

$$r_n = (n^2)\frac{a_0}{Z}$$

Equation 2

where r_n is the radius of the stationary orbit, a_0 is a constant, and Z is the atomic number. Further, the energy of the orbit is given by:

$$E_n = -\frac{ke^2}{2a_0}\left(\frac{Z^2}{n^2}\right)$$

Equation 3

where k is the coloumbic constant and e is the charge of the electron. A more complex model is necessary for systems with more than one electron. Adequate descriptions of an electron's energy require three quantum numbers. These quantum numbers map the location and energy of the electrons of an atom or ion. An orbital is typically described by the values of n and ℓ, where ℓ is the angular momentum quantum number. For example, an electron with $n = 2$ and $\ell = 0$ would be in a $2s$ orbital.

Scratch Paper

Equation 1

Equation 2

Equation 3

Paragraph

Scratch Paper

Stop:

Think:

Can this information be found in the passage?

Predict:

Match

Stop:

Think:

Can the answer be found in the passage?

Which of the answers states that electrons need to be uniquely identifiable?

Predict:

Match

Stop:

Think:

Can you use the answer choices to your advantage?

How does the energy of He^+ compare to H?

How does the radius of He^+ compare to H?

Predict:

Match

1. Which electron orbit, according to Niels Bohr, is expected to have the lowest energy?

   A. $n = 1$
   B. $n = 2$
   C. $n = 3$
   D. $n = 4$

2. Which of the following states that no two atomic electrons can have the same four quantum numbers?

   A. Pauli exclusion principle
   B. Hund's rule
   C. Aufbau principle
   D. Octet rule

3. How do the energy and radius of an electron orbit in He^+ compare to the energy and radius of an electron orbit in H, if each electron has the same value of n?

   A. The energy of the electron in orbit around He^+ is higher than the electron in orbit around H; the radius of the electron orbit in H is longer than the radius of the electron orbit in He^+.
   B. The energy of the electron in orbit around He^+ is higher than the electron in orbit around H; the radius of the electron orbit in H is shorter than the radius of the electron orbit in He^+.
   C. The energy of the electron in orbit around H is higher than the electron in orbit around He^+; the radius of the electron orbit in He^+ is longer than the radius of the electron orbit in H.
   D. The energy of the electron in orbit around H is higher than the electron in orbit around He^+; the radius of the electron orbit in He^+ is shorter than the radius of the electron orbit in H.

Directed Practice

- *Physical Sciences Review Notes*: Gen. Chem. Ch. 1
- *Diagnostic*: Physical Sciences (Passage I) Question 3

ATOMIC STRUCTURE

Quantum Numbers

n: _energy level (radius)_

l: _subshell (shape; $0-n-1$); s, p, d, f_

m_l: _# orbitals in subshell; $-l$ to l_

m_s: _spin; $\pm \frac{1}{2}$_

Hund's Rules

Add ~~plata~~ parellel 1st (fill all blank)
then pair up

Spectroscopic Notation

writing 4s

THE PERIODIC TABLE

What It Tells Us

1. Atomic number (z) → # protons

2. Atomic mass → average weights (isotopes)

3. Valence shell configuration

4. Chemical properties

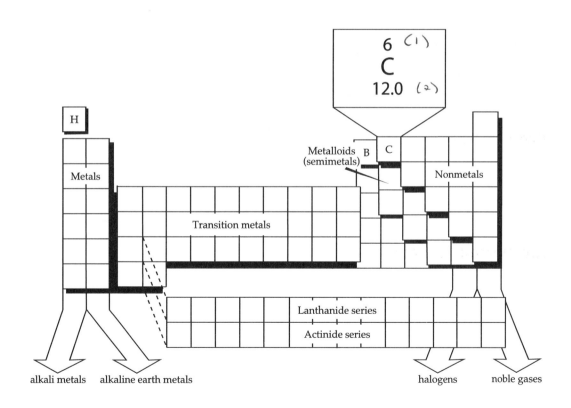

Fully _____ and _____ half subshells have exceptional stability.

PERIODIC AND GROUP TRENDS

Effective Nuclear Charge, Z_{eff}

Effective nuclear charge is the attractive, positive charge of the nucleus as perceived by a valence electron.

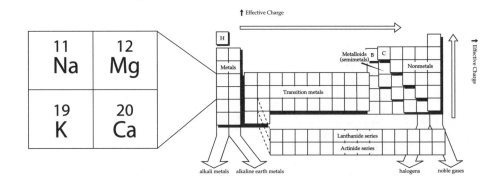

Atomic Radius

The atomic radius gives an indication of the size of an atom.

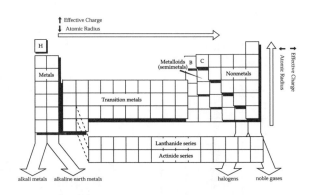

Critical Thinking Exercise

Which of the following has the larger radius: Sr or Rb?

Which of the following has the larger radius: K or K^+?

Which of the following has the larger radius: Ar or K^+?

Directed Practice

- *Physical Sciences Review Notes*: Gen. Chem. Ch. 2
- *Foundation Review*: pp. 1–8

Ionization Energy

$$X_{(g)} \rightarrow X_{(g)}^+ + e^-$$

Definition: <u>energy to remove</u>
<u>an e⁻ (+ requires ener)</u>

As Z_{eff} Increases,
Ionization Energy <u>increases</u>.

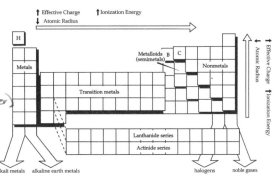

Critical Thinking Exercise

Scratch Paper

Stop:

Think:

Predict:

Match

4. The ionization energies below most likely correspond to which of the following elements?

First Ionization Energy	590 kJ/mol
Second Ionization Energy	1145 kJ/mol
Third Ionization Energy	4912 kJ/mol

 A. Na
 B. Ca
 C. N
 D. P

Electron Affinity

$$X_{(g)} + e^- \rightarrow X^-_{(g)}$$

Definition: <u>how much to</u> <u>form bond (– releases energy)</u>

As Z_{eff} Increases,
Electron Affinity <u>increase</u>.

Critical Thinking Exercise

Contrary to periodic trends, phosphorus has a lower electron affinity than silicon. Why?

Silicon	−135 kJ/mol
Phosphorus	−72 kJ/mol
Sulfur	−203 kJ/mol

Directed Practice

- *Topical Tests*: Electronic Structure Test (Passage I)
- *General Chemistry Subject Tests*: Test 1, Questions 7–12

Electronegativity

Electronegativity is the attraction of an atom for electrons **in a bond**.

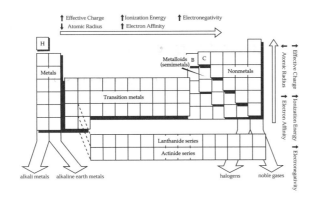

Metallic Character

Certain characteristics are associated with metals: relatively electropositive, good conductors of heat and electricity, malleable, etc.

Critical Thinking Exercise

Where do elements with good metallic character show up on the periodic table? (lower left)

Example Atom	Cesium	Fluorine
Location on Periodic Table	alkali metals	halogen
Effective Nuclear Charge	↓	↑
Atomic Radius	↑	↓
Ionization Energy	↓	↑
Electron Affinity	↓	↑
Electronegativity	↓	↑
Metallic Character	↑	↓

Directed Practice
- *General Chemistry Subject Test 1*: Questions 19–25, 28–30
- *General Chemistry Strategic Supplemental*
- *General Chemistry Subject Test 2*: Question 30

BONDING

Ionic

Ionic bonding involves transfer of electrons.

$$Na^+ \ Cl^- \quad \text{(two opposite elements)}$$

IE   ↓   ↑
EA   ↓   ↑
ENeg ↓   ↑

Covalent

Covalent bonding involves sharing of electrons.

1. polar → unequal sharing ; some ionic

2. Nonpolar → shared equally (pure)

3. coordinate cov. → both e's from ~~same~~ one atom

Lewis Structures

Lewis structures are used to depict covalent compounds and ions.

Octet Rule:

Critical Thinking Exercise

What are some instances to which the octet rule does not apply?   :N̈ = Ö:

Propose two different Lewis structures for a compound consisting of a carbon atom, a hydrogen atom, a nitrogen atom, and an oxygen atom.

Formal charge

Formal charge is the charge an atom would have if the valence electrons in the covalent bond were shared equally.

Formal charge = Valence Electrons − number of π and σ bonds attached − nonbonding electrons.

Question in Context

Two possible structures of *perchloric acid* are shown below. Which one of these is better, and why?

b/c want FC to be closest to O.

Resonance structures

Resonance structures differ only in the distribution of valence electrons.

Critical Thinking Exercise

Arrange the following in the order of decreasing bond strength between the nitrogen and oxygen atoms: nitrate ion (NO_3^-), hydroxylamine (NH_2OH), nitrosyl ion (NO^+), nitryl ion (NO_2^+).

Structures:

Nitrate Ion	Hydroxylamine	Nitrosyl Ion	Nitryl Ion

Directed Practice

- *Physical Sciences Review Notes*: Gen. Chem. Ch. 3
- *General Chemistry Foundation Review:* pp. 9–16
- *Topical Tests*: Bonding Test, Questions 1–11

MOLECULAR GEOMETRY AND VSEPR

VSEPR Stands for

V<u>alence</u> S<u>hare</u> E<u>lectron</u> P<u>air</u> R<u>epulsion</u>

The electron pairs of a molecule orient themselves to be as far apart from one another as possible in three-dimensional space, leading to characteristic geometries.

Nonbonding pairs vs. Bonding pairs

Electronic vs. Molecular geometry (elect= all , mg = w/out lone pair)

Number of Electron Pairs vs. Molecular Geometry

generic formula	molecular geometry	picture	example
AX_2	linear	X—H—X	CO_2
AX_3	trigonal planar		BF_3
AX_2E, AX_2E_2	bent		SO_2, H_2O
AX_4	tetrahedral		CH_4
AX_3E	trigonal pyramidal		NH_3
AX_5	trigonal bipyramidal		PCl_5
AX_6	octahedral		SF_6
AX_4E_2	square planar		XeF_4

Bond dipole vs. Molecular dipole

Molecular dipole depends on two factors:

electronegativity

Shape

Bond   vs.   Molecular

w/ respect to each bond

* where e's consentrated

Ortho-dichlorobenzen
*greatest

para-

meta-

Directed Practice

- *General Chemistry Foundation Review*: pp. 11–16
- *General Chemistry Subject Test 3*: Questions 12–18
- *Topical Tests*: Bonding Test, Questions 1–7

Unit 1

Passage II (Questions 5–7)

While living systems are composed predominantly of the nonmetallic elements carbon, hydrogen, nitrogen, and oxygen, many other elements, including several transition metals, are known to be essential for life. In the plant world, magnesium is an integral part of chlorophyll; among mammals, iron is required for the proper transport of oxygen by hemoglobin in the bloodstream.

The biochemical behavior of the essential transition metals in human beings is based upon their ability to form complexes with various biologically prevalent donor groups. For instance, the Fe^{2+} ions in the heme subunits of hemoglobin can be coordinated to six atoms: five nitrogen atoms (four from the heme porphyrin and one from the protein that composes the bulk of the hemoglobin molecule) and one oxygen atom (from O_2 in arterial blood).

Complex ions, such as $[Cr(NH_3)_6]^{3+}$ and $[Co(CN)_4]^-$, are composed of a central metal atom or ion bonded to a fixed number of anions or neutral molecules known as ligands. These ligands surround the central atom usually with either tetrahedral or octahedral geometry, although several square planar complexes are known. Common examples of ligands important in inorganic systems are neutral molecules such as NH_3, CO, and H_2O, and anions such as CN^-, SCN^-, and the halides. The ligands act as Lewis bases during complex ion formation, and the bonding within the complex ion is generally characterized as coordinate covalent.

The interaction between the complex ion and its counter ion(s), on the other hand, is predominantly coulombic. The number of complex ions and counterions determines the conductance of a solution: Conductance is the ability to carry a charge, and is thus a function of the total charge of the species present (as absolute values) and the number of ions. For example, a $CaCl_2$ solution should be expected to have a greater conductance than an equimolar NaCl solution because of the +2 charge on the calcium ion versus the +1 charge on sodium and to the total of three rather than two ions per formula unit.

-

Scratch Paper
Paragraph 1
Paragraph 2
Paragraph 3
Paragraph 4

Scratch Paper

Stop:

Think:

Where are the transition metals listed located on the periodic table?

Where are Sc and Ti located on the periodic table?

Are any of the elements in the answers similar to Sc or Ti? Can we eliminate these?

Predict:

Match

Stop:

Think:

What part of the passage mentions conductance of a solution?

What determines how good a conductor a solution is?

Predict:

Match

Stop:

Think:

How many electrons does neutral Fe have?

How does the number of electrons change since Fe is now an ion?

In what orbitals will the valance electrons be found?

Predict:

Match

5. Among the transition metals which are essential to life one finds V, Cr, Mn, Fe, Co, Ni, Cu, and Zn, but not Sc or Ti. Which one of the following elements is also likely to be biologically important?

   A. Zr
   B. La
   C. Hf
   D. Mo

6. Which of the following compounds will produce the strongest conductance in a 0.010 M aqueous solution at 25°C?

   A. $[Co(NH_3)_6]PO_4$
   B. $Na_3[CoCl_6]$
   C. $[Cr(NH_3)_4Cl_2]Cl$
   D. $[Cr(NH_3)_5Cl]SO_4$

7. What is the electronic configuration of a free Fe^{3+} ion?

   A. $[Ar]3d^5$
   B. $[Ar]3d^6$
   C. $[Ar]4s^23d^6$
   D. $[Ar]4s^14d^4$

Directed Practice

- *General Chemistry Strategic Supplemental*

INTERMOLECULAR FORCES

Intermolecular forces are a result of electrostatic interactions between different charges or partial charges on different molecules.

1. Ion-dipole

2. Hydrogen bonding

Increasing Strength

3. dipole-dipole

4. dispersion (induced)

Critical Thinking Exercise

Rank the following molecules in order of increasing boling point:

depends on mw and forces

water, acetone, methane, acetic acid, octane

Directed Practice

- *Physical Sciences Review Notes*: Gen. Chem. Chs. 3, 7
- *General Chemistry Subject Test 4*: Questions 11–16
- *High Yield Problem Solving Guide*: pp. 112–115

PROPERTIES OF GASES

Boyle's Law

Boyle's law states that at constant temperature, the pressure (P) and volume (V) of a gas are inversely proportional, or PV = C, where C is a constant.

$$P_1V_1 = P_2V_2$$

Charles' Law

Charles' law states that at constant pressure, the volume and temperature (T) of a gas are directly proportional, V = CT, where C is a constant.

$$\frac{V_1}{T_1} = \frac{V_2}{T_2}$$

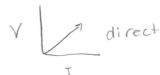

Ideal Gas Law

The ideal gas law incorporates Boyle's law, Charles' law, as well as Avogadro's principle into one equation, PV = nRT.

Critical Thinking Exercise

What is the volume occupied by 3.2 g of oxygen at STP (standard temperature and pressure)?

$$3.2g \times \frac{mol}{32g} = 0.10mol \times 22.4L/mol = 2.24L$$

STP = 273K
1 atm

When do gases deviate from ideal behavior? high pressure, low temp.
(b/c interaction)   (too slow to overcome interaction)

Directed Practice:

- *Physical Sciences Review Notes*: Gen. Chem. Ch. 7
- *General Chemistry Subject Test 1*: Questions 16–17 & 27
- *General Chemistry Discretes Test 2*: Question 22
- *General Chemistry Subject Test 5*: Questions 5 & 6

Unit 1

Dalton's Law

$$P_{total} = P_A + P_B + P_C + ...$$

mole fraction

$$P_A = X_A P_{total}$$

Critical Thinking Exercise

32 g of oxygen, 28 g of nitrogen, and 22 g of carbon dioxide are confined in a container. If the total pressure is 5 atm, what is the partial pressure of each gas?

$$\begin{array}{r} 3 \\ 11\overline{)41.00} \\ 33 \\ \hline \end{array}$$

$$\begin{array}{r} 32 \\ 28 \\ 22 \\ \hline 82 \end{array}$$

$O_2 \rightarrow \frac{32}{82} = \quad ; \quad 2 \text{ atm}$

$N_2 \rightarrow \frac{28}{82} = \quad ; \quad 2 \text{ atm}$

$CO_2 \rightarrow \frac{22}{82} = \quad ; \quad 1 \text{ atm}$

Graham's Law

The speed of gas particles is <u>inversely prop.</u> to the square root of their molecular weight at the same temperature. This is because at the same temperature the particles have <u>same KE</u>.

$$\frac{\text{rate } A}{\text{rate } B} = \sqrt{\frac{MM_B}{MM_A}}$$

Critical Thinking Exercise

Cotton at the ends of a closed tube is saturated with X at one end and Y at the other as shown. If the two vapors react to give a precipitate, where will the precipitate form, assuming that X has a higher molecular weight?

↑MW, ↓ Speed

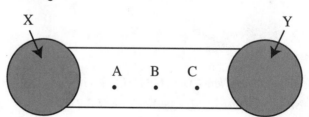

Van der Waals Equation of State

The van der Waals equation accounts for _non-ideal gases_ ; it corrects for the intermolecular forces that exist between gas molecules and the volume occupied by the molecules themselves. These deviations will be most apparent at _high pressure_ and _low volume_ .

$$(P + \frac{n^2a}{V^2})(V - nb) = nRT$$

ideal = smaller
non = greater

Critical Thinking Exercise

What kinds of molecules will have a larger value of a in the van der Waals equation of state, polar ones or nonpolar ones?

Polar (b/c corrects for attractive force)

What kinds of molecules do we expect to have a larger value of b, big ones or small ones?

big ones (b/c take up more space /account for space)

Directed Practice

- *High-Yield Problem Solving Guide*: pp. 132–133
- *General Chemistry Discretes Test 2*: Question 12
- *General Chemistry Subject Test 2*: Question 28
- *Diagnostic Test:* PS Question 1

Passage III (Questions 8–10)

In the 17th century, Robert Boyle performed a series of experiments that demonstrated the relationship between the pressure and volume of a gas at a constant temperature; Boyle discovered that the product of the pressure and volume is constant at a given temperature. His work formed a basis for the ideal gas law.

A chemistry student attempted to reproduce Boyle's experimental results. Each experiment was performed at room temperature, 298 K.

Experiment 1

The student fills a J-shaped tube with 0.05 moles of helium gas. The student then partially fills the tube with mercury and allows the system to equilibrate. The trapped helium occupies a volume and exerts a pressure in the tube that the student is able to measure. The student adds more mercury, decreasing the volume occupied by the gas, and observes an increase in the pressure of the gas. The student adds identical amounts of mercury four more times and records the volume and pressure after each addition. The results are summarized in Table 1.

Experiment 2

The student repeats Experiment 1, but fills the J-tube with 0.05 moles of carbon dioxide instead of helium. The results are summarized in Table 2.

Table 1

Volume occupied by He (L)	Pressure exerted by He (mm Hg)	Pressure × Volume (mm Hg × L)
0.40	2330	931 (± 1)
0.80	1154	931 (± 1)
1.2	775	930 (± 1)
1.6	581	930 (± 1)
2.0	465	930 (± 1)

Table 2

Volume occupied by CO_2 (L)	Pressure exerted by CO_2 (mm Hg)	Pressure × Volume (mm Hg × L)
0.40	2293	917 (± 1)
0.80	1154	923 (± 1)
1.2	771	925 (± 1)
1.6	579	926 (± 1)
2.0	463	927 (± 1)

Scratch Paper

Paragraphs

Experiment 1

Experiment 2

Table 1

Table 2

Scratch Paper

Stop:

Think:

What is the difference between Xe and He?

How would this difference affect the experimental results?

How would a higher temperature affect the experimental results?

Predict:

Match

Stop:

Think:

How is He different from CO_2?

What properties of real gases cause them to deviate from ideal behavior?

Predict:

Match

Stop:

Think:

How do changes in pressure affect ideal behavior?

How do changes in volume affect ideal behavior?

Predict:

Match

8. If the student repeats the experiment at a higher temperature using xenon instead of helium, how would the results be affected?

   A. Neither the larger size of xenon nor the higher temperature would affect the results.

   B. The larger size of xenon would have no effect on the results, but the higher temperature would cause deviation from ideal behavior.

   C. The larger size of xenon would result in deviation from ideal behavior, but the temperature change would not result in a deviation from ideal behavior.

   D. The larger size of xenon and the increased temperature would result in deviation from ideal behavior.

9. The student concludes that helium gas behaves more ideally than carbon dioxide. Which of the following accurately explain why this is so? *interact more Pt*

   I. CO_2 exerts a greater pressure because its molecules have greater volume.

   II. The intermolecular forces between CO_2 molecules are stronger than those in He.

   III. Helium molecules have greater kinetic energy, and therefore behave more ideally. *(always same)*

   A. I only
   B. II only
   C. II and III only
   D. I, II, and III

10. A gas behaves most like an ideal gas at which of the following conditions?

   A. Low pressure and low volume
   B. Low pressure and high volume
   C. High pressure and low volume
   D. High pressure and high volume

HOMEWORK

Review for General Chemistry 1

Topical Tests	❏ Electronic Structure and the Periodic Table Test 1 ❏ Bonding Test 1
Subject Tests	❏ Test 1 (Optional, DD3074) ❏ Test 2 (Optional, DD3075)

Preview for Verbal Reasoning & Writing Sample 1

Verbal Reasoning Strategy and Practice	❏ *Chapters 1–3
Writing Sample section in Verbal Reasoning Strategy and Practice	❏ *Chapters 1 and 2
Foundation Review	❏ Unit 1 (Optional, MM3261A)
Online Workshops	❏ *Critical Reading Skills

CRITICAL READING

Verbal Reasoning
and Writing Sample 1

CRITICAL READING: APPLYING THE PROCESS

- Critical Reading
- The Kaplan 5-Step Method for the Writing Sample
- Prewriting

VERBAL REASONING

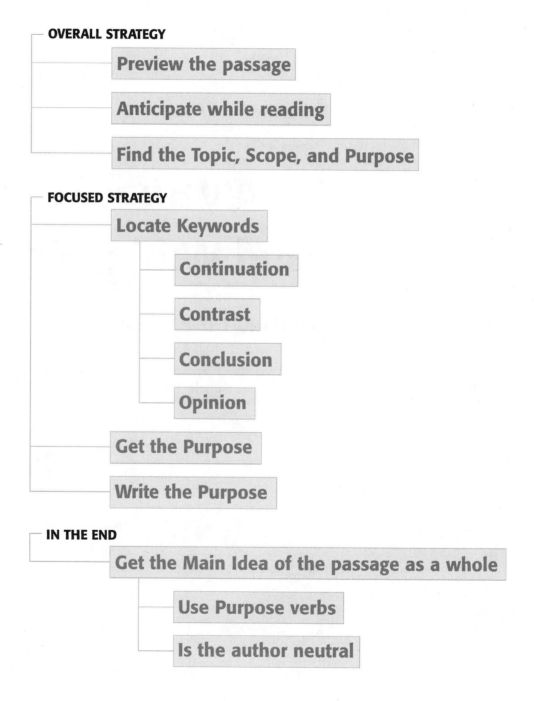

OVERALL STRATEGY

Preview the passage

Anticipate while reading

Find the Topic, Scope, and Purpose

FOCUSED STRATEGY

Locate Keywords

Continuation

Contrast

Conclusion

Opinion

Get the Purpose

Write the Purpose

IN THE END

Get the Main Idea of the passage as a whole

Use Purpose verbs

Is the author neutral

KEYWORDS

Continuation – more is coming ; and , more over, furthermore

Contrast – opposition;
        although
        but
        however
        despite

Conclusion – summary (end) ;
        in conclusion
        hence
        consequently

Opinion – clearify authors purpose (overall "vibe")

A HUMANITIES PASSAGE

The social novel has always presupposed a substantial amount of social stability. The ideal social novel had been written by Jane Austen, a great artist who enjoyed the luxury of being able to take society for granted; it was there, and seemed steady beneath her glass, Napoleon or no Napoleon. But soon it would not be steady beneath anyone's glass, and the novelist's attention had necessarily to shift from the gradations within society to the fate of society itself. It is at this point that the political novel comes to be written — the kind in which the idea of society, as distinct from the mere unquestioned workings of society, has penetrated the consciousness of the characters in all of its profoundly problematic aspects.

The political novel — I have in mind its ideal form — is peculiarly a work of internal tensions. To be a novel at all, it must contain the usual representation of human behavior and feeling; yet it must also absorb into its stream of movement the hard and perhaps insoluble pellets of modern ideology. The conflict is inescapable: the novel tries to confront experience in its immediacy and closeness, while ideology is by its nature general and inclusive. Yet it is precisely from this conflict that the political novel gains its interest and takes on the aura of high drama.

Scratch Paper

Paragraph 1 – Social vs. political Novel

Paragraph 2 – Political novel = study of conflict

Critical Thinking Exercise

Suppose Jane Austen had written in a letter to her sister, "My strongest characters were those forced by circumstance to confront basic questions about the society they lived in." What relevance would this have to the passage?

In opposition to authors view

Because it exposes the impersonal claims of ideology to the pressures of private emotion, the political novel must always be in a state of internal warfare, always on the verge of becoming something other than itself. The political novelist establishes a complex system of intellectual movements, in which his own opinion is one of the most active yet not entirely dominating movers. Are we not close here to one of the secrets of the novel in general? I mean the vast respect which the great novelist is ready to offer the whole idea of opposition, the opposition he needs to allow for in his book against his own predispositions and yearnings and fantasies.

Abstraction, then, is confronted with the flux of experience, the monolith of program with the *[set up contrast]* richness and diversity of motive, the purity of ideal with the contaminations of action. The political novel turns characteristically to an apolitical temptation: in *The Possessed* to the notion that redemption is possible only to sinners who have suffered greatly; in Conrad's *Nostromo* and *Under Western Eyes* to the resources of private affection and gentleness; in *Man's Fate* to the metaphysical allurements of heroism as they reveal themselves in a martyr's death; in Silone's *Bread and Wine* to the discovery of peasant simplicity as a foil to urban corruption; and in *Darkness at Noon* to the abandoned uses of the personal will. This, so to say, is the pastoral element that is indispensable to the political novel, indispensable for providing it with polarity and tension.

Scratch Paper

Paragraph 3 — opposition = major force in political novel

Paragraph 4 — Root of conflict; apolitical tension

Topic: Political novel

Scope: Characteristics

Purpose: To detail components of political novel

Critical Thinking Exercise

Some critics assert that political novels can serve as textbooks for the study of the writer's political views. Why might the author of this passage NOT agree?

active but not most dominate

THE PAYOFF

Scratch Paper

Stop:

Think:

What are "literary works that focus on ideological issues"?

Where can you find the author's attitude?

Predict:

Match

Stop:

Think:

Where is Jane Austen mentioned?

What is the author's purpose there?

Predict:

Match

1. The author's attitude toward literary works that focus on ideological issues can best be described as:

   A. appreciative of their ability to subordinate dramatic appeal to an exposition of serious themes.
   B. puzzled over their lack of acceptance by the general public.
   C. confident that their inherent tensions can be a source of strength.
   D. disappointed by their confusion of personal experiences with ideological arguments.

2. The author includes a discussion of Jane Austen primarily in order to:

   A. cite an example of a novelist who successfully combines elements of ideology and human experience.
   B. show the roots of the political novel in relation to earlier fiction traditions.
   C. criticize the social novel for presenting only stable social structures.
   D. argue that great novelists are not limited by their social backgrounds.

Scratch Paper

Stop:

Think:

What do the words "according to the passage" tell you?

Where is the "emergence of the political novel" mentioned?

How do you know what is "important" to the author?

Predict:

Match

Stop:

Think:

What does it mean to say that accepting the author's view requires endorsing a position?

Where do we find the author's overall views?

Predict:

Match

3. According to the passage, which of the following was an important factor in the emergence of the political novel?

   A. The critical success of novelists like Jane Austen.

   B. The development of the "pastoral" element in novels like *Darkness at Noon.*

   C. Increased awareness of the concept of societal change.

   D. Agreement among critics that every great novel involves some kind of [conflict].

4. Adopting the author's views as presented in the passage would most likely require endorsing which of the following positions?

   A. Human emotions and ideology are distinct categories that can conflict.

   B. Consciousness of societal conditions is necessary for the development of any new form of literature.

   C. The social novel owes much of its dramatic power to the conflict between rationality and human experience.

   D. Before the invention of the political novel, most novelists could not overcome their own prejudices.

A NATURAL SCIENCE PASSAGE

Astronomers noted more than 150 years ago that sunspots wax and wane in number in an 11-year cycle. Ever since, people have speculated that the solar cycle might exert some influence on the earth's weather. In the twentieth century, for example, workers linked the solar cycle to droughts in the American Midwest. Until recently, however, none of these correlations has held up under close scrutiny.

One problem is that sunspots themselves are so poorly understood. Observations have revealed that the swirly smudges represent areas of intense magnetic activity where the sun's radioactive energy has been blocked, and that they are considerably cooler than bright regions of the sun. Workers have not been able, however, to determine just how sunspots are created or what effect they have on the solar constant (a misnomer that refers to the sun's total radiance at any instant).

The latter question, at least, now seems to have been resolved by data from the Solar Maximum Mission satellite, which has monitored the solar constant since 1980, the peak of the last solar cycle. As the number of sunspots decreased through 1986, the satellite recorded a gradual dimming of the sun. Over the next year, as sunspots proliferated, the sun brightened. According to Richard C. Willson, the data suggest that the sun is .1 percent more luminous at the peak of the solar cycle, when the number of sunspots is greatest, than at its nadir.

Scratch Paper

Paragraph 1 — Solar cycle to weather

Paragraph 2 — Sunspots poorly understood + effect on suns radiance

Paragraph 3 — increase sunspots = increase ~~suns~~ radiance

The data show that sunspots do not themselves make the sun shine brighter. Quite the contrary. When a sunspot appears, it initially causes the sun to dim slightly, but then — after a period of weeks or months — islands of brilliance called faculas usually emerge near the sunspot and more than compensate for its dimming effect. Willson says faculas may represent regions where energy that initially was blocked beneath a sunspot has finally breached the surface.

Does the subtle fluctuation in the solar constant manifest itself in the earth's weather? Some recent reports offer statistical evidence that it does, albeit rather indirectly. The link seems to be mediated by a phenomenon known as the quasi-biennial oscillation (QBO), a 180-degree shift in the direction of stratospheric winds above the Tropics that occurs about every two years. Labitzke and van Loon were the first to uncover the QBO link. They gathered pressure readings from various latitudes and altitudes during three recent solar cycles. They found no correlation between the solar cycle and their data until they sorted the data into two categories: those gathered during the QBO's west phase (when stratospheric winds blow west) and those gathered during its east phase. A remarkable correlation appeared: temperatures and pressures coincident with the QBO's west phase rose and fell in accordance with the solar cycle.

Scratch Paper

Paragraph 4 → Faculas cause brightness

Paragraph 5 — correlation b/w solar constant + weather

Topic: Sunspots

Scope: How sunspots relate to weather

Purpose: ~~f P~~ Prove sunspots relate to weather

THE PAYOFF

Scratch Paper

Stop:

Think:

Where does the "Solar Maximum Mission" appear?

What is the author's purpose there?

Predict:

Match

Stop:

Think:

What are we told about the occurrence of faculas in the passage?

Where is there a reference to a solar cycle?

What relevance does the question's new information have there?

Predict:

Match

5. The author refers to data gathered by the Solar Maximum Mission satellite primarily in order to:

   A. illustrate that fluctuations in the solar constant are difficult to monitor.
   B. suggest that further research is needed to identify the causes of sunspots.
   C. demonstrate that sunspots have a verifiable effect on the solar constant.
   D. assert that changes in the solar constant are reflected in the earth's weather.

6. Suppose that researchers determine that the number of faculas on the sun's surface rises and falls in a 20-year cycle. This new information would most challenge the claim that:

   A. faculas represent energy regions formed in response to the appearance of sunspots.
   B. the initial appearance of sunspots causes the solar constant to drop temporarily.
   C. sunspots are areas that are cooler than the most luminous regions of the sun.
   D. the emergence of faculas increases the sun's total radiance.

Scratch Paper

Stop:

Think:

What is the context?

What is the author's purpose there?

Predict:

Match

Stop:

Think:

What are the author's overall opinions?

How would they apply to the QBO?

Predict:

Match

7. The author's reference to the solar constant as a "misnomer" (paragraph 2) indicates that:

   A.   the sun's radiance has not been accurately measured.
   B.   the sun's total radiance fluctuates.
   C.   solar radiance is dramatically affected by external forces.
   D.   the solar constant equals the average radiance of the sun over a long period of time.

8. The author of the passage would most likely argue that the solar cycle's influence on temperatures and pressures during the QBO's west phase is:

   A.   likely to be offset by the solar cycle's influence during the QBO's east phase.
   B.   due to the indirect link between the QBO's west phase and the weather.
   C.   limited to rainfall in the American Midwest.
   D.   likely to discourage further research into the relationship between sunspots and the earth's weather.

Unit 1

A SOCIAL SCIENCE PASSAGE

Divided power creates a built-in hurdle to making and carrying out fiscal policy. The hurdle is low when the president is articulating a policy that has broad support. It can lead to erratic shifts of policy when the president is leading in a direction in which the public and its representatives do not want to go. Deadlocks are rare, but can be serious. The failure to reduce the huge structural deficit of the mid-1980s largely reflects the fact that the president's solution — drastic reduction of the federal role in the domestic economy — did not command broad support.

The simple notion that the president proposes and Congress disposes is greatly complicated by the fragmentation of power within each branch. Moreover, efforts to make fiscal policy more coherent have added new power centers without consolidating old ones. Presidents have tried various coordination mechanisms including "troika" arrangements and an almost infinite variety of committees with varying responsibilities. The system works tolerably well or exceedingly creakily, depending on the president's personal style and the personalities involved. But it encourages battling over turf as well as substance. One wonders whether it is not time to give our president the equivalent of a finance minister charged with functions now diffused to our budget director, Council of Economic Advisers, and Treasury Secretary. The fragmentation of power and responsibility is, of course, even more extreme in the Congress. The legislative branch also has a long history of attempts to make taxing and spending policy more coherent by adding new coordinating institutions — appropriations committees, budget committees, a congressional budget office — without eliminating or consolidating any old ones.

Concern that the economic policy process is not working has spawned proposals for drastic change that move in two quite different directions: one toward circumscribing the discretion of elected officials by putting economic policy on automatic pilot and the other toward making elected officials more directly responsible to voters. The automatic pilot approach flows from the perspective that the decisions of elected officials cannot be counted on to produce economic policy in the social interest, but are likely to be biased toward excessive spending, growing deficits, special interest tax and spending programs, and easier money. A way to overcome these biases is to agree in advance on strict rules, such as a fixed monetary growth path, or constitutionally required budget balance. The other direction of reform reflects the contrasting view that the diffusion of responsibility in our government makes it too difficult for the electorate to enforce its will by holding elected officials responsible for their policies. The potential for deadlock would be reduced if the country moved toward a parliamentary system, or found a way to hold political parties more strictly accountable for proposing or carrying out policies.

Scratch Paper

Paragraph 1 – divided power hinders exec. of fiscal policy

Paragraph 2 – problems w/ divided power → authorsay consolidate

Paragraph 3 – 2 solutions: autopilot vs. responsibility

Topic: Divided power

Scope: How hinders fiscal policy

Purpose: To describe and give solution

Scratch Paper

Stop:

Think:

Is fiscal policy-making a detail, or part of the author's main idea?

What evidence supports the author's argument?

Predict:

Match

Stop:

Think:

What ideas does the author express just before this statement?

What ideas follow it?

Predict:

Match

9. Which of the following, if true, would most strengthen the author's argument about fiscal policy-making?

   A. Countries that lack coherent and efficient procedures for determining fiscal policy also tend to have unjust electoral systems.
   B. Presidents have only been successful in making new policies when their own party controls Congress.
   C. Members of Congress whose votes do not reflect the will of the people are typically not reelected.
   D. Public opinion is often sharply divided with regard to a president's policy proposals.

10. In the context of the passage, "The simple notion that the president proposes and Congress disposes" (paragraph 2) represents:

    A. an ideal that is often unattainable given the diffusion of responsibility in government.
    B. an example of the misperception that Congress is too divided to put forth its own proposals.
    C. evidence that government bureaucrats have added new power centers without removing old ones.
    D. an oversimplification of the fact that efforts have been made to make fiscal policy more coherent.

Critical Thinking Exercise

Do we know whether the author prefers the "automatic pilot" solution or "accountability"?

Scratch Paper

Stop:

Think:

Where are "the mid-1980s" mentioned in the passage?

What is the author's purpose?

What is the relevance of "governmental influence in the domestic economy"?

Predict:

Match

Stop

Think:

How can you quickly locate each claim?

Predict:

Match

Stop:

Think:

Where is the "automatic pilot approach" described?

What are the characteristics of a solution it might suggest?

Predict:

Match

11. Suppose that during the mid-1980s, Congress sought to lessen the extent of governmental influence in the domestic economy. What relevance would this have to the passage?

    A. It supports the author's claim that presidents are largely responsible for the system's inefficiency.
    B. It supports the author's claim that the system has worked tolerably well at times.
    C. It weakens the author's claim that the failure to reduce the deficit in the 1980s was the result of governmental deadlock.
    D. It weakens the author's claim that power is more fragmented in the legislative branch than in the executive branch.

12. Which of the following is a claim made in the passage but NOT supported by evidence, explanation, or example?

    A. Putting the economy on automatic pilot may circumvent the problems caused by elected officials.
    B. The proposals to revamp the economic policy process are based on very different assumptions.
    C. A president can have difficulty pushing through a fiscal policy when the public is opposed to it.
    D. There would be less deadlock if a parliamentary system were adopted.

13. An advocate of the "automatic pilot approach" to fiscal reform would probably support which of the following proposals?

    A. Legislating a limit on the size of the federal budget deficit
    B. Placing all power over economic policy in the hands of an official selected by the president
    C. Publicizing the voting records of those elected officials who are involved in making fiscal policy
    D. Relying on Supreme Court rulings to determine the constitutionality of new fiscal regulations

THE WRITING SAMPLE

Consider this statement:

To run a successful campaign, a political candidate must treat complex issues as if they were simple choices.

Write a unified essay in which you perform the following tasks: Explain what you think the above statement means. Describe a specific situation in which a political candidate could run a successful campaign by not treating complex issues as if they were simple choices. Discuss what you think determines when a political candidate should or should not simplify complex issues.

Task 1:

Task 2:

Task 3:

Goals:

TEN TYPICAL PROBLEMS IN STUDENT ESSAYS

	Symptom	Cause
1	They start without a clear sense of purpose.	Rushing → sol = prewrite
2	They focus on 1 or 2 tasks but neglect others.	didn't know → stick to plan / prewrite
3	They focus on personal opinion instead of tasks.	opinion → do not include
4	They are overly general lacking specific examples.	lack knowledge → read news paper
5	They fulfill tasks separately but fail to unify.	→ transitions ; keep ideas together
6	The best ideas are jammed at the end.	→ stick to plan
7	They include digressions.	→ stick to plan
8	They merely repeat ideas without deepening them.	→ Focused and breif
9	They end in mid-thought or with a hasty conclusion.	→ Time management
10	They are not proofread for obvious errors.	→ Time management

Crisis Prevention Tip

What two things do students fear most on the Writing Sample section of the MCAT?

1. Time
2. Ideas

THE KAPLAN 5-STEP METHOD FOR THE WRITING SAMPLE

STEP 1

Read and Annotate

locate terms to define
Statement for related ideas

STEP 2

Prewrite Each Task

STEP 3

Clarify Main Idea and Plan

Unify (open close)

Time: _____5 min._____

STEP 4

Write

Time: _____23 min._____

STEP 5

Proofread

Time: _____2 min._____

STEP 1

Read and Annotate

Consider this statement:

To run a successful campaign, a political candidate must treat complex issues as if they were simple choices.

Write a unified essay in which you perform the following tasks: Explain what you think the above statement means. Describe a specific situation in which a political candidate could run a successful campaign by not treating complex issues as if they were simple choices. Discuss what you think determines when a political candidate should or should not simplify complex issues.

Purpose: To clarify what the statement means and what the specific instructions require.

Meaning: Make complex issues simple

Definitions: Complex issues, simple choices, successful campaign

STEP 2

Prewrite Each Task

Consider this statement:

To run a successful campaign, a political candidate must treat complex issues as if they were simple choices.

Write a unified essay in which you perform the following tasks: Explain what you think the above statement means. Describe a specific situation in which a political candidate could run a successful campaign by not treating complex issues as if they were simple choices. Discuss what you think determines when a political candidate should or should not simplify complex issues.

Purpose: To develop a clear interpretation of the statement.

1	Provide an example Abraham Lincoln (slavery)

2	Counter Example
	  Healthcare policy (know specifics) when do we not make
	  Environment complex issue simple?

3	When / when not? ① equal rights (right and wrong) ② any education (benefits

STEP 3

Clarify Main Idea and Plan

Consider this statement:

To run a successful campaign, a political candidate must treat complex issues as if they were simple choices.

Write a unified essay in which you perform the following tasks: Explain what you think the above statement means. Describe a specific situation in which a political candidate could run a successful campaign by not treating complex issues as if they were simple choices. Discuss what you think determines when a political candidate should or should not simplify complex issues.

Purpose: To ensure that you have a main idea that runs through all paragraphs.

How all works together

STEP 4

Write

Consider this statement:

To run a successful campaign, a political candidate must treat complex issues as if they were simple choices.

Write a unified essay in which you perform the following tasks: Explain what you think the above statement means. Describe a specific situation in which a political candidate could run a successful campaign by not treating complex issues as if they were simple choices. Discuss what you think determines when a political candidate should or should not simplify complex issues.

Purpose: To build an essay based on your prewrite.

Crisis Prevention Tip

What can you do to improve your writing style and grammar?

A LOOK AT HOW YOUR SCORE IS DETERMINED

Unit 1

	6	5	4	3	2	1
Tasks	Fully addresses all tasks	Substantially addresses all tasks	Adequately addresses all tasks	Neglects or distorts one or more tasks	Seriously neglects or distorts one or more tasks	Does not address the tasks
Depth	Shows depth, synthesis, and complex thought	Shows some depth, synthesis and complex thought	Has ideas but lacks depth and synthesis	Has some ideas but is simplistic or superficial	Lacks sufficient ideas	Confuses ideas
Organization	Sharply focused, unified, and coherent	Coherently organized	Coherent, but has digressions	Weak organization	Confusing organization	Lacks organization
Writing	Superior vocabulary and sentence structure	Above-average vocabulary and sentence structure	Adequate vocabulary and sentence structure	Erratic vocabulary and sentence structure	Confusing language and recurrent errors	Seriously flawed and impossible to understand

Bottom line _____

_____

Crisis Prevention Tip

How can I hurt my score?

STEP 5

Proofread

Purpose: To detect errors that affect clarity.

In a real democracy all citizens have the right to vote, and a politician must appeal to a diverse populace with many different views. Most often the politician does this by running their campaign as if complex issues were simple choices instead of fairly complex issues, which campaigns are usually successful because most citizens cannot easily understand the complexity of a given issue or worse, do not even care, like in a presidencial, for example, a politician normally finds success discussing issues such as the economy or social security in simple terms. Most citizens are only concerned with pressing problems that effect their lives. If the politician attempts to educate the voters on the details of economic theory, they will not be as successful as they had stuck to a rudimentary discussion of how the economy or social security policy affects you.

But there are times when politicians are actually more likely to win if they treat complex issues as what they really are: compicated. If, for example, a country has built up a record national debt that is dragging down the economy, it may be that the politician is best off just leveling with the voters. To pay off the debt, the president will need to raise . . .

PRACTICING STEPS 1 THROUGH 3

Consider this statement:

Opportunity favors those who work hard.

Write a unified essay in which you perform the following tasks: Explain what you think the above statement means. Describe a specific situation in which a hard-working person might not be favored by opportunity. Discuss what you think determines when opportunity does or does not favor those who work hard.

Definitions: _oppurtunity , hardwork_

Meaning of statement: _hard work leads to oppurtunity_

1	Example Pilgrams education
2	Counter Example well connected
3	When /where ① ②

*money, time, edu

Unit 1

The Lesson Continues
on the Next Page →

HOMEWORK

Review for Verbal Reasoning & Writing Sample 1

Verbal Reasoning Strategy and Practice	❑ *Test 1
Writing Sample section in Verbal Reasoning Strategy and Practice	❑ *Chapter 3
Section Tests	❑ Verbal Reasoning Test 1
Online Workshops	❑ *Critical Reading Basics ❑ *Writing Sample Skills: Grammar and Usage ❑ *Writing Sample Skills: Writing ❑ *Diagnosing Questions Workshop ❑ *Arguments Dissection Basics Workshop

Preview for Organic Chemistry 1

Organic Chemistry Review Notes	❑ *Chapters 1–5
Foundation Review	❑ Unit 1 (Optional, MM3257A)
Online Workshops	❑ *Nomenclature and Functional Groups

* Required for Higher Score Guarantee.

UNIT ONE

CRITICAL READING

Organic Chemistry 1

CRITICAL READING: ANALYSIS

- Isomerism
- Substitution Reactions
- Elimination Reactions

KAPLAN PASSAGE STRATEGY

Unit 1

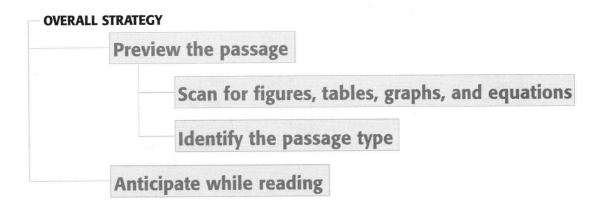

OVERALL STRATEGY

Preview the passage

Scan for figures, tables, graphs, and equations

Identify the passage type

Anticipate while reading

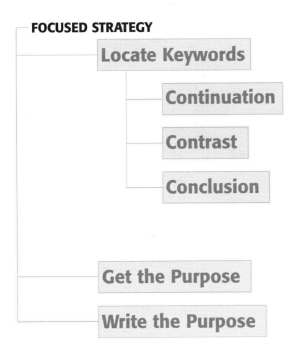

FOCUSED STRATEGY

Locate Keywords

Continuation

Contrast

Conclusion

Get the Purpose

Write the Purpose

Passage I (Questions 1–4)

Styrene is used extensively in the manufacture of plastics, rubber, and resins. It is a colorless liquid with a sweet, aromatic odor at low concentrations, but with a sharp, penetrating, disagreeable odor at high levels. Styrene is classified as a possible human carcinogen.

Styrene can be synthesized in the lab by either reacting sulfuric acid with compound A ($C_8H_{10}O$) or using zinc metal with compound B ($C_8H_8Br_2$) in ethanol. Compound B can be made from compound C (C_8H_9Br) by generating Br_2 gas *in situ* from the reaction of potassium bromate and hydrobromic acid and irradiation with a lamp. Compound A is characterized by its mild hyacinth odor and the ester, D ($C_{10}H_{12}O_2$), formed by the reaction of A with acetic acid and sulfuric acid, has a fruity smell.

Compound A, will undergo oxidation to E (C_8H_8O) in the presence of bleach and acetic acid. Compound E, which is characterized by its floral aroma, has a boiling point of 202°C and a refractive index of 1.5372. The semicarbazone derivative of E has a melting point of 198°C.

The following diagram summarizes the transformations mentioned above.

Figure 1

Scratch Paper
Paragraph 1
Paragraph 2
Paragraph 3
Figure 1

Directed Practice

• *Topical Tests*: Oxygen Containing Compounds Test 1 (Passage I)

Scratch Paper

Stop:

Think:

Circle the functional groups in compound **F**.

What's the difference between amino, amido and imino functional groups?

Predict:

Match

1. Compound **E** reacts with semicarbazide to form the semicarbazone **F** according to the following equation:

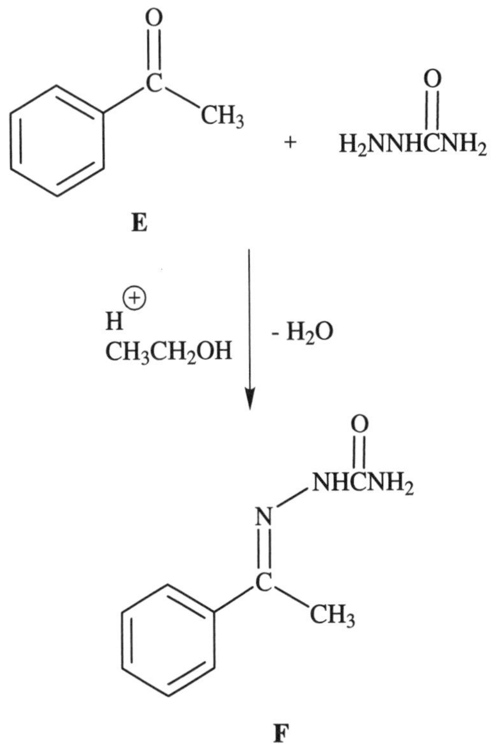

E

$+$

$H_2NNHCNH_2$

$$H^{\oplus}$$
CH_3CH_2OH | $- H_2O$

F

Compound **F** contains what functional groups?

A. imine, amine, amide
B. imine, amine, carbonyl
C. amine, amide, hydroxyl
D. phenyl, amide, imine

Stop:

Think:

What are the rules for IUPAC nomenclature?

What's the primary functional group in compound **A**?

Predict:

Match

2. What is the correct IUPAC name for compound **A**?

A. 1-phenylethanol
B. 2-ethylphenol
C. 2-phenylethanol
D. methyl phenyl ketone

Scratch Paper

Stop:

Think:

What's a dehydration reaction?

What's the geometry at the carbon atom before dehydration?

What's the geometry at the carbon atom after dehydration?

Predict:

Match

Stop:

Think:

Look at Figure 1 for a similar reaction.

What structure can be drawn to help answer the question?

Predict:

Match

3. During the dehydration reaction of Compound **A** with H_2SO_4, what change occurs in the hybridization of the carbon atom bearing the hydroxyl group?

   A. sp^3 to sp
   B. sp^3 to sp^2
   C. sp^2 to sp
   D. sp^2 to sp^3

4. If 3-phenyl-2-butanol were treated with NaOCl and CH_3COOH, the product would be:
   A. methyl phenyl ketone
   B. 1-phenyl-2-butanone
   C. 3-phenyl-2-butanone
   D. ethyl phenyl ketone

Unit 1

Critical Thinking Exercise

Scratch Paper

Stop:

Think:

Predict:

Match

5. According to the graph below, which straight chain alkanes exist in the liquid state at $-50°C$? *(n is the number of carbons)*

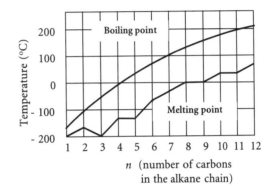

A. ethane, butane, pentane
B. pentane, hexane, octane
C. propane, butane, hexane
D. pentane, octane, urethane

Directed Practice

• *Biological Sciences Review Notes*: Orgo. Ch. 4

ISOMERISM

Isomer types and definitions

Same molecular formula differen structure

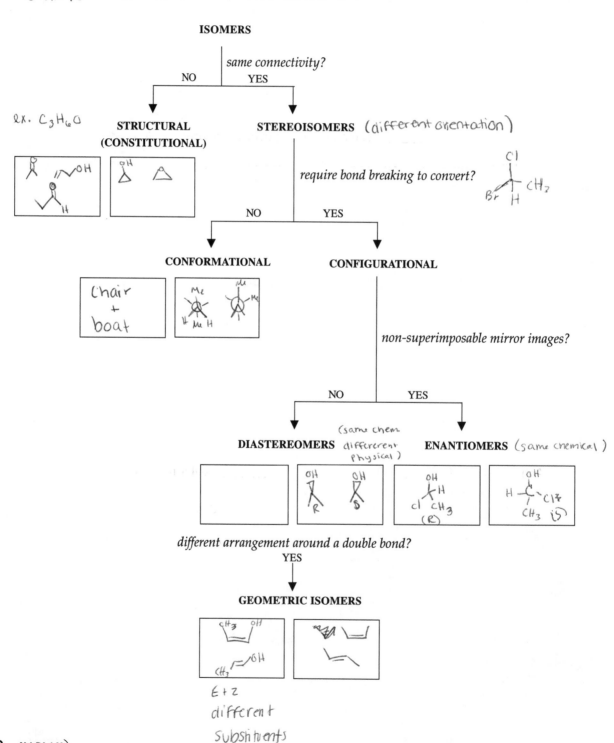

Conformational Isomers — rotation about single bond (w/out breaking)

Torsional Strain (aka)

Torsional strain is caused by the repulsion between <u>electron clouds (adjacent carbons)</u> when two or more atoms are in close proximity.

Staggered vs. Eclipsed

In <u>staggered</u> conformations, groups on adjacent carbons are as far apart as possible. In <u>eclipsed</u> conformations, groups are as close together as possible.

Ethane C_2H_6

<u>Staggered</u>

Ethane C_2H_6

<u>eclipsed</u>

Gauche vs. Anti

Gauche and Anti are types of <u>staggered</u> conformations.

Butane C_4H_{10}

<u>gauche</u>

Butane C_4H_{10}

<u>anti</u>

Unit 1

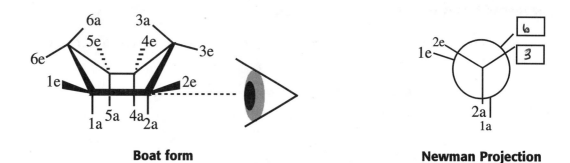

Boat form   **Newman Projection**

Torsional Strain in Cycloalkanes

boat = energetically unfavorable
chair = energetically favorable (staggered)

Angle strain

Angle strain occurs when bond angle deviates from that predicted by VSEPR theory.

Hybridization of Carbons				
Types	**Configuration**	**Hybrid**	**Angle**	**# of π bonds**
Alkanes	tetrahedral	Sp^3	109.5	0
Alkenes	planar	Sp^2	120	1
Alkynes	linear	Sp	180	2

Ring strain occurs from both angle and torsional strain.

deviation → ex. cyclopropane

Directed Practice

- *Topical Tests:* Hydrocarbons Test 1

Unit 1

Nonbonded Strain

Nonbonded strain refers to the __electron cloud__ [*repulsion*] between groups bonded to nonadjacent atoms.

[*non bonded strain*]

Chair form   **Boat form**

Cycloalkane Conformations

Critical Thinking Exercise

Do the following substituents of the following molecules occupy axial or equatorial positions?

[↳same   ↳opposite (*bigger equitorial*)]

[*equitorial*]   [*both equitorial*]   [*axial*] [*equitorial*]

Geometric Isomers

Cis–trans isomers

The *cis-trans* designation is used for relatively simple alkenes in which one non-hydrogen group is attached to each side of the double bond.

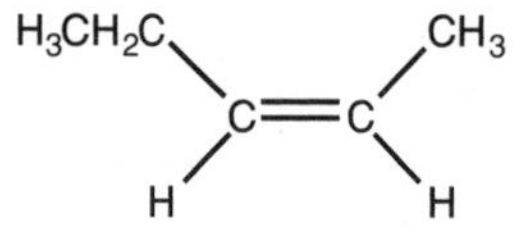

cis

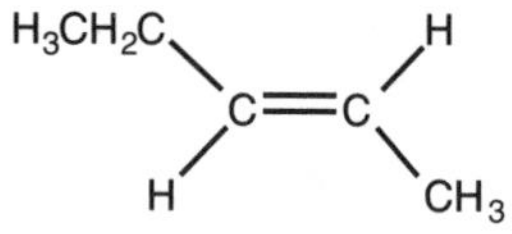

trans

(E)–(Z) isomers

The *(E)–(Z)* designation is used for more complex alkenes.

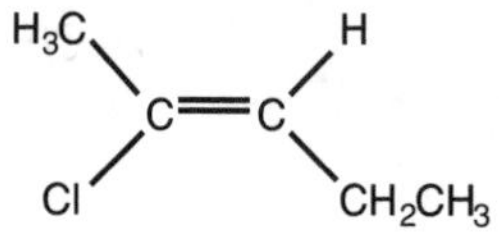

(Z)-2-chloro-2-pentene 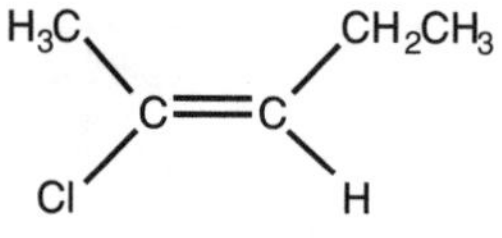   (E)-2-chloro-2-pentene

* Priority goes highest MW
  high
  2 on same side = Z
  2 on opposite side = E

Chiral centers

A carbon atom that has four different groups bonded to it is a chiral carbon. Chiral centers are named using the (R)/(S) system.

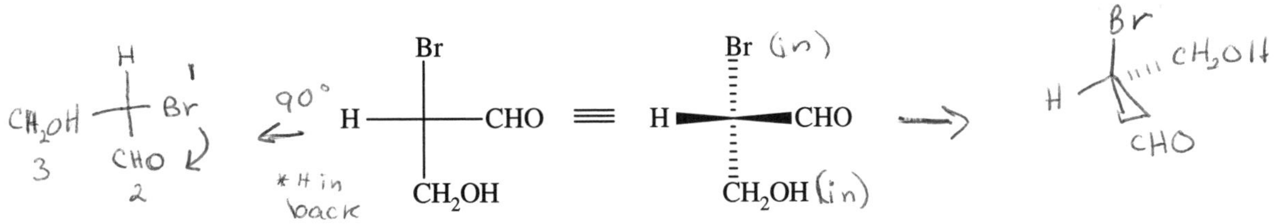

(handwritten) CH₂OH —|— Br   3   CHO   2   90°   *H in back   #then # priority

H —|— CHO   CH₂OH

Br (in)   H ▬|▬ CHO   CH₂OH (in)

Br   H ⟍ ‖ CH₂OH   CHO

(S) 2-bromo-3-hydroxypropanal

(handwritten) R = right , S = left → actual opposite what get w/ 90° rule so (S)

Critical Thinking Exercise

Scratch Paper

Stop:

Think:

Predict:

Match

6. Which molecule is an enantiomer to the others?

A.

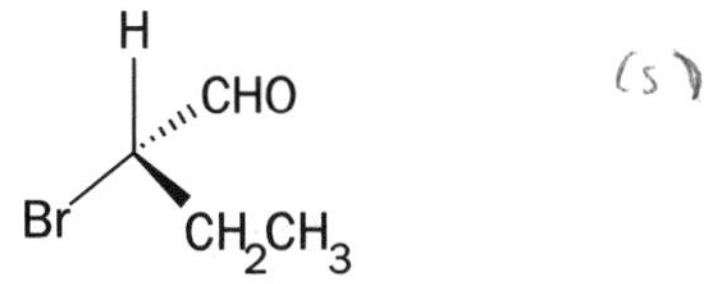

(s)

B.

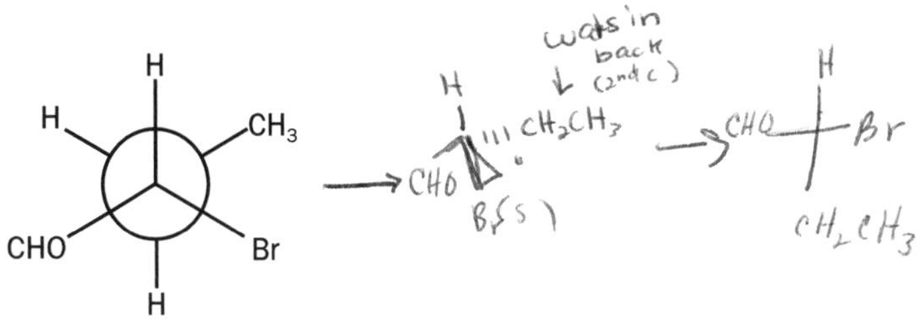

(handwritten) was in back ↓ (2nd c) CHO ⟍ ‖ CH₂CH₃ B(S) → CHO —|— Br CH₂CH₃

C.

(R)

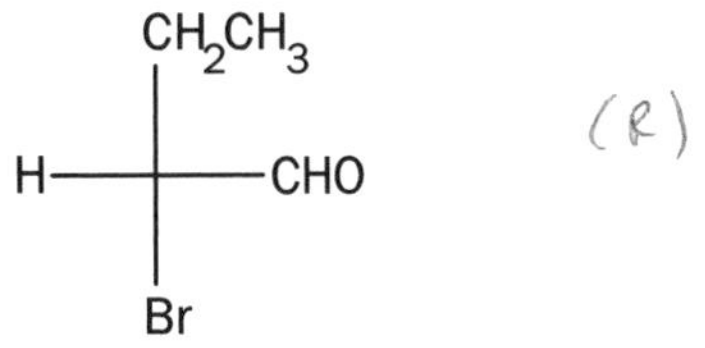

D.

(s)

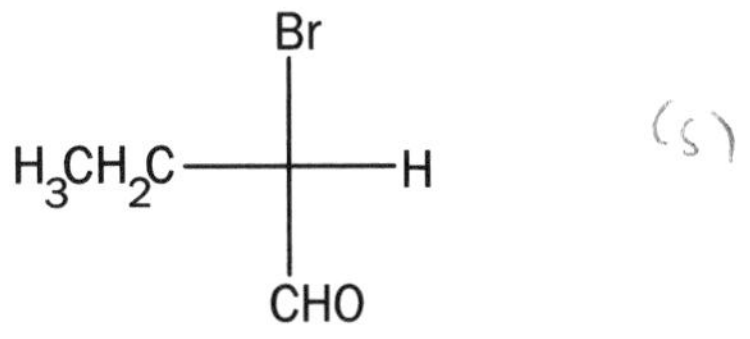

Meso Compounds - line & symetry in center

(dont rotate polarized light $\alpha_0 = 0$)

Diastereomers and Enantiomers

Isomerism and Physical Properties

Critical Thinking Exercise

Which has a higher boiling point, cis-2-butene or trans-2-butene?

cis → b/c dipole

The Lesson Continues
on the Next Page

Passage II (Questions 7–11)

A student performed an experiment in order to separate racemic α-phenylethylamine into its two enantiomeric components. This was accomplished through a chemical reaction of the amine with an optically active acid, (+)-mandelic acid.

The student added (+)-mandelic acid, 0.10 mol, to methanol, and heated the resulting solution to 60°C. Racemic α-phenylethylamine, 0.10 mol, was then added to the flask. A proton NMR spectrum of the resulting mixture gave peaks at 2.0, 5.0, 5.4 and 7.3 ppm. The mixture was left to stand overnight, during which time a white solid crystallized. The solid and solution were separated by vacuum filtration. The solvent was evaporated from the remaining solution, leaving behind a second solid residue. These solids were separately mixed with 50 mL of aqueous sodium hydroxide. In each case, an oily layer formed above the aqueous layer. The organic layers were each separated from the aqueous layers in a separatory funnel by two extractions with ether. The specific rotations of the organic layers, [α], were each measured and determined to be –153° and +153° for the organic layers from the first and second solids, respectively.

Scratch Paper

Paragraph 1

Paragraph 2

Scratch Paper

Stop:

Think:

In what ways do the solids behave similarly?

In what ways are they different?

In what ways do different kinds of isomers behave similarly?

Predict:

Match

Stop:

Think:

What is specific rotation?

How is it related to the actual measured rotation?

How does concentration come into play?

Predict:

Match

7. Based on the information in the passage, the two solids formed were:

    A.   the same compound.
    B.   (+)-mandelic acid and its phenylethylamine salt.
    C.   two diastereomeric phenylethylamine salts.
    D.   two enantiomeric phenylethylamine salts.

8. In trying to calculate the specific rotation of (+)- phenylethylamine from its observed rotation, a chemist had inadvertently recorded the concentration as twice what it actually was. How would his calculated value compare to the true specific rotation?

    A.   It would be the same.
    B.   It would be greater than the true value.
    C.   It would be less than the true value.
    D.   It would be less than the true value but only at a certain concentration.

Scratch Paper

Stop:

Think:

What kind of isomers are we trying to resolve?

What is needed to accomplish this?

Are racemic mixtures optically active or inactive?

Predict:

Match

Stop

Think:

What components do we expect to see in the name of this molecule?

Note that the structure of (+)-tartaric acid is given as a Fischer projection.

Predict:

Match

9. What would be the effect on the resolution process if racemic mandelic acid were used instead of (+)-mandelic acid?

   A. The racemic α-phenylethylamine mixture would separate in the same way.
   B. The enantiomers could not be separated.
   C. The amine mandelate salts would become optically inactive.
   D. Diastereomers would form but could not be separated.

10. Another common optical resolving agent is (+)-tartaric acid, whose structure is shown below:

$$\begin{array}{c} COOH \\ H \!-\!\!\!\mid\!\!\!-\! OH \\ HO \!-\!\!\!\mid\!\!\!-\! H \\ COOH \end{array}$$

   What is the correct IUPAC name for tartaric acid?

   A. 2,3-Dihydroxybutanedioic acid
   B. 1,2-Dicarboxy-1,2-ethanediol
   C. 2,3-Dihydroxybutanoic acid
   D. 1,2-Dicarboxyethanol

Scratch Paper

Stop:

Think:

What's the structure of (+)-tartaric acid?

What's the relationship between enantiomers of a compound?

Predict:

Match

11. Which of the following compounds is the enantiomer of (+)-tartaric acid?

A.

B.

C.

meso (perfect symetry)

D.

Directed Practice

- *Topical Tests*: Molecular Structure of Organic Compounds Test 1
   Oxygen Containing Compounds Test 1 (Passage I)
- Isomer chart on p. 112 of this book

REACTION MECHANISMS: SUBSTITUTION AND ELIMINATION REACTIONS

S$_N$2

S$_N$2 stands for **Bi**molecular **N**ucleophilic **S**ubstutution.

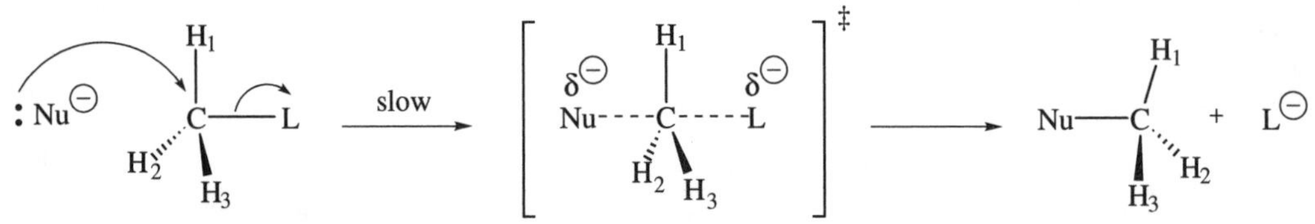

Substrate   Transition state   Substituted product

(L = leaving group)

Mechanism

S$_N$2 reactions proceed according to a ____One step____ mechanism.

Kinetics

S$_N$2 reactions exhibit bimolecular kinetics. That is, S$_N$2 reactions have rate laws that show the direct dependence of the reaction rate on the concentrations of both the electrophilic substrate and the nucleophile.

Rate = ____[R-L] [Nu]____

Sterics in substrate

$$CH_3X > RCH_2X > R_2CHX > R_3CX$$

Less substituted carbon substrates with a suitable leaving group will be most reactive toward S_N2 displacement reactions.

Nucleophiles

S_N2 reactions are favored by _Strong base_. A strong base is a _nucleophile_.

Leaving groups

A good leaving group needs to be able to stabilize the negative charge it carries via _resenonce_ or _induction_.

Critical Thinking Exercise

How is the free energy profile different when the reactant is a tertiary as opposed to a methyl halide?

PE [← tertiary (higher cause harder)]

Rxn coordinate

How is the free energy profile different with a good leaving group rather than a poor one?

good (after gone hard go back)

easy go back

CH₃ — C(=O) — CH₃ acetone → CH₃ — S(=O) — CH₃

Solvent effects

S_N2 reactions will proceed faster in _polar aprotic_ and slower in _protic solvent_ (require more energy).

Stereochemistry

S_N2 reactions involve backside bond formation between the nucleophile and the substrate, $180°$ away from the C–L bond that is breaking concomitantly. The local geometry of the S_N2 reaction product is the opposite of that of the starting material.

only not if Nu⁻ lower priority of L.G.

S$_N$1

S$_N$1 stands for **Uni**molecular **N**ucleophilic **S**ubstitution.

Substrate Carbocation intermediate Substituted product

Mechanism

S$_N$1 reactions occur in two steps. The first step is the ___*Slow step*___ (rate determining)
(carbocation formation).

Kinetics

S$_N$1 reactions exhibit *unimolecular* kinetics. The rate law shows the direct dependence of the reaction rate on the concentration of ___*molecule*___ only.

Rate = ___$[R-L]$___

Substrate

The more stable the carbocation intermediate formed in the first step, the faster the reaction.

$$R_3CX > R_2CHX > RCH_2X > CH_3X$$

Nucleophiles

S$_N$1 reactions don't require strong nucleophiles.

Leaving groups

A good leaving group is necessary because the departure of the leaving group is the _rate determing_ step.

Solvent effects

Protic solvents favor S_N1 reactions.

Stereochemistry

Since the carbocation intermediate is planar, it can be attacked from either side to give a _mixture_ of products.

Critical Thinking Exercise

Scratch Paper

Stop:

Think:

What kind of reaction do we expect to occur, given the reacting species and the solvent?

What is the attacking nucleophile? What is its priority relative to the other three substituent groups on the carbon atom?

Predict:

Match

12. (R)-1-fluoro-1-iodopropane is reacted with NaN_3 in HMPA. Which of the following is the major product of this reaction?

(R)-1-fluoro-1-iodopropane

A. (R)-1-azido-1-fluoropropane
B. (R)-1-azido-1-iodopropane
C. (S)-1-azido-fluoropropane
D. a racemic mixture of (R)-1-azido-1-fluoropropane and (S)-1-azido-1-fluoropropane

Nucleophilic Substitutions: S_N2 vs S_N1

	S_N2	S_N1
Kinetics		
Mechanism		
Stereochemistry	inverted	racemic
Sterics in substrate		
Leaving groups	weak base	weak base
Solvent effects		
Nucleophiles		

E1

E1 stands for **Uni**molecular **E**limination.

S_N1 and E1 reactions often occur simultaneously and __compete__ with another, under the same reaction conditions.

Base :⁻

H—C—C—L   slow   H—C—C ⊕   →   C=C   +   HL
— L ⊖

Substrate   Carbocation   Elimination product
                   intermediate

*add heat
↳ shift to E1*

Mechanism

E1 and S_N1 have the same rate-determining step (carbocation formation). The second step in E1 involves abstraction of __-hydrogen.
↳ *beta*

Kinetics

E1 reactions exhibit __unimolecular__ kinetics because only one molecule (the precursor of the carbocation) is involved in the rate-determining step.

Rate = ___[R-L]___

Substrate

As in S_N1 reactions, the more stable the *Carbon cation* formed in the first step, the faster the reaction.

Bases

A strong base is not required for E1.

Solvent effects

E1 and S_N1 reactions are favored in *polar protic* solvents, such as water and ethanol.

E2

E2 stands for **Bi**molecular **E**limination.

Substrate   Elimination product

Mechanism

E2 reactions are __1 step__. The base (B:) attacks a neighboring C–H bond and begins to remove the hydrogen at the same time as the alkene double bond starts to form and the leaving group starts to leave.

Kinetics

Like S_N2, E2 reactions exhibit __bimolecular__ kinetics. That is, two molecules must come together for the reaction to occur.

Rate = __[R–L][Nu⁻]__

Stereochemistry

↳ (staggered)

E2 reactions strongly prefer to occur via __anti__ ; that is, the atoms of the H–C–C–L group involved in the reaction must lie in the same plane. This will usually lead to Zaitsev elimination but Hoffman elimination occurs in a few cases.

(most sub)   (least sub)

Substrate

1°, 2°, and 3° alkyl halides can all participate in E2 reactions.

Bases

E2 reactions are favored by <u>strong</u>, <u>bulky</u> bases.

Solvent effects

E2 reactions are usually run in the _____ of the strong base used as the nucleophile.

Conj. acid nuc⁻

CORRELATION BETWEEN STRUCTURE AND REACTIVITY FOR SUBSTITUTION AND ELIMINATION REACTIONS

When predicting the reactivity of a substrate with respect to S_N2, S_N1, E2 and E1 reactions, the following questions should be asked:

1. Would the carbocation be stable if the leaving group dissociated?

   (If no, rule out S_N1 and E1.)

2. Is there are a good nucleophile?

   (If no, rule out S_N2.)

3. Does the nucleophile have easy access to the backside of the substrate opposite the leaving group?

   (If no, rule out S_N2.)

4. Is there a strong, bulky base available to attack the nucleophile?

   (If no, rule out E2.)

Predicting Reactivity in Substitutions and Eliminations

Substrate	Bad base, good nucleophile	Good base, good nucleophile	Good base, pour nucleophile	Protic/Acidic conditions
Methyl	SN_2	SN_2	NR	SN1
Primary	SN_2	SN_2	E2	NR
Secondary	SN_2	E2	E2	SN1/E1
Tertiary	NR	E2	E2	SN1/E1

Directed Practice

- *Biological Sciences Review Notes*: Orgo. Chs. 4, 5

Passage III (Questions 11–15)

The *cis* to *trans* isomerization of maleic acid to fumaric acid may be accomplished by reaction with hydrochloric acid. The rate of conversion is known to depend only on the concentration of maleic acid. The overall reaction is shown below.

Reaction 1

An organic chemistry instructor asked two students to convert maleic acid into fumaric acid.

Student #1 added aqueous hydrochloric acid to maleic acid and gently heated the resulting solution to dissolve any excess solid. She then heated the solution vigorously for 30 minutes, during which time a white precipitate formed. After cooling to room temperature, the precipitate was washed with two successive 25-mL aliquots of cold water. The crystalline residue was then dried. The melting point of the product revealed that it was slightly impure; therefore, the product was recrystallized in hydrochloric acid. The student obtained 78% yield of pure fumaric acid.

The proton NMR spectra of maleic acid and fumaric acid run in CD_3OD solvent revealed singlet peaks at 6.2 and 6.8 ppm respectively.

Student #2 followed a similar procedure but mistakenly added aqueous NaCl instead of aqueous HCl. Melting point determination of the solid she isolated confirmed it to be unreacted maleic acid.

Scratch Paper
Paragraph 1
Reaction 1
Paragraph 2
Paragraph 3
Paragraph 4

Scratch Paper

Stop:

Think:

What reaction has occurred?

What do we know about the reaction mechanism?

Predict:

Match

11. Which of the following is most probably the intermediate formed during the isomerization of maleic acid to fumaric acid?

    A.   A free radical
    B.   A carbocation
    C.   A carbanion
    D.   A carbene

Stop:

Think:

Note that we do not always have to be certain of the accuracy of every statement. Use the choices to help you eliminate answers!

Predict:

Match

12. Which of the following factors distinguish fumaric acid from maleic acid?

    I.   Fumaric acid is the thermodynamically favored product in the isomerization reaction.
    II.   Fumaric acid is a (Z)-isomer.
    III.   Fumaric acid possesses different physical properties than maleic acid.

    A.   I only
    B.   II only
    C.   II and III only
    D.   I and III only

Unit 1

Scratch Paper

Stop:

Think:

Are they mirror images?

Predict:

Match

Stop:

Think:

What characteristics must a plausible explanation possess?

Predict:

Match

Stop:

Think:

What is *syn* addition?

Predict:

Match

13. Maleic acid and fumaric acid differ in their spatial arrangement of carboxyl groups. As a result, they can be classified as:

    A. enantiomers.
    B. structural isomers.
    C. geometric isomers.
    D. *meso* compounds.

14. When maleic acid is heated, it loses water to form an anhydride. Why does this process not occur when fumaric acid is heated?

    A. Anhydride formation is not thermodynamically favored.
    B. The configuration of the hydroxyl groups about the double bond do not permit anhydride formation.
    C. Hydrogen bonding does not permit anhydride formation.
    D. No water is lost in the reaction.

15. Maleic acid and fumaric acid can both undergo *syn* addition. What would be the products formed if maleic acid was reacted with D_2?

    A. Racemic (2,3-D)-butanedioic acid
    B. *Meso*-(2,3-D)-butanedioic acid
    C. A diastereomeric mixture of deuterated butanedioic acid
    D. (1-D)-butanoic acid

The Lesson Continues
on the Next Page
$\longrightarrow$

HOMEWORK

Review for Organic Chemistry 1

Topical Tests	❏ Hydrocarbons Test 1 ❏ Molecular Structure of Organic Compounds Test 1
Subject Tests	❏ Test 1 (Optional, DD3080) ❏ Test 2 (Optional, DD3081) ❏ Test 3 (Optional, DD3082)

Preview for Biology 1

Biology Review Notes	❏ *Chapters 1–5 and 13
Foundation Review	❏ Unit 1 (Optional, MM3260A)
Online Workshops	❏ *Generalized Eukaryotic Cell ❏ *Microbiology

Biology 1

CRITICAL READING: SYNTHESIS

- Generalized Eukaryotic / Prokaryotic Cell
- Membrane Traffic
- Enzymes
- Metabolism
- Mitosis and Meiosis
- Embryogenesis and Genetics

KAPLAN PASSAGE STRATEGY

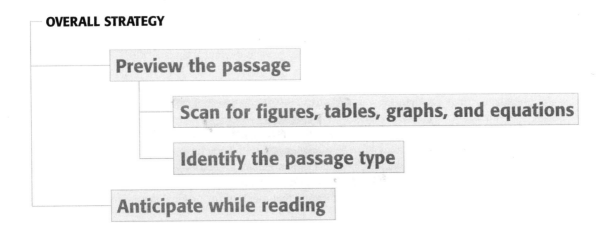

OVERALL STRATEGY

- Preview the passage
  - Scan for figures, tables, graphs, and equations
  - Identify the passage type
- Anticipate while reading

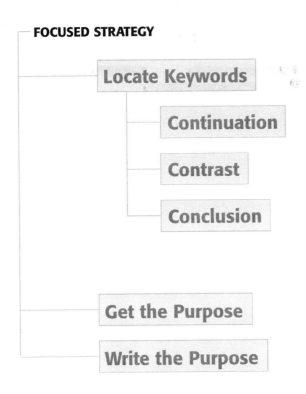

FOCUSED STRATEGY

- Locate Keywords
  - Continuation
  - Contrast
  - Conclusion
- Get the Purpose
- Write the Purpose

Passage I (Questions 1–3)

The Serial Endosymbiosis Theory (SET) provides the best explanation for the development of eukaryotic cells from prokaryotic ancestors, hypothesizing that organelles such as mitochondria, chloroplasts, and microtubular complexes originated from the invasion of anaerobic prokaryotic host cells by aerobic prokaryotes. The theory holds that these symbiotic events occurred about three billion years ago and led to the evolution of present day eukaryotes.

Mitochondria are theorized to have appeared first in the sequence of organelle development, when aerobic prokaryotes were engulfed by larger host prokaryotes that had been restricted to sugar fermentation. Mitochondria are very similar to prokaryotes in a number of respects: They are about the same size as bacteria, they possess their own genomes, which are structurally very similar to those of bacteria, and they have small ribosomes with bacteria-like antibiotic sensitivity. DNA sequencing of mitochondrial DNA has shown greater similarity with prokaryotic DNA than with eukaryotic nuclear DNA. However, many mitochondrial proteins are coded by nuclear DNA and translated in the cell cytoplasm, indicating that much of the original symbiont genome has been transferred to the host nucleus.

Chloroplasts (*plastids*) more closely resemble prokaryotes than do mitochondria, indicating that chloroplasts may have developed later in evolution. Chloroplasts, presumably, developed through invasion of a host cell by a cyanobacteria. There are many different types of chloroplasts; for example, the chloroplasts of plants have two membranes while those of the *Euglena* have three.

Organelles of motility (*undulipodia*) are composed of microtubules and are commonly referred to as flagella or cilia. The SET suggests that *undulipodia* developed from spirochetes which formed symbiotic attachments to the surface of nonmotile host cells. These spirochetes may have also given rise to centrioles, chromosomal kinetochores, and the spindle apparatus.

Scratch Paper

Paragraph 1

Paragraph 2

Paragraph 3

Paragraph 4

Scratch Paper

Stop:

Think:

Where are mitochondria discussed in the passage?

Does the passage provide relevant information?

Predict:

Match

Stop:

Think:

What is the SET?

Note that the question wants the <u>best</u> evidence.

Are there any answers that are similar to an example provided in the passage?

Predict:

Match

Stop:

Think:

Where does the passage discuss spirochete symbiosis?

Is the information provided relevant?

Predict:

Match

1. The mitochondrial genome consists of:
   - A. plasmids with histone protein cores.
   - B. a segment of single stranded RNA.
   - C. circular loop of double stranded DNA.
   - D. 24 chromosomes.

2. Which of the following observations provides the best evidence in support of the SET?
   - A. Luminescent bacteria living symbiotically in the extracellular space of fish are able to reproduce and live in the absence of their host.
   - B. The prokaryote *Mixotricha paradoxa* is covered by a shell of spirochetes which are responsible for its movement.
   - C. Bacteria reproduce by binary fission.
   - D. Bacteria present in the human gut are involved in the digestion and release of certain necessary vitamins.

3. Assuming the validity of the SET, which of the following cell phenomena would have been least likely to have evolved prior to spirochete symbiosis with the host cell?
   - A. Mitosis
   - B. The Krebs cycle
   - C. Nitrogen fixation
   - D. Budding

MEMBRANE TRAFFIC

The plasma membrane controls <u>movement in and out cell</u>.

Permeable	Nonpermeable
small (CH_2O) nonpolar (CO_2, fats)	large molecules (proteins Polar Ions

The membrane components

· <u>lipid bilayer</u>

· <u>proteins</u>

_____

Diffusion (high to low)

moves: <u>gases, small</u>

requires: <u>No energy</u>

Osmosis (low to high)

moves: <u>water</u>

requires: <u>No energy</u>

Facilitated Diffusion

moves: <u>Carrier protien</u>

requires: <u>No energy</u>

Active Transport

moves: _____

requires: <u>ATP (energy)</u>

Primary → use ATP

Secondary → use others energy

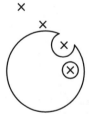

Endocytosis <u>into cell (take up)</u>

Exocytosis <u>expell something</u>

used when: <u>↳ in nervous</u>

<u>system (releasing</u>

<u>chemicals</u>

Directed Practice

- *Biological Sciences Review Notes*: Biology Ch. 1
- *Topical Tests*: Gen. Eukaryotic Cell Test 1 (Questions 14, 15) and Microbiology Test 1

Critical Thinking Exercise

What happens to an ocean (salt water) fish when it moves into a river (fresh water)?

Going to blow up →

NaCl
water go in

What role does osmosis play in diabetes mellitus?

Increases water cause increase sugar

What happens to the urine volume?

Increases

What happens when you have a container separated into two compartments by a semipermeable membrane, with 1.5 M NaCl in the left compartment and 2.0 M glucose in the right one?

1.5 M NaCl *2.0 M glucose*

* go to NaCl because
1.5 of Na > so really 3M
1.5 of Cl (go to high from lower
↳osmosis)

Scratch Paper

Stop:

Think:

What does hypotonic mean?

What is the purpose of the sodium potassium pump?

How does the pump affect concentration gradients in the cell?

Predict:

Match

---

4. The sodium potassium pump is an ATPase that pumps 3 Na^+ out of the cell and 2 K^+ into the cell for each ATP hydrolyzed. Cells can use the pump to help maintain cell volume. Which of the following would most likely happen to the rate of ATP consumption immediately after a cell is moved to a hypotonic environment?

    A. It would increase.
    B. It would decrease.
    C. It would increase, then decrease.
    D. It would remain the same.

ENZYMES: CATALYZE REACTIONS BY LOWERING ACTIVATION ENERGY

Structure

Most enzymes are proteins. The specific portion of the enzyme that binds the substrate is called the active site.

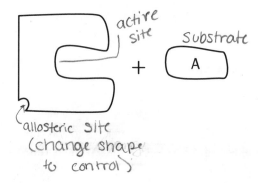

Enzyme-substrate complex

An enzyme will only catalyze one specific reaction (known as enzyme specificity). Molecules upon which an enzyme acts are called substrates; substrates bind to the active site.

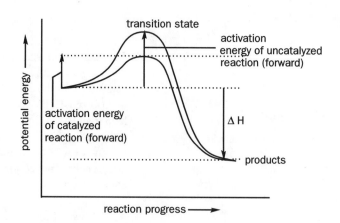

Directed Practice

- *Biological Sciences Review Notes*: Biology Ch. 2
- *Topical Tests*: Molecular Genetics Test 1 (Passage I)

Enzyme activity

Factors that may affect enzyme activity include: pH, concentration of substrate and enzyme, temperature, and cofactors.

Critical Thinking Exercise

Scratch Paper

Stop:

Think:

Where is pepsin found?

What are the conditions under which pepsin functions?

Predict:

Match

5. Which set of graphs best depicts the optimal temperature and pH range for pepsin activity?

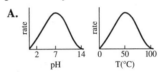

A.

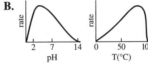

B.

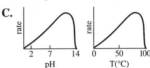

C.

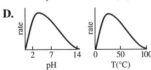

D.

Inhibition

— allosteric site

Two types of inhibition are competitive and noncompetitive inhibition.

↳ bound to active site so substrate can't (increase subrate)

Negative feedback

Negative feedback is a regulatory mechanism that serves to maintain homeostasis.

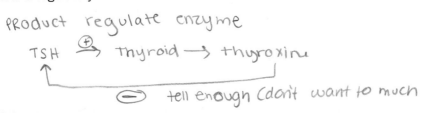

product regulate enzyme

TSH ⊕→ thyroid → thyroxine

⊖ tell enough (don't want to much

*Product
beneficial
aerobatic + anaerobatic*

CELLULAR METABOLISM: ENZYMATIC RELEASE OF ATP FROM ORGANIC COMPOUNDS

ATP

The source of ___energy___ for cellular activities is ATP.

* bond breaking (ATP → ADP)
b/c unstable w/ negative bonds
(opposite normal

Glycolysis (

Glycolysis is the ___anaerobic___ catabolism of glucose to pyruvic acid (pyruvate).

(not productive

Anaerobic respiration

Anaerobic respiration occurs in the absence of ___oxygen___ and results in ___2 ATP___ per molecule of glucose.

Fermentation

Fermentation begins with glycolysis and ends with the conversion of pyruvate to ___lactic acid___ (muscle cells) or ___ethanol___ (yeast).

Directed Practice

- *Biological Sciences Review Notes*: Biology Ch. 3
- *Topical Tests*: Molecular Biology Test 1, Question #9.

Aerobic respiration (midocondria matrix

Aerobic respiration occurs in the ___presence___ of O_2 and results in a net ___36___ ATP per molecule of glucose.

Pyruvate decarboxylation (mito matrix)

Pyruvate decarboxylation is the conversion of ___Pyruvate___ to _____.

Krebs cycle (Citric Acid Cycle) mito matrix

In the Krebs cycle, the breakdown of acetyl CoA generates ___NADH___, ___FAD___, and ___ATP___.

Electron transport chain/oxidative phosphorylation (mitocondria membrane)

___Oxygen___ is the final electron acceptor.

↳proton gradiant → ATP released

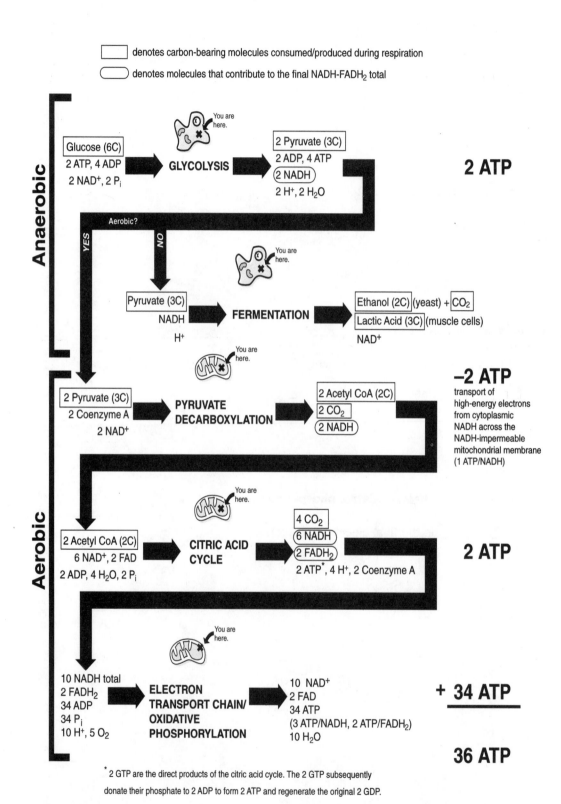

denotes carbon-bearing molecules consumed/produced during respiration

denotes molecules that contribute to the final NADH-FADH$_2$ total

Critical Thinking Exercise

During anaerobic conditions, why must pyruvate undergo fermentation for glycolysis to continue?   regenerate NAD+ (not consumed just carrier)

Scratch Paper

Stop:

Think:

Do I know the enzymes for this?

What do I know?

What is the last step?

Predict:

Match

6. Which is the last enzyme in cellular respiration?

 A. hexokinase
 B. pyruvate decarboxylase
 C. alcohol dehydrogenase
 D. cytochrome C oxidase

Passage II (Questions 7–9)

The final step in the aerobic utilization of glucose for energy, oxidative phosphorylation, depends on sufficient concentrations of various substrates. Insufficient concentrations of any of these "essential substrates" can limit the rate of oxidative phosphorylation. Specifically, the concentration of ADP present influences the extent of the mitochondrial activity within a cell: mitochondria increase their oxidative phosphorylation activity in the presence of high ADP concentrations. This increase in oxidative phosphorylation can be shown experimentally.

To study mitochondrial activity experimentally, a biochemist prepares a plate of mitochondria without the addition of external substrates. Initially, the biochemist records the basal rate of oxygen consumption by measuring the amount of oxygen present at different times. Then, the biochemist adds 1.0 μmol of glutamate, an amino acid, and records the change in oxygen consumption. The biochemist then adds 0.3 μmol of ADP. After this initial quantity of ADP is consumed, another 0.6 μmol of ADP is added. It is found that the amount of ADP present is directly proportional to the amount of oxygen taken up by the mitochondrion. Figure 1 summarizes the results.

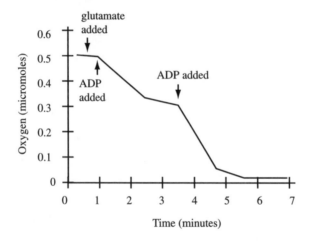

Figure 1

Scratch Paper
Paragraph 1
Paragraph 2
Figure 1

In another experiment, the biochemist repeats the preparation of a mitochondria rich plate. Initially, 1.0 μmol of glutamate is added, followed shortly by the addition of approximately 0.8 μmoles of ADP. Then the biochemist adds oligomycin, which inhibits oxidative phosphorylation. Finally, the biochemist adds dinitrophenol (DNP) to the plate, which acts to dissipate the proton gradient in the mitochondria. Figure 2 summarizes the results.

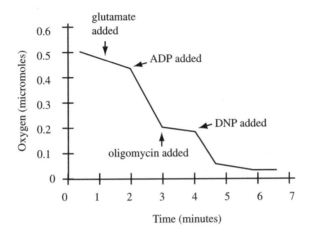

Figure 2

Scratch Paper

Paragraph 3

Figure 3

Scratch Paper

Stop:

Think:

Refer back to Figure 1!

What process produces acetyl coenzyme A?

Predict:

Match

Stop:

Think:

Where is oxygen consumption discussed in the passage?

What diagram(s) refer to oxygen consumption?

Predict:

Match

Stop:

Think:

Does the passage provide relevant information?

What is the role of each substance in oxidative phosphorylation?

Predict:

Match

7. Based on the data in Figure 1, between which times would the rate of acetyl coenzyme A production be lowest?

   A.   0.5 to 1.1 minutes
   B.   2.8 to 3.3 minutes
   C.   4.6 to 5.1 minutes
   D.   5.8 to 6.3 minutes

8. Suppose a biochemist begins an experiment by measuring 1.5 μmoles of oxygen in a plate of mitochondria. After adding 1.2 μmoles of ADP, the amount of oxygen left in the plate is:

   A.   0.31 μmoles.
   B.   0.56 μmoles.
   C.   0.94 μmoles.
   D.   1.19 μmoles.

9. The absence of which of the following substrates would not be expected to limit the rate of oxidative phosphorylation?

   A. NAD^+
   B. O_2
   C. $FADH_2$
   D.   inorganic phosphate

MITOSIS: CELL DIVISION WITH PRESERVATION OF CHROMOSOME NUMBER

Cell cycle

The cell cycle consists of the 4 stages of cell life (G_1, S, G_2, M).

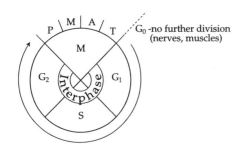

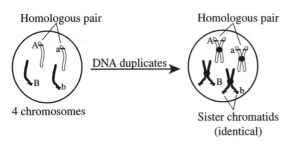

S phase

Mitotic phases

(PMAT)

Cell division

After cytokinesis, there are ___identide daughter___ cells.

Directed Practice

- *Biological Sciences Review Notes*: Biology Ch. 4

MEIOSIS: CELL DIVISION WITH HALVING OF CHROMOSOME NUMBER

Meiotic phases

In meiosis, there is only one round of chromosome replication, but there are two rounds of PMAT.

Mitosis	Meiosis
continuous process	discontinuous → eggs stay at Meiosis I until fertilized
2N chromosomes	N chr
2 daughter cells	4 daughter cells → sperm / 1 d.c + polar bodies
somatic cells underg	germ
PMAT once	PMAT twice (MI → cross over) (MII → mitosis)

Male/Female reproductive systems

Spermatogenesis

Spermatogenesis is the formation of sperm.

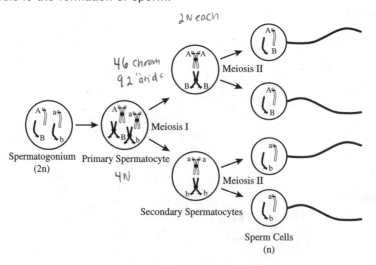

2N each

46 chrom
92 'tids

4N

Spermatogonium (2n) · Primary Spermatocyte · Meiosis I · Secondary Spermatocytes · Meiosis II · Sperm Cells (n)

Directed Practice

- *Biological Sciences Review Notes*: Biology Ch. 4

Unit 1

Oogenesis   *(In ovalries) → all eggs present at birth*

Oogenesis is the formation of eggs.

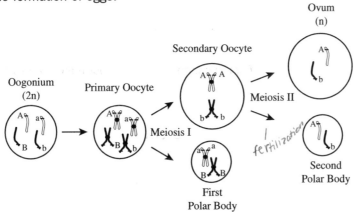

Spermatogenesis	Oogenesis
continuous	discon
1° spermate → 4 spermatid	oocyte → 1 ovum + polar bodies
NO Mitochondria DNA	Mitochondria DNA
NO RNA	RNA → RNA gradient (polarizes) → head tail

Critical Thinking Exercise

Scratch Paper

Stop:

Think:

How many copies of the mutation will end up in the primary spermatocyte?

How many copies of DNA does each gamete obtain?

Predict:

Match

10. A mutation has occurred in one strand of DNA in a spermatogonium. This mutation will show up in how many of the gametes produced from this cell?

   A.   None

   B.   Two

   C.   All four

   D.   It cannot be determined

EMBRYOGENESIS: FORMATION AND DEVELOPMENT OF EMBRYO

Fertilization

Fertilization is the joining of an ___~~Sp~~ ovum___ and a ___~~onom~~ sperm___.

Development

___Zygote___ (fertilized ovum) → ___~~ovotata~~ morula~~ovg~~___ (a solid ball of cells) → ___blastula___
(a hollow ball of cells with a fluid-filled center) → ___gastrula___ (three cell layers)

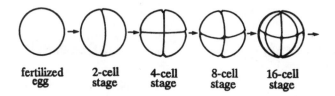

| fertilized egg | 2-cell stage | 4-cell stage | 8-cell stage | 16-cell stage |

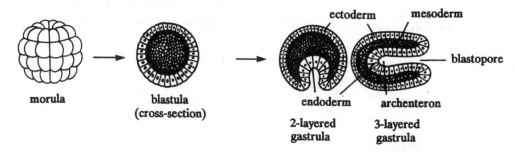

morula   blastula (cross-section)   ectoderm   mesoderm   blastopore   endoderm   archenteron
2-layered gastrula   3-layered gastrula

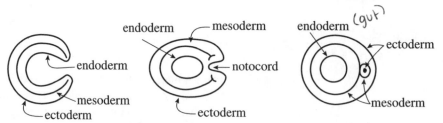

endoderm — mesoderm — endoderm (gut) — ectoderm
endoderm — notocord — mesoderm
mesoderm — ectoderm

Differentiation

Cells specialize (can be anything when start)

Induction

one is induced by another
cells causing inducing of other cell formation

Primary germ layers and their derivatives

Ectoderm: nervous system (brain and spinal cord), epidermis, lens of eye, inner ear

Endoderm: epithelial lining of digestive tract, lungs, liver, pancreas (gut)

Mesoderm: muscles, skeleton, circulatory system, gonads, kidneys

Unit 1

Critical Thinking Exercise

Scratch Paper

Stop:

Think:

What are the three primary germ layers?

What structures form from each germ layer?

Predict:

Match

11. Congenital defects in both the circulatory system and excretory system can be traced back to embryonic development. Such defects are likely to have come from which primary germ layer?

    A.   Notochord
    B.   Ectoderm
    C.   Endoderm
    D.   Mesoderm

Directed Practice

- *Topical Tests*: Reproductive System and Development (Passage I) and discretes
- *Biological Sciences Review Notes*: Biology Ch. 4

Unit 1

GENETICS AND PEDIGREE ANALYSIS

Dominant – only need 1 to show up

Recessive – need two copies to show

Autosomal Recessive – not sex linked
(skips generation)

(cause shows up 2nd generation)

Key:

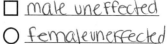

□ male uneffected
○ female uneffected
■ effected male
● effected female

Rr x Rr

Genotype: actual genetic make up (genes read)

Phenotype: physical make up

What if you see ◧ or ◑? Carrier

Autosomal Dominant – skips a ger always show up
(every generation)

Rr x rr

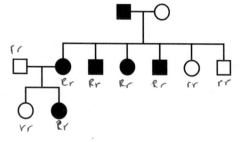

Directed Practice

• *Biological Sciences Review Notes*: Biology Ch. 13

Is This Autosomal Recessive? ~~Skips a generation~~

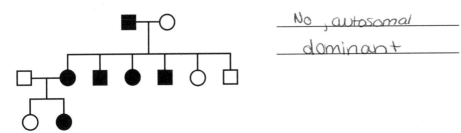

No, autosomal
dominant

You can prove ___recessivity___ but you can't prove ___dominance___
from the pedigree.

Remember: ___prevalace ≠ dominant___

Sex Linked Recessive Inheritance – occurs on X chromosome → so only males
(in females only 1 X will
be expressed)

XY by $X_c X$

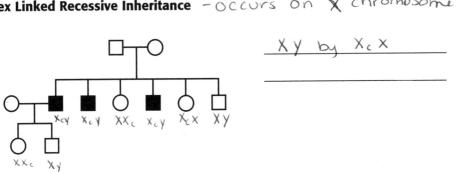

$X_c Y$ $X_c Y$ XX_c $X_c Y$ $X_c X$ XY

XX_c XY

Punnett Squares/Probabilities

AB   **O**

	A	B
O	A_o	B_o
O	A_o	B_o

% O → 0
% A → 50
% B → 50
% AB – 0

Rr   **Rr**

	R	r
R	RR	Rr
Rr	Rr	rr

What's the likelihood that the offspring is a carrier?

~~50%~~

66% → out of 3 possible

(all who contain ~~letter~~
except rr cause would show
as dark)

Penetrance

Critical Thinking Exercise

can't give x's

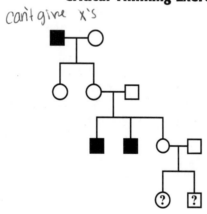

What type of pedigree is this? Sex linked

Who, in Gen4, should be tested? male

What is the likelihood of each Gen4 offspring
   –having the disease? male (50%)
   –being a carrier? female (50%)

Directed Practice

• *Biological Sciences Review Notes*: Biology Ch. 13

Chromosomal Mutations *— miss or duplication*

nondisjunction → chromosomes fail to seperate (more less than need)

Critical Thinking Exercise

What type of pedigree is this? *recessive*

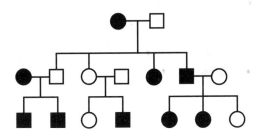

What is monosomy and how does it occur? Is a zygote that is monosomic for a particular chromosome viable?

−1

What is trisomy? *+1*

three

What are the most common trisomies?

down syndrome

Passage III (Questions 12–15)

Many genetically inherited disorders result from chromosomal abnormalities involving autosomes, sex chromosomes, or both. The abnormalities can be classified as either structural or numerical.

Structural abnormalities result from chromosome breakage and subsequent reconstitution in an abnormal combination. This often results in a translocation—the rearrangement of genetic material from one chromosome to another. The most common type of translocation is a balanced translocation leading to chromosome sets which contain the normal complement of genetic information arranged in different positions. In contrast, an unbalanced translocation describes a structural abnormality in which the chromosome set contains additional or missing genetic information. Unbalanced translocations are thus more likely to produce abnormal phenotypes. Translocations can further be classified as either stable or unstable. A stable translocation is one in which the rearranged chromosome is capable of progressing through normal cell division unaltered. Translocations are written in the following way: 45, XY, t(14q22q). This describes a male individual with 45 chromosomes and a balanced translocation between chromosomes 14 and 22 (they are attached).

Numerical abnormalities are more common than structural abnormalities. Any chromosome set which differs in number from the normal diploid set is termed heteroploid. Euploid describes a heteroploid state that is an exact multiple of the haploid chromosome number. Aneuploidy, the most clinically significant chromosome abnormality, describes any chromosome number that is not an exact multiple of the haploid. Most aneuploid patients have either trisomy, three representatives of a particular chromosome, or monosomy, only one representative of a particular chromosome. The causes of aneuploidy are not entirely understood. It is supposed that most cases of aneuploidy result from meiotic nondisjunction, the failure of a pair of chromosomes to separate normally during one of the two meiotic divisions, most often during meiosis I.

Trisomy or monosomy for a whole chromosome rarely results in a viable phenotype. In fact, most instances of aneuploidy are eliminated before birth by spontaneous abortion (Table 1). Trisomy 21 (Down syndrome), trisomy 18, and trisomy 13 are the only well-defined instances of trisomy that are observed in postnatal infants (Table 2). Each of these autosomal trisomies result in phenotypes which include reduced growth development, mental retardation, and congenital deformities. Monosomy for an entire chromosome in a live birth is only observed for the X chromosome, a condition known as Turner's syndrome. It is interesting to note that although the great majority of Down syndrome cases have 47 chromosomes due to trisomy 21, approximately 5% of Down syndrome cases have the normal chromosome number (46 chromosomes) with the extra chromosomal material from chromosome 21 translocated onto one of these. This is known as a Robertsonian translocation and is shown in Figure 1.

Scratch Paper
Paragraph 1
Paragraph 2
Paragraph 3
Paragraph 4

Table 1 Major types of chromosome abnormality in spontaneous abortions

	%
Trisomies	52
45,X	18
Triploidy	17
Translocations	2–4

Table 2 Frequency of cytogenic abnormalities in newborns

Autosomal abnormalities	%
Trisomy 13	0.05–0.27
Trisomy 18	0.10–0.27
Trisomy 21	0.69–1.44
14/21 translocations	0.18–0.27

Sex chromosome abnormalities	
XXY	0.50–1.60
XXX	0.50–1.68
XYY	0.50–1.07

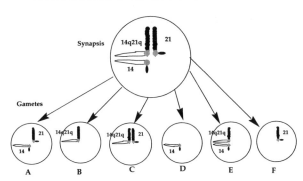

Figure 1. Diagram of abnormal segregation of translocation (Robertsonian)

Figure 1

Scratch Paper

Table 1

Table 2

Figure 1

Scratch Paper

Stop:

Think:

What is another name for an unstable rearrangement?

Which of the structures listed in the choices are actually found on individual chromosomes?

Predict:

Match

Stop:

Think:

What is partial trisomy?

Does the passage refer to partial trisomy?

Predict:

Match

12. Which of the following might be absent in a chromosome with an unstable rearrangement?

    A. Centromere
    B. Nucleus
    C. Chiasmata
    D. TATA box

13. Which of the following events could lead to partial trisomy?

    A. A balanced rearrangement
    B. An unbalanced rearrangement
    C. Absence of crossing over
    D. Replication error during mitosis

Scratch Paper

Stop:

Think:

What is Down Syndrome?

How does Down Syndrome result?

Predict:

Match

Stop:

Think:

Refer back to Figure 1!

What must be present in a gamete for it to be viable and normal?

Predict:

Match

14. Which of the following hypotheses might explain the disproportionate number of babies with Down Syndrome born to mothers over 35 years of age?

    A. Older eggs require fertilization by multiple sperm.

    B. Older eggs contain a higher percentage of mutated chromosomes.

    C. Older eggs are more likely to disjoin incorrectly.

    D. Older eggs are not susceptible to translocations.

15. In Figure 1, which of the gametes (A, B, C, D, E, or F) will most likely produce a viable, normal phenotype?

    A. A and C

    B. A and B

    C. A, B, and C

    D. A, B, and D

HOMEWORK

Review for Biology 1

Topical Tests	❏ Generalized Eukaryotic Cell Test 1 ❏ Reproductive System and Development Test 1 ❏ Microbiology Test 1
Subject Tests	❏ Test 1 (Optional, MM3211) ❏ Test 2 (Optional, MM3212) ❏ Test 3 (Optional, MM3213)

Preview for Physics 2

Physics Review Notes	❏ *Chapters 4, 6–9
Foundation Review	❏ Unit 2 (Optional, MM3259A)
Online Workshops	❏ *DC and AC Circuits ❏ *Thermodynamics ❏ *Magnetism

UNIT TWO

QUESTIONS AND ANSWERS

Physics 2

QUESTIONS AND ANSWERS: FOUNDATION

- Simple Harmonic Motion
- Waves
- Electrostatics
- Magnetism
- Circuits

THE KAPLAN MCAT TRAINING PROGRAM

Unit 1: Critical Reading

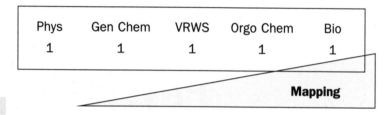

Unit 2: Attacking Questions

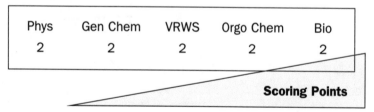

Unit 3: Integrated Practice

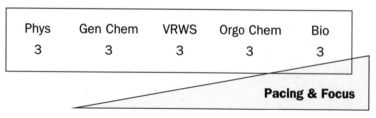

Unit 4: Test Day Simulation

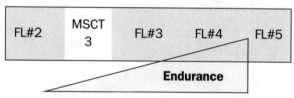

✱ YOU ARE HERE

THE KAPLAN QUESTION STRATEGY

STOP

Characterize the answer choices

THINK

What is the question really asking

What topic is being tested

What relevant information do you need

PREDICT

Formulate a framework or prediction for your answer

MATCH

Which answer truly meets the requirements of the prediction

Unit 2

Passage I (Questions 1–4)

When placed in a container with a movable piston at the top, a gas with a high temperature and pressure will push the piston upward, doing work on it. If the gas and its container are thermally isolated, and if no heat is allowed to enter or leave the system, then the gas is said to undergo adiabatic expansion. Adiabatic expansion is used frequently in steam and automobile engines, an example of the conversion of thermal energy into mechanical energy.

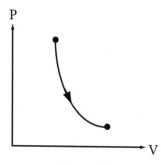

Figure 1

The pressure versus volume curve for an adiabatic expansion drops off more quickly than an isotherm starting from the same state.

If an ideal gas undergoes adiabatic expansion, the relationship between the pressure and the volume of the gas is constant throughout:

$$PV^{\gamma} = \text{constant,}$$

where $\gamma = 5/3$ for a monatomic ideal gas, and $\gamma = 7/5$ for a diatomic ideal gas.

Scratch Paper

Scratch Paper

Stop:

Think:

Which thermodynamic concept connects the answer choices?

Predict:

Match

1. Which of the following would NOT be true if an adiabatic compression, the process in Figure 1 taken in reverse, were applied to an ideal gas?

   A. The internal energy of the gas decreases.
   B. Work is done on the gas.
   C. No heat is exchanged between the gas and the environment outside the container.
   D. The temperature of the gas increases.

Stop:

Think:

Is this relationship discussed in the passage?

What equation do we know that helps us predict the nature of the relationship between temperature and internal energy of an ideal gas?

Predict:

Match

2. If the temperature of an ideal gas is doubled, what is the effect on the gas's internal energy?

   A. The internal energy of the gas is halved.
   B. The internal energy of the gas remains unchanged.
   C. The internal energy of the gas is doubled.
   D. There isn't enough information to determine the change in internal energy.

Unit 2

Scratch Paper

Stop:

Think:

What do the form of the answer choices remind you of?

Predict:

Match

3. If a volume of hydrogen gas inside the cylinder is reduced by two thirds via an adiabatic process, by what factor is the pressure increased?

A. $\left(\dfrac{1}{3}\right)^{7/5}$

B. 3

C. $3^{5/3}$

D. $3^{7/5}$

Stop:

Think:

What is the best way to keep track of the information in this problem?

What information in the passage does our passage map direct us to?

Predict:

Match

4. A sample of monatomic ideal gas is taken through an adiabatic expansion, and then is isothermally compressed until the gas returns to its original pressure. Which of the following is true of this process?

A. The net heat input into the gas is zero.
B. The net work done by the gas is zero.
C. The final state of the gas has a lower volume than the initial state does.
D. The final state of the gas has a higher temperature than the initial state.

SIMPLE HARMONIC MOTION

Springs, pendulums, waves

Frequency and Period (time per cycle)

$f = \frac{1}{T}$ ($\frac{1}{s}$ or Hertz)

$\omega = 2\pi f$ (angular frequency - rate of change of angle of wave)

$\rightarrow$ radians/second

$V = f\lambda$

Hooke's Law

$\frac{N}{m} \cdot m = N$

(force = spring constant · distance)

$\vec{F} = -k\vec{x}$

$\omega = \sqrt{\frac{k}{m}}$

$KE = \frac{1}{2}mv^2$ (max at equilibrium)
$\searrow$ total = KE + PE

$PE = \frac{1}{2}kx^2$

(max = max displacement)
$\hookrightarrow$ greatest a b/c greatest force)

Unit 2

Pendulum Motion

$$\omega = \sqrt{\frac{g}{l}}$$

$$f = \frac{\omega}{2\pi}$$

restoring force → gravity (bring back and forth)

* does not change w/ mass just gravity
   and length

Critical Thinking Exercise

Scratch Paper

Stop:

Think:

Predict:

Match

5. Two children are on separate swings of the same length. One weighs twice as much as the other. The swing with the lighter child is pulled back to an initial angular displacement of 5°, while the swing with the heavier child is pulled back to 10°. Both are then let go to swing back and forth. What is the ratio of the angular frequency of the lighter swing to the heavier swing?

   A. 1:2
   B. 2:1
   C. 1:1
   D. 2π:1

Waves

Fundamentals

Snapshot at a particular point in space

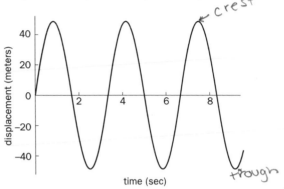

← crest

trough

Amplitude = 50 (max displacement)

Period = 3.3

Frequency = $\frac{1}{3}$

Snapshot in time

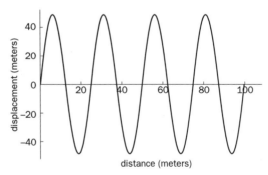

Wavelength = 25 m

$V = f\lambda$

Speed = 7.5

Unit 2

Directed Practice

- *Topical Tests*: Wave Characteristics and Periodic Motion Test 1 (Passage I)
- *Physical Sciences Review Notes*: Physics Ch. 9

transverse → perpendicular to

longitudinal → same direction (ex. slinky)

Examples of Waves

Type of Wave	Transverse vs. Longitudinal	Oscillation of What?	Frequency
Sound	longitudinal	air molecules	↑f = ↑ pitch
Light	transverse	E & B field	↑f = Red to blue
Water	transverse	water	↑f = faster waves

Interference

Type of Interference	Path length difference	Phase Difference
(add to each other) constructive interference	$0, \lambda, 2\lambda, 3\lambda$	$0°, 360°, 720°$
(cancel out) destructive interference	$\frac{\lambda}{2}, \frac{3\lambda}{2}$	$180°, 540°$
partially constructive interference	in between	in between

Directed Practice

- *Topical Tests*: Wave Characteristics and Periodic Motion Test 1 (Passage 1)
- *Physical Sciences Review Notes*: Physics Ch. 9

Unit 2

logs → for very big differences

$$\log_x y = z \rightarrow x^z = y$$

SOUND

Intensity and the decibel scale

ratio of sound (I) *to threshold* $(I_0 = 10^{-12}\ W/m^2)$

$$\beta = 10\log\left(\frac{I}{I_0}\right)$$

Beat frequency *(same amplitude out of phase)*

$$f_{beat} = |f_1 - f_2|$$

Doppler Effect

- f' (heard frequency)

f^x = actual frequency

V = speed sound
V_d = detector
V_s = source

$F' =$ higher when approaching $(\pm)$

f' softer = $\mp$

$$f' = f\frac{(v \pm v_d)}{(v \mp v_s)}$$

Critical Thinking Exercise

Scratch Paper

Stop:

Think:

Predict:

Match

6. A train is moving at 80 mph. A car in front of it is moving in the same direction at 50 mph. If the frequency of a whistle on the train is f, what is the frequency heard by a passenger riding in the car? (v = speed of sound in air in mph)

A. $f\dfrac{(v + 50)}{(v + 80)}$

B. $f\dfrac{(v - 50)}{(v + 80)}$

C. $f\dfrac{(v + 50)}{(v - 80)}$

D. $f\dfrac{(v - 50)}{(v - 80)}$

Directed Practice

- *Physical Sciences Review Notes*: Physics Ch. 9
- *Topical Test*: Sound Test 1 (Passage II)

Standing waves (boundary conditions)

At a closed end: __node__

At an open end: __anti-node__

ex. jump rope, organ

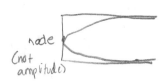

node
(not
amplitude)

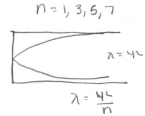

closed pipe

$n = 1, 3, 5, 7$

$\lambda = 4L$

$\lambda = \dfrac{4L}{n}$

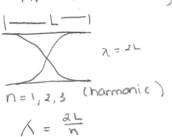

pipe (open) or string

|—— L ——|

$\lambda = 2L$

$n = 1, 2, 3$ (harmonic)

$\lambda = \dfrac{2L}{n}$

Critical Thinking Exercise

Scratch Paper
Stop:
Think:
Predict:
Match

7. A pipe with one closed end has a ~~third~~ 2nd harmonic with a frequency of 165 Hz. What is the length of the pipe? (the speed of sound is 330 m/sec)

   A. 0.5 m
   B. 1.5 m
   C. 2.0 m
   D. cannot be determined from the given information

Directed Practice

- *Physical Sciences Review Notes*: Physics Ch. 9
- *Topical Tests*: Sound Test 1 (Passage I)
            Wave Characteristics and Periodic Motion Test 1 (Passage II)

Unit 2

ELECTROSTATICS

Coulomb's law (inverse square law)

$$F = \frac{kQq}{r^2}$$

k = proportionality constant

Q, q = point charges   (equal and opposite force)

Electric field (E)   - force waiting to do work

$$\vec{F} = q\vec{E}$$

(go from (+) to (−))

E = greater as lines get closer

Unit 2

Principle of Superposition

• at any point in space, figure at where field is

Electrical Potential Energy

Similar to: __gravitational__

Units: __Joules__

further= highest potential
(two negatives want to be farther)

m_3

m_1

$\widehat{Eart}$

$V_{m_2} > V_{m_1}$

$q_2 +$

$q_1 +$

$\boxed{q-}$

$V_{q_2} > V_{q_1}$

Electric Potential (Voltage)

1 volt = Joules/coulomb

$$V = \frac{U}{q}$$

Units: _____

Lines of constant voltage around a point charge

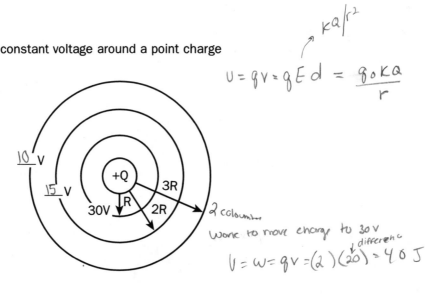

$\nearrow kq/r^2$

$$U = qv = qEd = \frac{q \circ kq}{r}$$

2 coloumbs
Work to move charge to 30 v

difference
$$V = W = qv = (2)(20) = 40 J$$

Directed Practice

- *Physical Sciences Review Notes*: Physics Ch. 6
- *Topical Tests*: Electrostatics and Electromagnetism Test 1 (Passage II)

Unit 2

$$r_1 \begin{bmatrix} q^- \\ \\ q^- \end{bmatrix} \qquad r_2 \begin{bmatrix} q^- \\ q^- \end{bmatrix}$$

$$V_{r_2} > V_{r_1}$$

(r₁ close to want to be (part))

The Lesson Continues on the Next Page →

Passage II (Questions 8–11)

To understand the effects of an electric field on a neutral atom, one can use a simple atomic model: a point nucleus with charge $+q$, surrounded by a uniformly charged spherical cloud of electrons with charge $-q$, centered on the nucleus. When an external uniform electric field, E, is applied to the atom, the nucleus and the electron cloud shift, moving in opposite directions and forming an induced dipole moment $p = qd$.

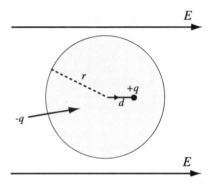

Figure 1

Eventually, the nucleus and the cloud reach translational equilibrium, separated by distance d, as the force on each due to the electric field is balanced by their mutual electrostatic attraction.

The induced dipole moment is directly proportional to the external field:

$$p = \alpha E,$$

where α is the atomic polarizability, the degree to which an atom polarizes in an external electric field. Using this simplified atomic model, $\alpha = 4\pi\varepsilon_0 r^3$.

Scratch Paper

Stop:

Think:

What is the relationship between electric fields and potential difference?

Predict:

Match

Stop:

Think:

Where does the passage discuss atomic polarizability?

What equations are used?

Predict:

Match

8. If two oppositely charged conducting plates are to be used to generate an 500,000 N/C electric field, how far apart should the plates be separated if the potential difference between them is 2,000 volts?

   A.   2 mm
   B.   4 mm
   C.   5 mm
   D.   10 mm

9. The atomic polarizability has the SI units:

   A. $\dfrac{C^2 \cdot s^2 \cdot m^3}{kg}$

   B. $\dfrac{C^2 \cdot s^2}{kg}$

   C. $\dfrac{C^2 \cdot s^2}{kg \cdot m^3}$

   D. $\dfrac{kg \cdot s^2}{C^2}$

Unit 2

Scratch Paper

Stop:

Think:

What is the relationship between Force and Work?

What is the magnitude of the force that each charge is exerting on the other?

Predict:

Match

Stop:

Draw a picture of the dipole.

Think:

What direction do the forces point in that are exerted on each charge within the dipole?

Predict:

Match

10. If the external electric field causes the nucleus and the electron cloud to shift the same distance, what is the work done on the nucleus by the electric field during this process?

    A. $-qEd$

    B. $-\dfrac{qEd}{2}$

    C. $+\dfrac{qEd}{2}$

    D. $+qEd$

11. An electric dipole is initially at rest in a uniform external electric field. Its dipole moment makes an angle θ with the direction of the field. What is the resulting motion of the dipole due to the field?

    A. Rotation, no translation
    B. No rotation, translation
    C. Both rotation and translation
    D. Neither rotation nor translation

MAGNETISM

Magnetic Field *(moving charge)*

SI unit: Tesla; $1T = 1 \dfrac{N \cdot s}{m \cdot C} = 1 \dfrac{N}{A \cdot m}$

Straight wire

$B = \mu_0 I / 2\pi r$

right hand rule

Center of circular wire

$B = \mu_0 I / 2r$

How to recognize magnetic fields

_____ $\rightarrow$ E $\underset{charge}{moving}$ _____ $\rightarrow$ B

Magnetic Force *(has to be charged) (perpendicular to E not parrallel)*

A magnetic field exerts a force on a moving charge or a current.

For moving charges

$F = qvB \sin \theta$; when $\theta = 90°$, $F = qvB$; when $\theta = 0°$ or $180°$, $F = 0$.

For a current-carrying wire

$F = ILB \sin \theta$

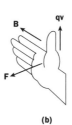

(a)   (b)

Unit 2

Unit 2

Critical Thinking Exercise

Consider a uniform magnetic field directed from left to right. In which direction will a stationary neutron be accelerated? A stationary proton? A proton moving at a speed v from left to right? A proton moving upwards at a speed v?

Critical Thinking Exercise

Scratch Paper
Stop:
Think:
Predict:
Match

12. A neutron decays into a proton, electron and anti-neutrino as shown in the bubble track photograph below. If there is a magnetic field but no electric field, what is the direction of the magnetic field?

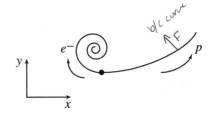

A. into the page
B. out of the page
C. along the positive *x*-axis
D. along the negative *y*-axis

Directed Practice

- *Physical Sciences Review Notes*: Physics Ch. 7
- *Topical Tests*: Electrostatics and Electromagnetism Test 1 (Passage I)

CIRCUITS

Current and Voltage

Current in = current out
Voltage drops = voltage gains

Resistance

$R \propto \dfrac{\frac{1}{A}}{}$

$R \propto \dfrac{\rho L}{}$

$\rightarrow$ resistivity (material)

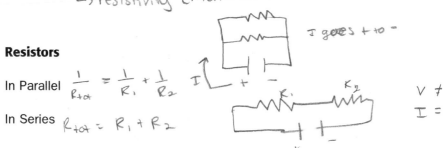

J goes + to –

$V =$
$I \neq$

$\boxed{V = IR}$

Resistors

In Parallel $\dfrac{1}{R_{tot}} = \dfrac{1}{R_1} + \dfrac{1}{R_2}$

In Series $R_{tot} = R_1 + R_2$

$V \neq$
$I =$

Ohm's Law

Example Circuit

Rₐ
15 Ω   25 Ω

R_b
40 Ω

30 Ω R_c

10 V

1) $R_a = [15 + 25] = 40$
   $\dfrac{1}{R_b} = \dfrac{1}{40} + \dfrac{1}{40} = \dfrac{\frac{2}{}}{40} = 20$
   $R_{tot} = 20 + 30 = 50$

2) current bat = 0.2 A
3) voltage drop in 30Ω = 6 V
4) voltage drop in 40Ω = 4 V
5) I of 40Ω = 0.1
6) I of 15Ω = 0.1
7) V of 15Ω = 1.5
8) V of 25Ω = 2.5
9) Power 15Ω = 0.15 W   (P = IV)

Electric Power

Capacitors and Dielectrics

Capacitor $\rightarrow$ storage charge

capacitance $= C = \dfrac{q}{V} = \dfrac{q}{Ed} = \dfrac{A E_0}{d}$

Dielectric $\rightarrow$ drops voltage difference to increase capacitance

$C' = KC$

Insert dielectric	Capacitance	charge	voltage
1) battery connected	↑	↑	=
			↓
2) Bat disconnected	↑	=	

AC Current and RMS

apply DC rules to AC

Directed Practice

- *Topical Tests*: Electric Circuits Test 1 (Passages 1 and 2)
- *Physical Sciences Review Notes*: Physics Ch. 8

Unit 2

The Lesson Continues
on the Next Page

Unit 2

Passage III (Questions 13–17)

Figure 1 shows an electromagnetic device designed to measure the strength of a magnetic field. The device accomplishes this task by balancing the magnetic force against a known force generated by the spring with spring constant k. The circuit consists of a D.C. battery supplying 100 V connected through a 2.5-Ω resistor and a metal rod. The metal rod is 30 cm long, has a mass of 0.7 kg, and slides with negligible friction along the arms of the circuit. The circuit is fixed in the plane of the page, and a permanent magnetic field B points out of the page (the generator is not shown). A spring is connected to the metal rod on one end and to an immobile piece of nonconducting material on the other.

In the configuration shown below, the metal rod experiences a force generated by the spring and a magnetic force $F = iLB$, where i is the current through the rod, L is the length of the rod, and B is the magnitude of the external magnetic field. The spring's equilibrium length x_{eq} is defined as the spring length for which the rod experiences no net force. In Figure 1, the switch is open, the spring is at its relaxed length x_0, and the metal rod is at rest.

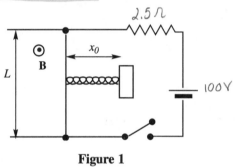

Figure 1

Stop:

Think:

What concept would explain the motion of the spring?

Predict:

Match

Stop:

Will this question require extensive calculations?

Think:

Predict:

Match

Stop:

Think:

What forces act on the rod?

Predict:

Match

13. After the switch has been closed, which best describes what happens to the spring?

    A. The spring compresses.
    B. The spring stretches.
    C. The length of the spring doesn't change.
    D. The spring will either stretch or compress depending upon the strength of the magnetic field.

14. If another 2.5-Ω resistor is added in series with the resistor and the battery in the circuit, how will the magnetic force on the rod change?

    A. It will decrease by a factor of 2.
    B. It will not change.
    C. It will increase by a factor of 2.
    D. It will increase by a factor of 4.

15. If the spring is removed from the apparatus when the switch is in the closed position, what will happen to the metal rod?

    A. It will remain motionless.
    B. It will accelerate.
    C. It will move with constant speed.
    D. It will oscillate with simple harmonic motion.

Unit 2

Scratch Paper

Stop:

How do we approach physics questions with wordy answer choices?

Think:

Predict:

Match

Stop:

Will this question require any intensive calculations?

Think:

Predict:

Match

16. After the switch is closed, the spring is displaced from equilibrium and released. The rod subsequently oscillates harmonically with a frequency of f cycles/sec. Which of the following will increase f?

A. Increasing the magnitude of the permanent magnetic field.
B. Decreasing the resistance of the resistor.
C. Decreasing the spring constant of the spring.
D. Decreasing the mass of the rod.

17. If the switch is closed, and the permanent magnetic field is reoriented so that it points toward the top of the page, which of the following will be true?

A. There will be no current flowing through the metal rod.
B. There will be current flowing through the spring.
C. The metal rod will not experience a magnetic force.
D. The current will flow clockwise around the circuit.

The Lesson Continues
on the Next Page

HOMEWORK

Review for Physics 2

Topical Tests	❏ Wave Characteristics and Periodic Motion Test 1
	❏ Electric Circuits Test 1
	❏ Sound Test 1
	❏ Electrostatics and Electromagnetism Test 1
Subject Tests	❏ Test 4 (Optional, DF3018)
	❏ Test 5 (Optional, DF3019)

Preview for General Chemistry 2

General Chemistry Review Notes	❏ *Chapters 4–6, 8 and 9
Foundation Review	❏ Unit 2 (Optional, MM3258A)
Online Workshops	❏ *Reaction Types
	❏ *Chemical Kinetics

General

Chemistry 2

QUESTIONS AND ANSWERS: COMPREHENSION

- Thermodynamics
- Equilibrium
- Solution Equilibria
- Phase Changes and Phase Equilibria

Passage I (Questions 1–5)

Hydrogen peroxide decomposes into oxygen and water according to Equation 1:

$$2H_2O_2(aq) \longrightarrow O_2(g) + 2H_2O(l)$$

Equation 1

Iodide catalyzes the decomposition of hydrogen peroxide by Mechanism 1:

$$H_2O_2(aq) + I^-(aq) \longrightarrow IO^-(aq) + H_2O(l)$$
$$H_2O_2(aq) + IO^-(aq) \longrightarrow I^-(aq) + H_2O(l) + O_2(g)$$

Mechanism 1

A chemistry student decides to study the kinetics of hydrogen peroxide decomposition.

Experiment 1

The student prepares two stock solutions of 0.060 M and 0.090 M KI in water, as well as stock solutions of 0.040 M and 0.080 M H_2O_2 in water. The student stores the hydrogen peroxide solutions in the freezer until beginning the experiment. He adds 100 mL of each hydrogen peroxide solution to 100 mL of each KI solution. The student measures the rate of oxygen formation for each trial. The results are summarized in Table 1.

Experiment 2

The student repeats Experiment 1, but uses flasks that were not properly cleaned. He observes the formation of molecular iodine, but no oxygen formation.

The student suspects that acid was present in the reaction vessel. In order to test his hypothesis, the student performs a third experiment.

Experiment 3

The student repeats Experiment 1, except he adds 100 mL of nitric acid to each reaction vessel before he adds the hydrogen peroxide solutions. He measures the initial rate of I_2 formation for the various concentrations of reactants. The results are summarized in Table 2.

Trial No.	Initial KI concentration (M)	Initial H_2O_2 concentration (M)	Initial rate of O_2 formation $(mol \cdot L^{-1} \cdot sec^{-1})$
1	0.060	0.040	3.61×10^{-8}
2	0.060	0.080	7.25×10^{-8}
3	0.090	0.040	5.39×10^{-8}
4	0.090	0.080	1.08×10^{-7}

Table 1

Trial No.	Initial KI concentration (M)	Initial H_2O_2 concentration (M)	Initial HNO_3 concentration (M)	Initial rate of I_2 formation $(mol \cdot L^{-1} \cdot sec^{-1})$
1	0.060	0.040	0.250	4.09×10^{-6}
2	0.060	0.080	0.250	8.23×10^{-6}
3	0.090	0.040	0.250	6.17×10^{-6}
4	0.060	0.040	0.500	8.21×10^{-6}

Table 2

After analyzing the experimental results, the student determines that $k_{obs}[H^+][I^-][H_2O_2]$ is the rate expression that governs the reactions of Experiments 2 and 3. The student proposes a mechanism consistent with this rate law, as shown in Mechanism 2.

$$H_2O_2 + H^+ \rightleftharpoons H_3O_2^+ \qquad \textbf{Step 1}$$

$$I^- + H_3O_2^+ \longrightarrow HOI + H_2O \qquad \textbf{Step 2}$$

$$I^- + HOI \longrightarrow I_2 + OH^- \qquad \textbf{Step 3}$$

$$H^+ + OH^- \longrightarrow H_2O \qquad \textbf{Step 4}$$

Mechanism 2

Unit 2

Scratch Paper

Scratch Paper

Stop:

Think:

Where is the information to answer this question?

Predict:

Match

Stop:

Think:

What is the rate-determining step for the reaction?

How is this step related to the rate expression?

Predict:

Match

Stop:

Think:

Remember to predict the answer before looking at the answer choices.

What kind of reactants do we have in step 4?

Predict:

Match

1. What is the rate expression for the reaction in Experiment 1?

   A. Rate = $k[\text{I}^-][\text{H}_2\text{O}_2]$
   B. Rate = $k[\text{H}^+][\text{I}^-][\text{H}_2\text{O}_2]$
   C. Rate = $k[\text{I}^-]^2[\text{H}_2\text{O}_2]$
   D. Rate = $k[\text{I}^-][\text{H}_2\text{O}_2]^2$

2. What is the slowest step in the mechanism proposed for Experiments 2 and 3?

   A. Step 1
   B. Step 2
   C. Step 3
   D. Step 4

3. What type of reaction is Step 4 of Mechanism 2?

   A. Precipitation
   B. Reduction-oxidation
   C. Neutralization
   D. Displacement

Scratch Paper

Stop:

Think:

What is the stoichiometry of the reaction?

Is there a limiting reagent?

Predict:

Match

Stop:

Think:

How does a catalyst affect a reaction?

What is the role of nitric acid in this reaction?

Predict:

Match

4. What is the maximum mass of $I_2(s)$ that the student can obtain from Trial 2 of Experiment 3?

   A.   0.20 g
   B.   0.76 g
   C.   2.03 g
   D.   3.18 g

5. Assuming Mechanism 2 is correct, is nitric acid acting as a catalyst in Experiment 3?

   A.   Yes, because it lowers the activation energy of the reaction.
   B.   Yes, because it makes the reaction proceed faster.
   C.   No, because in the absence of nitric acid, the same reaction would occur at the same rate.
   D.   No, because the H^+ is not regenerated.

Unit 2

Directed Practice

- *Physical Sciences Review Notes*: Gen. Chem. Ch. 5
- *High–Yield Problem Solving Guide*: pp. 116–117, pp. 118–119
- *Topical Tests*: Kinetics and Equilibrium Test 1 (Passage I)

THERMODYNAMICS

Enthalpy, *H* (heat content)

A reaction that leads to a decrease in enthalpy ($\Delta H < 0$) is exothermic. A reaction that leads to an increase in enthalpy ($\Delta H > 0$) is endothermic.

gases → highest enthalpy

State Functions – *path independent (only beginning and end matter)*

Critical Thinking Exercise

Scratch Paper

Stop:

Think:

What is bond enthalpy?

Is bond-breaking an exothermic or endothermic process?

What about bond-forming?

What bonds are broken and what bonds are formed in the reaction?

Predict:

Match

6. Given the following chemical reaction, what is the bond enthalpy of O–H?

$$4NH_3 + 3O_2 \rightarrow 2N_2 + 6H_2O$$
$$\Delta H = -1266 \text{ kJ}$$

(The bond enthalpy of the N–H bond is 389 kJ/mol; the bond enthalpy of O=O is 498 kJ/mol; the bond enthalpy of N≡N is 941 kJ/mol.)

A. 71 kJ/mol
B. 251 kJ/mol
C. 462 kJ/mol
D. 1033 kJ/mol

Unit 2

Entropy, S (disorder) → highest = gases , look highest # moles gases

Free energy, G – whether spontaneous (– G = spontaneous, no energy needed)

$$\Delta G = \Delta H - T\Delta S$$

Critical Thinking Exercise

x (*l*) → x (g)

$\Delta H = 44$ kJ

$\Delta S = 118$ J/K

Describe the system at low T: $\Delta G = 44 - T(118) \rightarrow \Delta G > 0$ non spontaneous

Describe the system at high T:
          $\Delta G < 0$, spontaneous

At what temperature is the system at equilibrium?
          when G = 0

What is the mystery substance?
          water

Directed Practice

- *Physical Sciences Review Notes*: Gen. Chem. Ch. 6, Physics Ch. 4
- *Topical Tests*: Thermodynamics and Thermochemistry Test 1, Questions 9–12
- *High–Yield Problem Solving Guide*: pp. 122–131

Critical Thinking Exercise

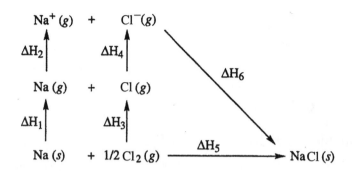

What would we call the quantity ΔH_5?

heat formation of NaCl

What is ΔH_1? Will it be positive or negative?

Heat of sublimation ; positive (need energy)

What is ΔH_2? Will it be positive or negative?

Ionization ; positive (need energy to take e^-)

What is ΔH_3? Will it be positive or negative?

½ bond enthalphy ; positive

What is ΔH_4? Will it be positive or negative?

electron affinity ; negative (gaing e^- and energy)

Would we expect ΔH_6 to be positive or negative?

negative (forming bond)

What does Hess's law say about these ΔHs?

$\Delta H_5 = H_1 + H_2 + H_3 + H_4 + H_6$

What do we know about the entropy change for the formation reaction?

decreasing (cause gas to solid)

The Lesson Continues
on the Next Page
$\longrightarrow$

Unit 2

Passage II (Questions 7–10)

Reactions result in enthalpy changes that represent the heat absorbed or lost by a system at constant pressure. The standard enthalpy of formation (ΔH_f°) is a specific case of enthalpy describing the heat lost or gained when a substance in its standard state is formed from the appropriate elements in their standard states. Enthalpy values are commonly in kJ/mol.

The enthalpy change of a reaction is often found by adding the enthalpy changes of simpler reactions that comprise the net reaction. For example, since Reaction 3 = Reaction 1 + Reaction 2 (below), $\Delta H_3 = \Delta H_1 + \Delta H_2$.

$$2H_2(g) \rightarrow 4H(g)$$

Reaction 1

$$C(g) + 4H(g) \rightarrow CH_4(g)$$

Reaction 2

$$C(g) + 2H_2(g) \rightarrow CH_4(g)$$

Reaction 3

Enthalpy is important in finding the free energy of a system, which can help determine the spontaneity of the reaction. Free energy is defined by the following formula:

$$\Delta G = \Delta H - T\Delta S$$

where ΔG = the free energy change of the reaction
ΔH = the enthalpy change of the reaction
T = the absolute temperature of the reaction
ΔS = the entropy change of the reaction

The following enthalpy values were gathered to study the energies of different hydrocarbons.

Fuel	Formula	ΔH_{comb} (kJ/mol)
Hydrogen	H_2	−241.8
Ethanol	CH_3CH_2OH	−1235.4
Acetylene	C_2H_2	−1255.5
Ethane	C_2H_6	−1427.7
Glucose	$C_6H_{12}O_6$	−2537.3

Scratch Paper

Stop:

Think:

What is the reaction that is taking place?

What equation do you need to use?

Predict:

Match

Stop:

Think:

What kinds of reactions can lead to an entropy increase?

What is the difference between the answer choices?

Predict:

Match

7. If the ΔH°_f of $CO_2(g)$ is –393.5 kJ/mol, and the ΔH°_f of $H_2O(g)$ is –241.8 kJ/mol, what is the ΔH°_f of acetylene?

    A.   –620.1 kJ/mol
    B.   –226.6 kJ/mol
    C.   226.6 kJ/mol
    D.   620.1 kJ/mol

8. Which of the following reactions would produce the greatest increase in entropy?

    A.   Combustion of hydrogen
    B.   Combustion of acetylene
    C.   Combustion of ethane
    D.   Combustion of glucose

Unit 2

Scratch Paper

Stop:

Think:

What equation do you need to use?

Predict:

Match

Stop:

Think:

How does temperature affect the spontaneity of a reaction?

Predict:

Match

9. Given that ΔS for the combustion of ethanol is 0.217 kJ/mol·K at 25°C, what is the value of the change in the Gibbs free energy for this reaction?

   A.   −64.7 kJ/mol of ethanol
   B.   −1170 kJ/mol of ethanol
   C.   −1235 kJ/mol of ethanol
   D.   −1300 kJ/mol of ethanol

10. Which of the following pairs of characteristics defines a reaction that is temperature-dependent?

    I.   Positive ΔH, positive ΔS
    II.   Positive ΔH, negative ΔS
    III. Negative ΔH, positive ΔS
    IV.   Negative ΔH, negative ΔS

    A.   I and II only
    B.   I and III only
    C.   I and IV only
    D.   II and III only

Directed Practice

- *Topical Tests*: Thermodynamics and Thermochemistry Test 1 (Passage II)

Unit 2

EQUILIBRIUM

Chemical Equilibrium

Chemical equilibrium is a dynamic state that exists when the net change in reactants and products is zero.

Rate of Forward Reaction = Rate of Reverse reaction

At Equilibrium, $\Delta G = 0$

The reaction quotient (Q)

The reaction quotient is a measure of where the reactants and products are at any given moment in time (given as a ratio).

The value of Q changes during the course of the reaction until the system reaches equilibrium.

The equilibrium constant (K_{eq})

The equilibrium constant, K_{eq} is constant for a certain ratio of the product and reactant concentrations for a reversible reaction at equilibrium.

At equilibrium, $Q = K_{eq}$.

$$\Delta G = RT \ln\left(\frac{Q}{K_{eq}}\right)$$

$$\Delta G° = -RT \ln K_{eq} \qquad (standard °; 1\ atm,\ 25°C)$$

Critical Thinking Exercise

When Q is less than K_{eq}, the ratio $\frac{Q}{K_{eq}}$ becomes a fraction between 0 and 1. What does this mean in terms of the ΔG of the reaction?

Directed Practice

- *Math Foundation Review*
- *Topical Tests*: Kinetics and Equilibrium Test 1 (Passage II)

Unit 2

Le Châtelier's Principle

Le Châtelier's Principle states that when an equilibrated system is placed under stress, it will react in a direction to reduce that stress.

Types of stress on a system: (increase or decrease)

Concentration

Temperature

Pressure

For	To Shift to the Right (forward)	To Shift to the Left (reverse)
Any reaction	Add: Reactants	Remove: Reactants
Any reaction	Remove: Product	Add: Product
Exothermic rxns	↓ Heat	↑ Heat
Endothermic rxns	↑ Heat	↓ Heat
Rxns that ↓ the number of gas moles	↑ Pressure ↓ Volume	↓ Pressure ↑ Volume
Rxns that ↑ the number of gas moles	↑ Volume ↓ Pressure	↓ Volume ↑ Pressure

Unit 2

Critical Thinking Exercise

System 1

3 moles of N_2O_4 is placed in a 0.5 L glass container. After a while the following equilibrium is established.

$$N_2O_4\ (g) \rightleftharpoons 2NO_2\ (g) \qquad \Delta H = 63\ \text{J/mole}$$
$$\text{colorless} \qquad\qquad \text{red}$$

What is the expression for the equilibrium constant for system #1? $\quad K_{eq.} = \dfrac{[NO_2]^2}{[N_2O_4]}$

At a certain temperature, the equilibrium constant is 6×10^{-6}. What is the concentration of NO_2 at this temperature?

What would happen if the temperature were increased in the vessel containing system #1?

What would happen if the pressure were increased in system 1?

System 2

$$2PbSo_4(s) + 2H_2O(l) \rightleftharpoons Pb(s) + PbO_2(s) + 2HSO_4^-\ (aq) + 2H^+\ (aq)$$

What effect would increasing the amount of $Pb(s)$ have on system 2?

What would happen if the pH of system 2 were increasing?

System 3

$$H_2O\ (g) \rightleftharpoons H_2O\ (l)$$

What would happen to system 3 if the pressure were increased?

Directed Practice

- *Topical Tests*: Kinetics and Equilibrium Test 1, Questions 15–18
- *High–Yield Problem Solving Guide*: pp. 120–121

SOLUTION EQUILIBRIA

Solubility product constant (K_{sp}) *solubility constant*
* (can not change)

This equilibrium constant is given the special name solubility product constant because it tells how soluble a solid is.

K_{eq} for a dissolution reaction is called the K_{sp} of the reaction.

Reaction Example:

Ion product

The ion product of a reaction has the same form as the K_{sp}. However, its value can be calculated at any concentration.

Q, the reaction Quotient for a dissociation reaction, is called the Ion Product, IP.

Saturation

Just like the Q and K_{eq}, the IP and the K_{sp} tell us where the products are in relation to where they're supposed to be at equilibrium.

IP < K_{sp} : _unsaturated_

IP = K_{sp} : _saturated (at equilibrium)_

IP > K_{sp} : _super saturated_

Molar solubility *(can change* w/ temp) *, x dissolve in y)*

Molar solubility is the molar concentration; i.e., molarity (M) of a solute in a saturated solution.

Common ion effect

The common ion effect occurs when one of the ions of a dissolved solid is present in solution from another source.

The common ion effect hinders the dissociation of solids and changes the molar solubility of the reaction.

Kaplan's Method for Molar Solubility Questions

1) Write down a balanced reaction for the dissociation reaction (if it's not given to you).

$$PbSO_4 (s) \rightleftharpoons Pb^{+2} (aq) + SO_4^{-2} (aq.)$$

2) Find an expression for the K_{sp}.

$$K_{sp} = [Pb^{+2}][SO_4^{-2}]$$

3) Plug into the K_{sp} expression.

$$K_{sp} = [x][x] = x^2$$

Examples:

What is the molar solubility of silver chloride solution in a 0.1 M solution of table salt? ($K_{sp} = \underline{1.6 \times 10^{-10}}$)

The molar solubility of ZnF_2 in water is $\underline{1.57 \times 10^{-1}}$ M. What is ZnF_2's K_{sp}?

Directed Practice
- *Physical Sciences Review Notes*: Gen. Chem. Ch. 9
- *High–Yield Problem Solving Guide*: pp. 136–137

Unit 2

PHASE CHANGES AND PHASE EQUILIBRIA

Heating curves

Specific heat

Specific heat, c, is the amount of heat required to raise the temperature of one unit mass of a material by one degree Celsius.

$q = mc\Delta T$

does not change phase

C for water = 1

Critical Thinking Exercise

Is it possible to add heat to a system without changing its temperature?

yes; phase change, gas expand (do work)

Heat of transformation

The heat of transformation is the heat necessary to cause a phase change in a substance.

$q = m\Delta H_L$

(latent heat)

Critical Thinking Exercise

Scratch Paper

12. The figure below shows plots of the vapor pressure of several compounds as a function of temperature. Which of them has the lowest boiling point if the ambient pressure is 0.5 atm?

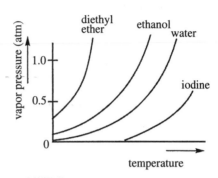

   A.   Diethyl ether
   B.   Ethanol
   C.   Water
   D.   Iodine

Directed Practice

- *Physical Sciences Review Notes*: Gen. Chem. Ch. 8
- *Topical Tests*: Thermodynamics and Thermochemistry Test 1 (Passage I)

Phase diagrams

A phase diagram shows the conditions at which a specific substance exists as a solid, liquid, or gas.

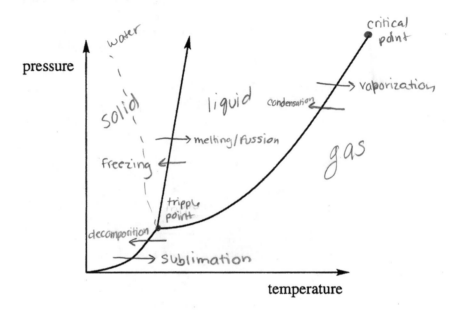

Critical Thinking Exercise

How does the phase diagram look different for water? What properties of water account for this difference?

negative slope b/w solid liquid
    b/c Hydrogen bonding
↑ Pressure = turns liquid
    freezes = crystalized (loss H bonding)

Unit 2

COLLIGATIVE PROPERTIES – properties dependent on concentration of solute

Molality – $\dfrac{\text{mols solute}}{\text{kg solvent}}$

ex. $NaCl \longrightarrow Na^+ Cl^-$ = 2 molals

Vapor Pressure Depression (Raoult's Law)

$P_A = X_A P_A^\circ$

Add solute to solvent, VP decreases ↓

BP increases ↑

Boiling Point Elevation

$\Delta T_b = K_b m$

Add solute to solvent, BP ↑

Freezing Point Depression

$\Delta T_f = K_f m$

Add solute to solvent, FP ↓

Critical Thinking Exercise

Imagine cooking identical frozen pizzas (at the same tempearture) in Denver and Los Angeles. Which would be cooked faster?

LA, b/c ↓ Pressure ↑ BP

Unit 2

Passage III (Questions 13–16)

The exact concentration of silver ion in solution can be determined experimentally by titrating with the thiocyanate ion, SCN^-. This method for silver determination is called the *Volhard method* and uses iron (III) as an indicator because it gives a deep red color at the first excess of thiocyanate ion in solution. The solution must be kept fairly acidic to prevent $Fe(OH)_3$ formation. The most useful application of the Volhard method is in the determination of halide ion concentration. After a halide solution has been titrated with silver ion to precipitate out insoluble silver halide salts, the solution can be back-titrated with thiocyanate to determine the amount of excess silver ion. This gives a more accurate reading of the halide endpoint. Relevant solubility products for the precipitates involved are given below.

A student planned to determine the concentration of chloride ion in an unknown solution. In order to obtain the best possible endpoint of silver, he filtered out the silver chloride precipitate and titrated the solution with 0.001M sodium thiocyanate. The sodium thiocyanate was contaminated with NaOH and the red $FeSCN^{2+}$ indicator never formed.

Compound	K_{sp}
AgSCN	1.0×10^{-12}
AgCl	1.8×10^{-10}
$Fe(OH)_3$	2.6×10^{-39}

Table 1

Scratch Paper

Scratch Paper

Stop:

Think:

Predict:

Match

Stop:

Think:

Predict:

Match

13. If 1.0 mL of a 1.0×10^{-5} M NaSCN solution is added to 3.0 mL of a 1.0×10^{-5} M $AgNO_3$ solution, will there be any precipitate?

 A. No, both NaSCN and $AgNO_3$ are completely soluble.
 B. No, all ion concentrations are at or below saturation levels.
 C. Yes, both AgSCN and $NaNO_3$ are completely insoluble.
 D. Yes, Ag^+ and SCN^- concentrations are above saturation levels.

14. In a Volhard titration, why does AgSCN precipitate before any $FeSCN^{2+}$ forms?

 A. The anion to cation bond in silver thiocyanate has more ionic character.
 B. Silver thiocyanate is the less stable of the two compounds.
 C. Silver thiocyanate reaches equilibrium in solution at lower concentrations.
 D. Silver thiocyanate is the heavier of the two compounds.

Unit 2

Scratch Paper

Stop:

Think:

Predict:

Match

Stop:

Think:

Predict:

Match

15. Which of the following has the highest molar solubility?

    A. $BaCrO_4$ ($K_{sp} = 2.1 \times 10^{-10}$)
    B. $AgCl$ ($K_{sp} = 1.6 \times 10^{-10}$)
    C. $Al(OH)_3$ ($K_{sp} = 3.7 \times 10^{-15}$)
    D. $PbCO_3$ ($K_{sp} = 3.3 \times 10^{-14}$)

16. Why was the endpoint never indicated in the student's Volhard titration?

    A.   The presence of NaOH prevented NaSCN dissociation.
    B.   A hydrated AgOH complex formed which is almost completely soluble.
    C.   A hydrated $Fe(OH)_3$ complex formed which is almost completely insoluble.
    D.   The NaOH neutralized the cations in the solution.

Scratch Paper

Stop:

Think:

Predict:

Match

Stop:

Think:

Predict:

Match

Stop:

Think:

Predict:

Match

Questions 17 through 19 are NOT based on a descriptive passage.

17. Copper oxide may be prepared by the following reaction:

$$2\ Cu(NO_3)_2 \rightarrow 2\ CuO + 4\ NO_2 + O_2$$

This is best characterized as:

   A.   a combustion reaction.
   B.   a neutralization reaction.
   C.   a Lewis acid-base reaction.
   D.   a decomposition and redox reaction.

18. What is the maximum possible concentration of calcium in a 0.7 M solution of NaF(aq) at 25°C? ($K_{sp} = 4.9 \times 10^{-11}$ for CaF_2 at 25°C)

   A. 1.0×10^{-11} M
   B. 1.0×10^{-10} M
   C. 7.0×10^{-6} M
   D. 2.3×10^{-4} M

19. For the reaction below, what would be the effect of decreasing the volume of the system?

$$2NaHCO_3(s) \rightleftharpoons Na_2CO_3(s) + CO_2(g) + H_2O(g)$$

   A.   The formation of reactants would be favored.
   B.   There would be no change.
   C.   The formation of products would be favored.
   D.   The effect cannot be determined.

HOMEWORK

Review for General Chemistry 2

Topical Tests	❏ Kinetics and Equilibrium Test 1 ❏ Thermodynamics and Thermochemistry Test 1 ❏ Stoichiometry Test 1
Subject Tests	❏ Test 3 (Optional, DD3076) ❏ Test 4 (Optional, DD3077) ❏ Test 5 (Optional, DD3078)

Preview for Verbal Reasoning & Writing Sample 2

Verbal Reasoning Strategy and Practice	❏ *Chapter 4
Writing Sample section in Verbal Reasoning Strategy and Practice	❏ *Chapters 2 and 4
Foundation Review	❏ Unit 2 (Optional, MM3261A)

Unit 2

QUESTIONS AND ANSWERS

Verbal Reasoning and Writing Sample 2

QUESTIONS AND ANSWERS: APPLYING THE PROCESS

- The Kaplan Question Strategy
- Question Types
- Wrong Answer Pathologies
- How Essays Are Scored
- Sample Essays
- Writing Sample Databases

THE KAPLAN QUESTION STRATEGY

STOP

> Characterize the question type

THINK

> What is the question really asking

> How does the passage map help answer the question

> What is the relevant information in the passage

PREDICT

> Formulate a framework or prediction for your answer

MATCH

> Which answer truly meets the requirements of the prediction

Unit 2

PHILOSOPHICAL PASSAGE

According to our traditional understanding of responsibility, we are primarily or directly responsible for our "voluntary" actions, the things we do, and (at most) only indirectly responsible for the things that happen to us. It is held, for instance, that "I can't help" the surge of anger, say, that I feel when objects in the environment present themselves to my senses in certain ways; however, I am supposed to govern my subsequent thoughts and activities regarding these objects by the force of my will. When we look inside ourselves with the goal of sorting our mental events into these two morally important categories, something peculiar happens. Events near the input and output "peripheries" fall unproblematically into place. Thus, feeling pain in my foot and seeing the desk are clearly not acts "in my control," but things that happen to me as a result of impingements from the world. And moving my finger or saying these words are obviously things that I do—voluntary actions *par excellence*.

But as we move away from those peripheries toward the presumptive center, the events we try to examine exhibit a strange flickering back and forth, like the illusion drawing of a transparent cube. It no longer seems so clear that perception is a passive matter. Do I not voluntarily contribute something to my perception, even to my recognition or "acceptance" of the desk as a desk? For after all, can I not suspend judgment in the face of any perceptual presentation, and withhold conviction? And on the other side of the center, when we look more closely at action, is my voluntary act really moving my finger, or is it more properly trying to move my finger? A familiar [thought experiment] about someone willing actions while totally paralyzed attests that I am not in control of all the conditions in the world (or in my body) that are necessary for my finger actually to move.

Faced with our inability to "see" (by "introspection") where the center or source of our free actions is, and loath to abandon our conviction that we really do things (for which we are responsible), we exploit the cognitive vacuum, the gaps in our self-knowledge, by filling it with a rather magical and mysterious entity, the unmoved mover, the active self.

This theoretical leap is nowhere more evident than in our reaction to our failures of "will power". "I'm going to get out of bed and get to work right now!" I say to myself, and go right on lying drowsily in bed. Did I or did I not just make a decision to get up? Can't I tell when I've really made a decision? Perhaps I just seem to myself to have made a decision. Once we recognize that our conscious access to our own decisions is problematic, we may go on to note how many of the important turning points in our lives were unaccompanied, so far as retrospective memory of conscious experience goes, by conscious decisions. "I have decided to take the job," one says. And very clearly one takes oneself to be reporting on something one had done recently, but reminiscence shows only that yesterday one was undecided, and today one is no longer undecided; at some moment in the interval the decision must have happened, without fanfare. Where did it happen? At Central Headquarters, of course.

But such a deduction reveals that we are building a psychological theory of "decision" by idealizing and extending our actual practice, by inserting decisions where theory demands them, not where we have any first-hand experience of them. I must have made a decision, one reasons, since I see that I have definitely made up my mind, and hadn't made up my mind yesterday. The mysterious inner sanctum of the central agent begins to take on a mysterious life of its own.

Scratch Paper

THE VERBAL REASONING QUESTION TYPES

Type	Task	Sub-types	Frequency	Keywords
Global	*Know purpose*	None	1–3 per section	Central thesis/primary purpose, title
Detail	*what's stated in passage*	Scattered detail (Roman Numeral questions or Least/Except/Not)	1–2 per passage	According to, Stated in the passage
Deduction	*Not in passage but must be true*	Inference, Assumption, Definition-in-context	3+ per passage	Infer, suggest, author would most likely agree/disagree, implicit in
Evaluation	*Foundation authors arguement*	Structure, Function	2–3 per passage	In order to (function)
Application	*apply new info to different situations*	None	2+ per passage	Vary. Questions tend to contain short paragraphs that seem to have no relation to text
Incorporation		Strengthen/Weaken	1–2 per passage	Strengthen, Weaken, The following, if true…

What type of passage information is ripe for MCAT questions?

author's opinion

evidence

arguements

APPLYING THE PROCESS

Scratch Paper

Stop:

Think:

Where should you expect to find the answer to this global question?

What was the author's overall point?

Predict:

Match

Stop:

Think:

Where does the passage refer to "making decisions"?

What is the gist of that paragraph?

Predict:

Match

1. The passage's central thesis is that:

   A. can't classify as voluntar
   B. or involuntary
   C.
   D.

2. According to the passage, if an individual has made a decision in the past, it:

   A. don't know when make
   B. decision or how process works
   C.
   D.

Scratch Paper

Stop:

Think:

Where should you expect to find the answer to this global question?

What was the author's overall point?

Predict:

Match

Stop:

Think:

Where does the passage refer to "making decisions"?

What is the purpose of that paragraph?

Predict:

Match

1. The passage's central thesis is that:

   A. one should not be held responsible for actions over which one exerts no control.
   B. our sense that we can act voluntarily is an illusion.
   C. decisions are the instants in which we exercise our volition to the fullest.
   D. many actions cannot be classified precisely as either voluntary or involuntary.

2. Based on information in the passage, if an individual has made a decision in the past, it:

   A. automatically follows that the individual must assume full responsibility.
   B. is sufficient proof that the individual possesses free will.
   C. often cannot be ascertained how the individual knows he made the decision.
   D. may not seem to the individual that there was any decision made at all.

Unit 2

Crisis Prevention Tip

What will you do on Test Day if one question seems impossible to answer quickly?

Scratch Paper

Stop:

Think:

What opinions are expressed by the author in the passage?

Predict:

Match

Stop:

Think:

How does the context define this phrase?

Predict:

Match

Stop:

Think:

How much of the passage must you read to understand this quote?

What does it contribute to the author's overall point?

Predict:

Match

3. Which of the following is a statement with which the author would most probably agree?

 A. People often exaggerate how much conscious thought went into their actions.
 B. A decision usually takes longer to make than one anticipates.
 C. Certain problems are better addressed through philosophical analysis than through science.
 D. More careful thought should go into decision-making.

4. Judging from the context, the "unmoved mover" (paragraph 3) could best be described as:

 A. the divine being that many think guides one's actions.
 B. the inherent core of irrationality in human behavior.
 C. the part of the human psyche that governs decision-making.
 D. the natural tendency to pursue one's self-interest.

5. The author most probably cites "our failures of 'will power'" (paragraph 4) in order to show that:

 A. some people have more will power than others.
 B. one could possibly make a decision and yet not act on it.
 C. some decisions are much more difficult to make than others.
 D. the concept of will power makes sense in theory but not in real life.

Unit 2

Scratch Paper

Stop:

Think:

Where does the author mention voluntary and involuntary acts?

What is the author's view?

Predict:

Match

Stop:

Think:

What is the author's view on voluntary and involuntary acts?

How does this example relate to the author's point?

Predict:

Match

6. Aristotle characterized a voluntary act as one whose source was "within the agent" and an involuntary act as "one of which the moving principle is outside." Based on the passage, the author would most likely respond to this by pointing out that:

   A. we are only responsible for our voluntary actions.
   B. many actions contain elements of both categories.
   C. there is no conscious judgment involved in an involuntary act.
   D. the external moving principle is actually our own creation.

7. Suppose that a person heats a kettle of water on a stove, takes it off the stove, and then accidentally spills some of the hot water on his or her skin. According to the passage, which of the following perceptions has a voluntary element?

   I. Perceiving that the hot stove caused the water to become hot
   II. Perceiving that the kettle is made of steel
   III. Perceiving the hot water as painful

   A. I only
   B. III only
   C. I and II only
   D. I, II, and III

Unit 2

Critical Thinking Exercise

In paragraph 4, the author claims that "many of the important turning points in our lives [are] unaccompanied, so far as retrospective memory of the conscious experience goes, by conscious decisions." Is this claim supported by information in the passage?

WRONG ANSWER PATHOLOGIES

Pathology		Why It's Wrong	Why It's Seductive	Where It Shows Up
Faulty Use of Detail		Not relevant to the answer (often a direct quote from the wrong part of passage or a fact about a concept other than the one the question is asking about)		Detail, Global
	Opposite	The opposite of the credited answer		Detail, Global, Deduction, Evaluation
	Distortion	Close to the credited answer, but distorted (often too extreme)		Detail, Global, Deduction, Evaluation
Out of Scope		Not relevant to the credited answer (outside the scope of the passage or question)		Detail, Global, Deduction, Evaluation (esp. Inference & Assumption), Incorporation, Application

The Lesson Continues
on the Next Page

#relationships

ABSTRACT PASSAGE

Those who consider the Devil to be a partisan of Evil and angels to be warriors for Good accept the demagogy of the angels. Things are clearly more complicated. Angels are partisans not of Good, but of Divine creation. The Devil, on the other hand, denies all rational meaning to God's world.

World domination, as everyone knows, is divided between demons and angels. But the good of the world does not require the latter to gain precedence over the former (as I thought when I was young); all it needs is a certain equilibrium of power. If there is too much uncontested meaning on earth (the reign of the angels), man collapses under the burden; if the world loses all its meaning (the reign of the demons), life is every bit as impossible.

Things deprived suddenly of their putative meaning, the place assigned to them in the ostensible order of things, make us laugh. Initially, therefore, laughter is the province of the Devil. It has a certain malice to it (things have turned out differently from the way they tried to seem), but a certain beneficent relief as well (things are looser than they seemed, we have greater latitude in living with them, their gravity does not oppress us).

The first time an angel heard the Devil's laughter he was horrified. It was in the middle of a feast with a lot of people around, and one after the other they joined the Devil's laughter. It was terribly contagious. The angel was all too aware that the laughter was aimed against God and the wonder of His works. He knew he had to act fast, but felt weak and defenseless. And unable to fabricate anything of his own, he simply turned his enemy's tactics against him. He opened his mouth and let out a wobbly, breathy sound in the upper reaches of his vocal register and endowed it with the opposite meaning. Whereas the Devil's laughter pointed up the meaninglessness of things, the angel's shout rejoiced in how rationally organized, well conceived, beautiful, good, and sensible everything on earth was.

There they stood, Devil and angel, face to face, mouths open, both making more or less the same sound, but each expressing himself in a unique timbre—absolute opposites. And seeing the laughing angel, the Devil laughed all the harder, all the louder, all the more openly, because the laughing angel was infinitely laughable.

Laughable laughter is cataclysmic. And even so, the angels have gained something by it. They have tricked us all with their semantic hoax. Their imitation laughter and its original (the Devil's) have the same name. People nowadays do not even realize that one and the same external phenomenon embraces two completely contradictory internal attitudes. There are two kinds of laughter, and we lack the words to distinguish them.

Scratch Paper

Scratch Paper

Stop:

Think:

Predict:

Match

8. What does the author's conception of laughter imply about language?

   A. Language is capable of concealing distinct meanings.
   B. Language cannot be suddenly deprived of all meaning.
   C. Language is always precise and unambiguous.
   D. Language is unnecessary for spiritual beings.

Stop:

Think:

Predict:

Match

9. In the context of the passage, which of the following forms of laughter is most similar to the Devil's laughter?

   A. Laughing nervously in a tense situation
   B. Laughing at a joke in which the meaning of a word is twisted
   C. Laughing in satisfaction when a complicated task is completed
   D. Laughing to conceal one's true intentions

Stop:

Think:

Predict:

Match

10. Based on information in the passage, with which of the following statements would the author most likely NOT agree?

    A. A balance must be struck in the world between rationality and irrationality.
    B. The Devil serves an important function for the good of the world.
    C. Laughter is the simultaneous expression of two contradictory attitudes.
    D. It is possible to laugh without having seen something deprived of meaning.

Unit 2

Scratch Paper

Stop:

Think:

Predict:

Match

Stop:

Think:

Predict:

Match

11. Based on information in the passage, which of the following opinions could most reasonably be ascribed to the author?

   A. Myths about the origin of phenomena can give insight into their nature.
   B. We are misguided in assuming that things in our world are at all rational or ordered.
   C. One should be horrified at laughter that contains an element of malice.
   D. Traditional religious conceptions of angels and demons should not be taken seriously.

12. According to the passage, which of the following is true about the relationship between laughter and meaning?

   A. Laughter would not have come about if the meaning of everything was immutable.
   B. Without laughter, there would be no way to contest the meaning of things.
   C. The word we use to denote laughter itself has no meaning.
   D. There are only two possible types of laughter that have meaning.

The Lesson Continues
on the Next Page
→

Unit 2

"EXPLAIN THE PHENOMENA" PASSAGE

Since it was proposed in 1980, the Alvarezes' theory that the mass extinction of plant and animal species at the end of the Cretaceous period 65 million years ago resulted from a devastating extraterrestrial impact has won increasing support, although even today there is no consensus for it among scientists. In the Alvarezes' scenario, an asteroid 10 kilometers in diameter struck the earth at high velocity, forming a crater 150 kilometers wide. In addition to the immediate devastation of tidal waves, global fires, and giant storms, impact debris hurled into the atmosphere at high altitude spread around the earth, preventing sunlight from reaching the ground. With photosynthesis blocked, herbivorous and carnivorous species died as the food chain was snapped at its base.

The Alvarezes' primary evidence is a superabundance of iridium in the "Cretaceous/Tertiary boundary" (KT boundary), a thin rock stratum dividing Cretaceous rocks from those of the later Tertiary period. Iridium, relatively rare in the earth's crust, comes mainly from the slow fall of interplanetary debris; in some KT boundary strata, iridium is 10–100 times as abundant as normal, suggesting a rapid, massive deposition. Coincident with the boundary, whole species of pollens and unicellular animals vanished from the fossil record, strongly supporting the idea of a catastrophic event. Later studies have shown that some KT boundary samples also contain osmium isotopes typical of meteorites, basalt spherules that may have melted on impact and rapidly cooled in the atmosphere, and quartz grains deformed in a manner typical of high velocity impacts.

Initially, paleontologists dismissed the theory, arguing that fossils of large animals such as dinosaurs showed a gradual extinction lasting millions of years. But recent intensive exploration of the Hell Creek formation of North Dakota and Montana, aimed at collecting all available dinosaur remnants rather than selectively searching for rare or well-preserved fossils, has shown an abundance of dinosaurs right up to the KT boundary. As a result, opposition to catastrophic mass extinction has substantially weakened among paleontologists.

Given the lack of a known impact crater of the necessary age and size, and the fact that the theory requires the extinctions to have occurred in an extremely short time, some scientists have proposed alternative catastrophe scenarios. Courtillot and others have argued that massive volcanic eruptions, lasting hundreds of thousands of years, pumped enough debris into the atmosphere to cause the darkness and chemical changes that devastated life on the planet. Courtillot's evidence includes huge volcanic flows in India that coincide with the KT boundary, and analyses of KT boundary rocks that seem to show that the excess iridium was laid down over 10,000–100,000 years, too long for the impact hypothesis.

Walter Alvarez and Frank Asaro reply that the shock wave caused by an impact could have melted mantle rocks, triggering the volcanic activity. They concede, though, that the exact mechanism is unclear. Meanwhile, drillings at a 150-kilometer-wide circular geologic formation in Yucatan, found in 1978 but not carefully examined until 1990, have shown a composition consistent with extraterrestrial impact. However, there is still no conclusive evidence that the Yucatan formation is the long-sought impact site.

Scratch Paper

Unit 2

Scratch Paper

Stop:

Think:

What evidence supports the Alvarezes' theory?

Predict:

Match

Stop:

Think:

What, briefly, is the Alvarezes' theory? What is Courtillot's?

Is the later proliferation of life forms relevant?

Predict:

Match

Stop:

Think:

What does the beginning of that sentence say?

How does it relate to the rest of the paragraph?

Predict:

Match

13. Which of the following statements, if true, would most strengthen the Alvarezes' theory?

   A. Geologists have determined that the Yucatan formation is in fact a 30-million-year-old asteroid impact site.
   B. Courtillot's analyses of KT boundary rocks overestimated the length of time over which iridium was laid down.
   C. The extinction of animal species accompanied the disappearance of plant life.
   D. The number of scientists that have proposed and now defend alternative catastrophe scenarios is very small.

14. According to a recent study, plant and animal species did not begin to proliferate again until several million years after the end of the Cretaceous period. If true, this would:

   A. provide support for the Alvarezes' theory, but not for Courtillot's theory.
   B. provide support for Courtillot's theory, but not for the Alvarezes' theory.
   C. provide support for both the Alvarezes' theory and Courtillot's theory.
   D. provide support for neither the Alvarezes' theory nor Courtillot's theory.

15. Judging from the context, the statement "the food chain was snapped at its base" (paragraph 1) means that:

   A. plants could not survive in the aftermath of the impact.
   B. even unicellular organisms vanished from the fossil record.
   C. normally herbivorous species were forced by disaster to become carnivorous.
   D. predators had difficulty hunting their prey in a darkened environment.

Unit 2

Scratch Paper

Stop:

Think:

Where is the Hell Creek exploration mentioned?

What does the passage tell us about it?

Predict:

Match

Stop:

Think:

What are the details given about this impact?

What must the Alvarezes believe, if this supports their theory?

Predict:

Match

Stop:

Think:

What are we told about the Alvarezes' views?

What do we know about Courtillot's?

Predict:

Match

16. With which of the following statements about the Hell Creek exploration would the author most probably NOT agree with?

   A. The conclusions of the Hell Creek exploration cannot be generalized to areas outside North Dakota and Montana.
   B. The conclusions of the Hell Creek exploration were based on a more suitable method than those of previous studies.
   C. Searching only for well-preserved fossils would have provided an artificially low estimate of species abundance.
   D. Data from the study indicate that there was a mass extinction of plant and animal species at the KT boundary.

17. Implicit in the Alvarezes' theory about the extraterrestrial impact at the KT boundary is the assumption that:

   A. similar extraterrestrial impacts had occurred at earlier points in the earth's history.
   B. an asteroid 10 kilometers in diameter would be of sufficient size to precipitate a catastrophic event.
   C. superabundance of iridium is the best evidence one could obtain to show that an impact took place.
   D. volcanic eruptions are not capable of altering atmospheric conditions.

18. It can be inferred that supporters of the Alvarezes' and Courtillot's theories hold which of the following views in common?

   A. The iridium layer was deposited over tens of thousands of years.
   B. Large animals such as the dinosaurs died out gradually over millions of years.
   C. Mass extinction occurred as an indirect result of debris in the atmosphere.
   D. It is unlikely that the specific cause of the extinctions will ever be determined.

19. Of the following, which is the most likely reason that the superabundance of iridium in the KT boundary is taken as evidence of an asteroid impact?

   A. Most of the iridium on earth is not of extraterrestrial origin.
   B. Iridium is never found in quantities greater than trace amounts on the earth.
   C. There is no other likely source of such massive amounts of iridium.
   D. Elevated levels of iridium are extremely uncommon geological findings.

20. Which of the following claims is best supported by evidence from the passage?

   A. An asteroid struck the earth in Yucatan, causing widespread devastation and mass extinction.
   B. Dinosaur species were flourishing prior to the end of the Cretaceous era.
   C. Dinosaurs became extinct as the direct result of massive volcanic eruptions.
   D. The main value of the asteroid impact theory is that it will eventually lead to another theory.

Unit 2

VERBAL REASONING PRACTICE STRATEGIES

Practice Tests

Practice at the same time of day that you will take the Verbal Reasoning section on Test Day.

When you take section-length practice tests, don't neglect passage and question triage strategies.

Don't just look at the answer choices and explanations; if you're having trouble, maybe you're not critically reading the passage.

Outside Reading

Read *The Economist, The Atlantic Monthly, The New York Review of Books, Civilization*, or other popular journals with articles by scholars. Focus on topics that you find troublesome.

Don't read the whole article if it's too difficult—just a few paragraphs, applying your critical reading skills.

Learn to keep your attention focused even when surrounded by distractions (in a train station, for example). Focused reading is essential to scoring well.

Crisis Prevention Tip

Are you reviewing wrong answer choices effectively?

Which Question	Question Type	Why I Missed It

Unit 2

THE WRITING SAMPLE

Consider this statement:

It is each citizen's duty to obey the laws of the nation.

Write a unified essay in which you perform the following tasks. Explain what you think the above statement means. Describe a specific situation in which a citizen might not have a duty to obey a law. Discuss what you think determines when citizens have a duty to obey the laws of the nation and when they do not.

Comments Legend

Def	define terms	Awk	awkward
Ex?	give an example	Gr	grammar error
Exp	explain further	Sp	spelling error
Rel?	state relevance	Wd	wrong word
Dig	digression(s)	Other	
Con	controversial		
Op	opinion, not the task		
Tr?	transitions not clear		

Writing Sample Scoring Sheet
☐ Must be in black ink; come see me for grading.
☐ Must be legible; come see me for grading.

Essay 1　　　　　　　　　　　　　　　　　　　**Essay 2**

Essay 1 Low Medium High		Task		Essay 2 Low Medium High
☐ ☐ ☐ ☐ ☐ ☐		**Explanation**		☐ ☐ ☐ ☐ ☐ ☐
☐ ☐ ☐ ☐ ☐ ☐	Task 1	Depth (e.g. example)		☐ ☐ ☐ ☐ ☐ ☐
☐ ☐ ☐ ☐ ☐ ☐		Organization		☐ ☐ ☐ ☐ ☐ ☐
☐ ☐ ☐ ☐ ☐ ☐		Writing		☐ ☐ ☐ ☐ ☐ ☐
☐ ☐ ☐ ☐ ☐ ☐		**Counter-example**		☐ ☐ ☐ ☐ ☐ ☐
☐ ☐ ☐ ☐ ☐ ☐	Task 2	Depth (e.g. relevance)		☐ ☐ ☐ ☐ ☐ ☐
☐ ☐ ☐ ☐ ☐ ☐		Organization		☐ ☐ ☐ ☐ ☐ ☐
☐ ☐ ☐ ☐ ☐ ☐		Writing		☐ ☐ ☐ ☐ ☐ ☐
☐ ☐ ☐ ☐ ☐ ☐		**Criteria**		☐ ☐ ☐ ☐ ☐ ☐
☐ ☐ ☐ ☐ ☐ ☐	Task 3	Depth (e.g. resolution)		☐ ☐ ☐ ☐ ☐ ☐
☐ ☐ ☐ ☐ ☐ ☐		Organization		☐ ☐ ☐ ☐ ☐ ☐
☐ ☐ ☐ ☐ ☐ ☐		Writing		☐ ☐ ☐ ☐ ☐ ☐
☐ ☐ ☐ ☐ ☐ ☐	Task 0	**Unity**		☐ ☐ ☐ ☐ ☐ ☐
1　2　3　4　5　6				1　2　3　4　5　6

Recommendations:

____	Avoid using an absolute in Task 1; a good counter-example is impossible.	____
____	Explain the statement; don't merely restate it.	____
____	Tasks 1 and 2 should clearly discuss 2 sides of the issue.	____
____	You misread task 2; read more carefully.	____
____	Provide depth with examples, definitions, and background.	____
____	Use the 3-paragraph structure and/or give the tasks more equal treatment.	____
____	Amplify examples with concrete imagery ("our mayor" v. "some politicians").	____
____	Your first sentences should introduce your main idea.	____
____	You need a strong opening and/or concluding sentence.	____

Score
/6

Score
/6

Unit 2

FOCUS ON HOW THE ESSAYS ARE SCORED

	6	5	4	3	2	1
Tasks	Fully addresses all tasks	Substantially addresses all tasks	Adequately addresses all tasks	Neglects or distorts one or more tasks	Seriously neglects or distorts one or more tasks	Does not address the tasks
Depth	Shows depth, synthesis, and complex thought	Shows some depth, synthesis and complex thought	Has ideas but lacks depth and synthesis	Has some ideas but is simplistic or superficial	Lacks sufficient ideas	Confuses ideas
Organization	Sharply focused, unified, and coherent	Coherently organized	Coherent, but has digressions	Weak organization	Confusing organization	Lacks organization
Writing	Superior vocabulary and sentence structure	Above-average vocabulary and sentence structure	Adequate vocabulary and sentence structure	Erratic vocabulary and sentence structure	Confusing language and recurrent errors	Seriously flawed and impossible to understand

Critical Thinking Exercise

What are the important differences between a 3 essay and a 4 essay?

What about between a 4 and a 5?

JASON'S ESSAY

People should obey the law in order to insure that people don't get killed or robbed. The statement that "It is the citizen's duty to obey the laws of a nation." is to say that if people expect to live in a particular country then they have to be sure to obey the laws, even if they don't seem to make sense to them. Take England for example, even though they seem to drive on the wrong side of the road, if you go to England to live you will have to do it in order to be safe. After all, "When in Rome..."

On the other hand, with all the accidents and deaths on the roads today, it is pretty evident that people are not obeying the law. Because they don't obey the law, people get killed and maimed on the highways every year. For example, if there was a taxi driver named John who was speeding through traffic in order to get somewhere faster, it might be okay as long as he didn't kill anybody in the process, but if he did kill somebody, then he should be tried and punished for second degree manslaughter for the accident.

What determines when someone should obey the laws of a nation is safety. After all, if a person can get away with killing somebody on the road, then everybody would be in danger of getting killed by reckless drivers. In the above example with the taxi driver, that person could be speeding because he has a pregnant woman in the car and that would be a good reason why he should be speeding, but if he kills somebody while doing it he should probably be punished for it.

	High	Medium	Low
Task 1			X
Task 2			X
Task 3			X
Unified			X
Depth			X
Organization		X	
Language			X

Unit 2

SALLY'S ESSAY

It is the citizen's duty to obey the laws of a nation. It is evident that if a citizen does not obey the laws, that he or she is not operating within the society for which the laws were created and thus are deviants from that society. It is important to understand that the law is created to be just and good for all the people in that society and if a citizen decides to disobey the law, then he or she is subject to the penalties and punishments accorded by the law. A nation's foundations are based on its laws; the Constitution provides us with rules and regulations that have to be followed to maintain justice and order in the country. There are laws against theft and graft in order to protect unsuspecting citizens from the criminal element. There are laws protecting the right to free speech and the right to vote in order to insure the voice of the citizenry. In the end, it is the law that provides the framework with which we conduct our lives.

However, sometimes the law must be broken. For example, if a pregnant woman was to be speeding in a taxi, a policeman would not give that person a ticket because there is a justifiable reason to break the speed limit. The cab driver was not driving recklessly for no reason at all; he was speeding to protect the mother and the child within his vehicle and to get them to the hospital on time. This stands as an example of when it is important to understand the circumstances for when it is all right to break the law. Another example might be in the case of war where not only is killing not punished, but even rewarded. *→ no need for second example*

There are many circumstances that can determine when it is justifiable or not to either obey or break a nation's law. Many times it hinges around the unwritten law of safety. The written law may be only the guideline for a range of situations and it is necessary to interpret the law in each circumstance. In the case of war, a nation's law against killing people is suspended in the need to protect its borders. In the case of traffic laws, when it is the safety of the individual at stake, such as in the pregnant woman scenario, or in an ambulance or even a fire truck, it may be appropriate to *not through in extra →* bend the rules and break the written law in favor of the unwritten law of safety.

	High	Medium	Low
Task 1		X	
Task 2	X		
Task 3	X		
Unified		X	
Depth		X	
Organization		X	
Language		X	

ATTACKING THE ESSAY: TASKS 1 AND 2

What makes the essay difficult?

examples in short time

How can we make it easier?

database

What's a database?

pre-thought out examples

How are databases used?

manipulate to situation

Where do ideas come from?

experiences, newspapers, etc.

BUILDING DATABASES

> It is each citizen's duty to obey the laws of the nation.

Choose a topic.	Civil Rights . (MLK)
Why did it happen?	Slavery → people demand change → good leader
Exactly what happened?	Pro - MLK, Rosa Parks Con - goveners (south) ↓
Who was involved?	
What were the results?	equal rights, changed views
Why was it important?	Changed society towards constitution

BUILDING DATABASES

Prompt Categories

Advertising/Media:

_____

Business:

_____

Education:

_____

Government:

_____

History:

_____

International Politics:

_____

National Politics:

_____

Law:

_____

Science/Technology:

_____

Sociology:

_____

Unit 2

ATTACKING THE ESSAY: TASK 3

The Kaplan Standard Criteria

1. Survival/Safety
2. Time
3. Size/Demographics
4. Education

How the Criteria Work

Issue: **Is it good to burn leaves?**

Based on Survival/Safety:

good → needed for warmth

bad → in forest

Based on Time:

good → care times

bad → modern

Based on Size/Demographics:

good → mild no where

bad →

Based on Education:

good → proper fire safety (parks)

bad → everyday kid

Unit 2

The Lesson Continues
on the Next Page
→

Unit 2

YOU BE THE JUDGE: LUCY'S ESSAY

It seems evident that a citizen should obey the laws of a country if he or she should wish to live within the borders of that nation. After all, laws are the evident product of a society's mores, ideology and guidelines for the safety and sanctity of its people. The creation of legislature is to define rules and regulations to insure the possibility of coexistence amongst the people for which those laws were defined. Ideally, laws are provisioned to be fair and just to everyone that they effect and to provide common guidelines for which people can live in relative safety. Traffic laws are clearly designed to provide guidelines such that there can be safe and expedient means of travel on the roads of a nation. The laws may differ between nations, however if the citizenry understand the conventions of those laws, such as the difference between the right of way in Great Britain and the United States, or that a red light means to stop and a double yellow line means to stay to your own side, then the population of that nation can be assured of travel and safety upon the roadways. Though it is evident through the number of accidents and fatalities reported that laws are not always being obeyed, the low proportion of those incidents in ratio to the actual number of drivers on the road is evidence that, for the most part, the citizens of the nation are indeed obeying the law.

And yet there are times when the deliberate defiance of the law is justified. Either through extraordinary circumstance or social acclimation, there are situations in which the adherence to the law is questionable, and even times when the outright defiance of the law is necessary. If an emergency situation should arise such as transporting a pregnant woman to the hospital, so long as appropriate caution is taken while speeding and running red lights, there can be an agreed justification that it was necessary to disobey the law in the interests of the mother's and the child's safety. Even in a situation as pedantic as speeding, there is justification for the action if the situation should require it. On freeways everyday, there are times during the day when the flow of traffic exceeds seventy, even eighty miles per hour; in this situation adhering to a sixty-five mile per hour speed limit would actually make the driver a hazard on the road. Like driving above the speed limit, driving below the minimum speed limit has justification that is even more evident: during inclement weather or even during heavy traffic, it is safer to follow the relative flow of traffic than to strictly adhere to the letter of the law.

An understanding of why the reasons the laws are created lets us understand why it is possible or when it is important to defy, in specific circumstances, a given law. In order to prevent chaos on the streets and to insure the safety of the people, we have rules that keep us to the correct side of the road, or stop in regular intervals or even to prevent us from driving at unsafe speeds. Once we understand the spirit of the law, we can understand that there are situations that require us to bend or even break the law. If a baby is trapped in a burning building, "breaking and entering" that building to save that infant would most probably be justified. It is important to understand that it is, many times, the circumstance around the situation that allows the law to be interpreted. Our society has provisioned for these circumstances; generally, a highway patrolman will not stop you if you are following the flow of traffic at eighty miles an hour, he or she will stop you only if you are presenting a hazard on the road. A policeman will not sit there and give you a ticket if your wife is pregnant in the car, more likely than not, he will escort you through traffic, breaking the letter of the law, to insure your safe arrival at the hospital. In the end, it is the spirit of the law that must be obeyed in order for the continuity of a society's just and peaceful coexistence.

Does Lucy:

Fulfill all three tasks?   yes

Offer an in-depth consideration of the statement?   yes

Organize ideas with coherence and unity?   yes

Show a sophisticated use of language that clearly articulates ideas?   yes

What score would you give Lucy's essay?

	High	**Medium**	**Low**
Task 1 complete	X		
Task 2 complete	X		
Task 3 complete	X		
Unified	X		
Depth	X		
Organization	X		
Language	X		

Unit 2

HOMEWORK

Review for Verbal Reasoning & Writing Sample 2

Verbal Reasoning Strategy and Practice	❏ *Test 2
Writing Sample section in Verbal Reasoning Strategy and Practice	❏ *Chapter 5, Part 1
Section Tests	❏ Test 2 ❏ Test 3 ❏ Test 4
Online Workshops	❏ *Argument Dissection Basics ❏ *Writing Sample: Advanced

Preview for Organic Chemistry 2

Organic Chemistry Review Notes	❏ *Chapters 6–10, 13
Foundation Review	❏ Unit 2 (Optional, MM3257A)
Online Workshops	❏ *Addition and Elimination Reactions ❏ *Spectroscopy

QUESTIONS AND ANSWERS

Organic
Chemistry 2

QUESTIONS AND ANSWERS: ANALYSIS

- Aromatic Compounds
- Spectroscopy Review
- Aldehydes and Ketones
- Carboxylic Acids
- Carboxylic Acid Derivatives

Passage I (Questions 1–4)

Cyclohexanol undergoes the acid-catalyzed elimination of water to form cyclohexene.

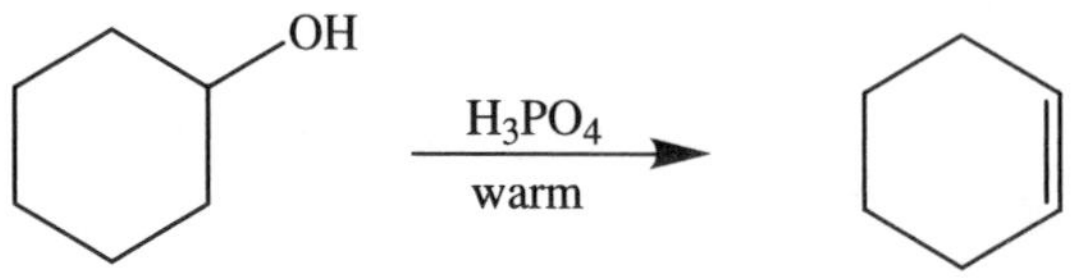

$$\text{Cyclohexanol} \xrightarrow[\text{warm}]{H_3PO_4} \text{Cyclohexene}$$

Cyclohexanol   Cyclohexene

Figure 1

The reaction takes place *via* the conjugate acid of cyclohexanol, which then loses a molecule of water in the rate-limiting step to form the secondary carbocation, which then transfers a proton to the solvent to give the alkene.

In contrast to the dehydration of cyclohexanol, which can give only a single alkene upon dehydration, a mixture of as many as four alkenes results from the dehydration of 2-methylcyclohexanol.

2-methylcyclohexanol

85% H_3PO_4
distill

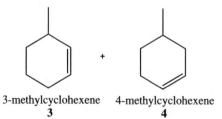

methylenecyclohexane   1-methylcyclohexene
1   2

3-methylcyclohexene   4-methylcyclohexene
3   4

Figure 2

A chemistry student wishing to investigate elimination reactions studied the dehydration of 2-methylcyclohexanol. In the reaction, the student heated 2-methylcyclohexanol with 85% phosphoric acid to produce a mixture of alkenes that was subjected to gas chromatographic analysis. A summary of the starting materials used and the results obtained is shown in Table 1.

Table 1. Dehydration of 2-Methylcyclohexanol

Compound	2-methylcyclohexanol	1	2	3	4
mmol used	50				
bp (°C)	161	103	110	103	102
% yield		5	73	20	3

Scratch Paper

Scratch Paper

Stop:

Think:

What's the mechanism of formation of 1-methyl-cyclohexene from 2-methylcyclohexanol?

Predict:

Match

Stop:

Think:

Do cis/trans isomers have different chemical properties?

What is the structure of the intermediate?

Predict:

Match

1. Compound **2**, 1-methylcyclohexene, is the major product of the dehydration of 2-methylcyclohexanol because:

   A. the secondary carbocation formed in the rate-determining step transfers a proton to the solvent.

   B. the primary carbocation formed in the rate-determining step transfers a proton to the solvent.

   C. the secondary carbocation formed in the rate-determining step rearranges to a more stable tertiary carbocation which transfers a proton to the solvent.

   D. the tertiary carbocation formed in the rate-determining step rearranges to a more stable secondary carbocation which transfers a proton to the solvent.

2. The 2-methylcyclohexanol used in this experiment is actually a mixture of two diastereomers, *cis*-2-methylcyclohexanol and *trans*-2-methylcyclohexanol. Does this fact make any difference in the product composition?

   A. Yes, because the *cis* isomer will react preferentially over the *trans*.

   B. Yes, because the *trans* isomer will react preferentially over the *cis*.

   C. No, because the same intermediate carbocation is formed from either isomer.

   D. No, because the intermediate carbocation will undergo rearrangement.

Scratch Paper

Stop:

Will the MCAT ever be this obvious?

Think:

What does the question stem say about Zaitsev's Rule?

Predict:

Match

Stop:

Think:

What kind of reaction is the bromination of 3-methylcyclohexene with Br_2?

What is the stereochemistry of the reaction?

Predict:

Match

3. The dehydration of 2-methylcyclohexanol is an illustration of Zaitsev's Rule, which states: In a β-elimination reaction, the most highly substituted alkene will be the major product. Assuming the following reaction follows an E2 mechanism, predict the product distribution.

A.   **1** will be the major product and **2** will be the minor product.
B.   **2** will be the major product and **1** will be the minor product.
C.   Both products will be formed in equal amounts.
D.   The product distribution is impossible to predict without experimental evidence.

4. If Compound 2, 1-methylcyclohexene, were treated with Br_2, the product of the reaction would be:

A.

B.

C.

D.

Unit 2

Directed Practice

- *Biological Sciences Review Notes*: Orgo. Chs. 5, 6, 7
- *Topical Tests*: Molecular structure of Organic Compunds Test 1 (Passage I)
- *Topical Tests*: Hydrocarbons Test 1 (Passage I)

AROMATICITY AND ELECTROPHILIC AROMATIC SUBSTITUTIONS

Stability

Benzene contains a conjugated delocalized system of pi electrons which imparts stability to the molecule.

Addition reactions that occur readily in alkenes aren't observed in aromatic rings, since they would disrupt the stable aromatic structure. Aromatic compounds undergo electrophilic substitution reactions.

Characteristics of Aromatic Compounds:

planar

_____

_____

_____

Critical Thinking Exercise

Predict the product(s) of the following reactions:

$$CH_3 - CH = CH_2 + Br_2 \longrightarrow CH_3 - \underset{\underset{Br}{|}}{CH} - \underset{\underset{Br}{|}}{CH_2}$$

$$\text{(benzene)} + Br_2 \longrightarrow \text{N.R. (need Lewis acid catalyst) } (AlCl_3)$$

Hückel's Rule

The criterion of $\underline{4n+2}$ pi electrons (n = 0, 1, 2, 3, etc.) is known as Hückel's rule. In general, if a cyclic conjugated polyene follows Hückel's rule, then it is an aromatic compound. Neutral compounds, anions, and cations may all be aromatic.

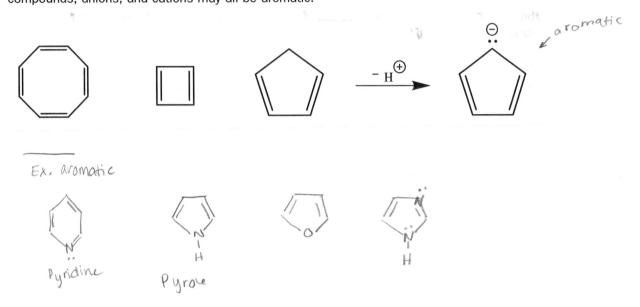

Ex. aromatic

Pyridine   Pyrole

Electrophilic Aromatic Substitutions (EAS)

In an EAS reaction, an electrophile reacts with an alkene ring, forming a new bond to a ring carbon with the loss of one hydrogen. In general, these reactions require a ___L A___ catalyst. The general mechanism for an EAS reaction is shown below:

Step 1: Attack on the electrophile.

Step 2: Loss of Hydrogen.

Unit 2

Substituent Effects in EAS Reactions

When EAS occurs on a ring already bearing a substituent, the nature of that substituent will impact both the rate of the reaction and where on the ring the substitution occurs (regiochemistry).

Activating substituents will react faster than benzene itself, and deactivating substituents will react more slowly. Substituents are grouped into 2 categories: *ortho-para*-directing and *meta*-directing.

activating

—NH_2

—OH

—OCH_3

—CH_3

—H

—X   (X = Cl, Br, I)

- - - - - - - - - - - - - -

—CHO

—COOR

—COOH

—COR

—SO_3H

—CN   —NO_2

deactivating

—$NR_3^{\oplus}$

activating/donating
(resonance, (-))

ortho-para- - directing

meta - directing
(loose (-) charge)

Critical Thinking Exercise

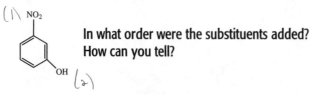

(1) NO_2

(2) OH

In what order were the substituents added?
How can you tell?

Unit 2

Polysubstituted Aromatic Rings

(draw towards)

A substituent is __activating__ if it releases electron density to the ring either inductively or through resonance. The orientation effect is seen by considering the family of resonance forms which can be drawn for a given substituent (e.g. NO_2 group).

NO_2 acts as a ring _____.

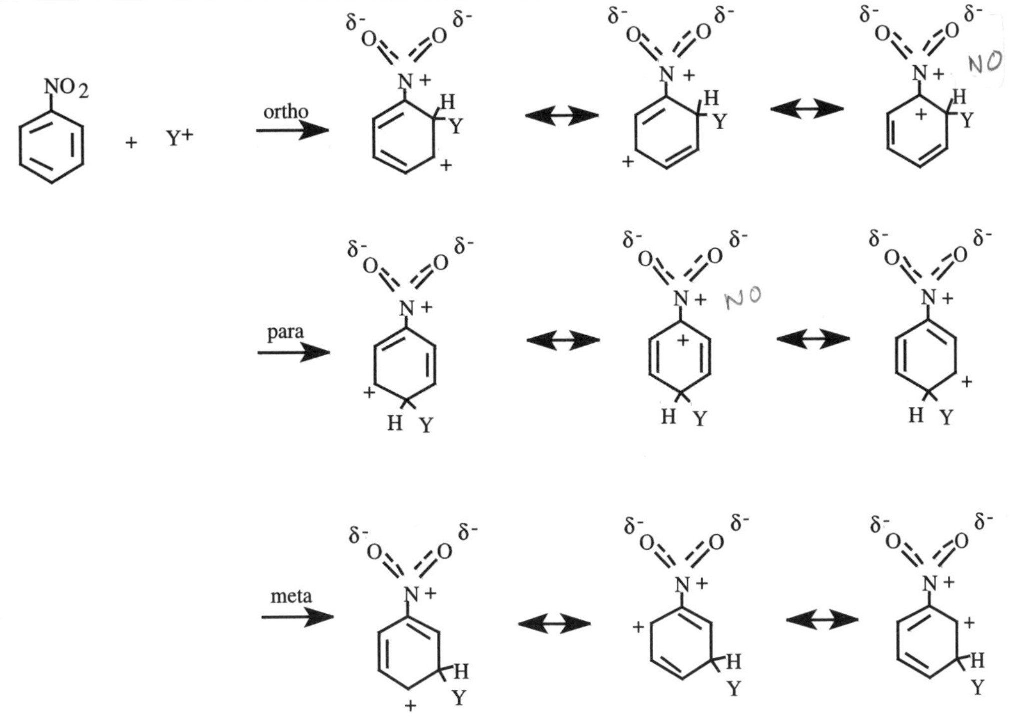

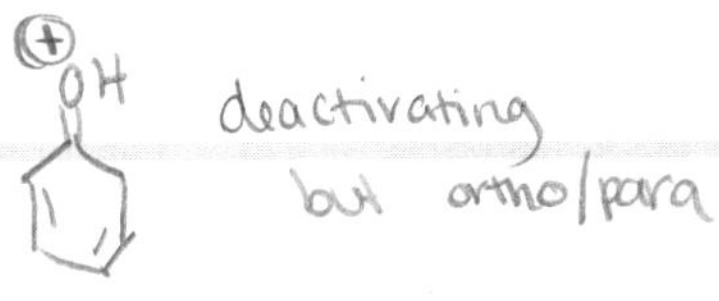

Critical Thinking Exercise

Does phenol have the same pattern of substitution as nitro benzene? What about a halogen substituted benzene?

deactivating but ortho/para

SPECTROSCOPY

IR ~ Tells functional groups ; measure vibrations of bonds

Critical Thinking Exercise

A student attempting to determine the identity of an unknown sample employs IR spectroscopy to analyze it and obtains the following spectrum.

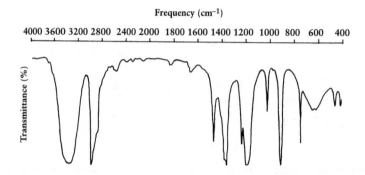

Based on the spectrum, the identity of the unknown compound is most likely to be:

A.   butanamine
B.   benzaldehyde
C.   hexane
D.   propanol

A chemist performs an organic synthesis where the oxidation of *sec*-butanol to 2-butanone is a necessary step. Based on the following IR spectrum, which of the following would provide the best evidence that he successfully completed this conversion?

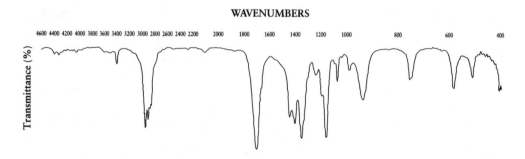

A.   Noting the appearance of a broad absorption peak in the region of 1000–800 cm^{-1}.
B.   Noting the appearance of a strong absorption peak in the region of 1700 cm^{-1}.
C.   Noting the appearance of two sharp peaks at 3000 cm^{-1}.
D.   Noting the appearance of multiple peaks in the fingerprint region.

SPECTROSCOPY

NMR — by frequency they flip (need odd #), to -½ spin (don't count if neighbors same)

sp³ _____ 0 - 3 (added group = 3 - 5)

sp/sp² _____ 4 - 8

aromatic _____ 6 - 8

ewg's _____ 3 - 5 (w/ sp³)

peaks = n +1

peaks = 4

CH₃ - CH₂ - CH₃ ② → peaks = 3

highest magnetic field

(less dense) deshielded

shielded (more dense)

11 10 9 8 7 6 5 4 3 2 1 6

Critical Thinking Exercise

Which of the following compounds will produce the given ^{1}H NMR spectrum?

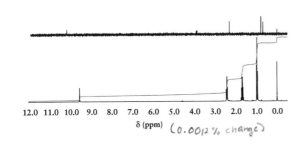

δ (ppm) (0.0012 % change)

A.   2 chloropentane
B.   butanal
C.   benzoic acid
D.   methanal

Which of the following compounds will produce the given ^{1}H NMR spectrum?

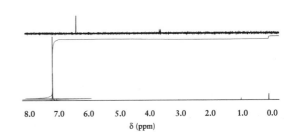

δ (ppm)

A.   benzene
B.   benzoic acid
C.   acetone
D.   methane

Unit 2

Passage II (Questions 5–8)

One of the most important reactions that aromatic compounds such as benzene undergo is electrophilic aromatic substitution, in which a proton on the ring system is replaced by an electrophile.

For example, benzene reacts with bromine in the presence of $AlBr_3$ to give primarily bromobenzene.

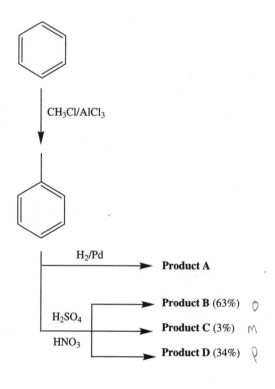

Reaction 1

A student carried out the following synthesis:

Toluene was synthesized by reacting benzene with chloromethane. Reacting toluene with hydrogen gas in the presence of palladium yielded one product (Product A). Reaction of toluene with nitric acid in concentrated sulfuric acid produced three products (Products B, C, and D). This procedure is outlined in Figure 1.

Figure 1

The ^{1}H NMR spectrum of toluene revealed singlet peaks at 2.4 ppm and 7.3 ppm. The ^{1}H NMR spectrum of Product A gave no peaks in the region of 6.5–8 ppm. The infrared spectrum of Products B, C, and D showed two strong absorption bands in the region of 1600 and 1450 cm^{-1}.

Scratch Paper

Unit 2

Scratch Paper

Stop:

Think:

What are products B, C, and D?

Predict:

Match

Stop:

Think:

What are products B, C, and D?

What type of reagent is Zn/HCl?

Predict:

Match

5. The best explanation for the fact that the reaction of toluene with HNO_3/H_2SO_4 yields three different products in the ratio indicated in Figure 1 is that the methyl substituent:

   A. is an *ortho-/para-* directing deactivator.
   B. is a *meta*-directing activator.
   C. sterically hinders the incoming electrophile.
   D. is an *ortho-/para-* directing activator.

6. Products B, C, and D can all react equally in the presence of Zn/HCl to form:

   A. an amide.
   B. an amine.
   C. a cyclic alkene.
   D. a cyclic alkane.

Directed Practice

- *Biological Sciences Review Notes*: Orgo. Ch. 6

Scratch Paper

Stop:

Think:

What is product A?

What factors determine stability in cyclohexanes?

Predict:

Match

Stop:

Think:

What is a conjugated system?

What are the structures of the compounds in the answer choices?

Predict:

Match

7. What is the most stable conformation of product A?

A.
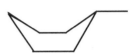

B.

C.

D.

8. Benzene can be described as a conjugated system. Which of the following is NOT a conjugated system?

A. 3-penten-1-yne
B. styrene ($C_6H_5CH=CH_2$)
C. 1,2-butadiene
D. 3-buten-2-one

Unit 2

ALDEHYDES AND KETONES

Nomenclature

Common Names

2-propanone   Phenylmethanal   ethanal   methanal

Synthesis

Aldehydes are usually synthesized by ___oxidation___ from the appropriate 1° alcohol.
Ketones are usually synthesized by ___oxidation___ from the appropriate 2° alcohol.

Oxidation Scheme

$$RCH_2OH \xrightarrow{PCC} RCHO \xrightarrow[\text{reagent}]{\text{Tollens'}} RCO_2H$$

$$KMnO_4 \text{ -or- } H^+/Cr_2O_7^{2-}{}_{(aq)} \text{ -or- } H^+/CrO_{3(aq)}$$

$$R-CH-OH \xrightarrow[\text{(except Tollens')}]{\text{any oxidizing agent}} R-\overset{O}{\underset{}{C}}-R'$$
      |
      R'

Reduction Scheme

$$RCO_2H \xrightarrow[\text{LiAlH}_4]{\text{no direct route}} RCHO \xrightarrow[\text{NaBH}_4]{\text{LiAlH}_4 \text{ or }} RCH_2OH$$

$$R-\overset{O}{\underset{}{C}}-R' \xrightarrow[\text{NaBH}_4]{\text{LiAlH}_4 \text{ or}} R-CH-OH$$
                              |
                              R'

Directed Practice

- *Biological Sciences Review Notes*: Orgo. Ch. 8

Key Reaction

Because the carbonyl carbon is an electrophile, a key reaction of aldehydes and ketones involves nucleophilic addition by a strong nucleophile.

Critical Thinking Exercise

What question should you always ask yourself after an attack on a carbonyl?

can reform carbonyle carbon (have Leaving group)

Acid-catalyzed formation of a Hemiketal from a ketone

hemiketal

Similary Properties to carbonyles

Acid-catalyzed reaction of hemiacetals to make acetals

acetal

Unit 2

Directed Practice

- *Biological Sciences Review Notes*: Orgo. Ch. 8

Critical Thinking Exercise

Scratch Paper

Stop:

Think:

Where is the electrophile in the reaction below? What about the nucleophile?

What reaction will take place between the nucleophile and electrophile?

Predict:

Match

Stop:

Think:

What are the structures of acetone and methylmagnesium chloride?

Which is the nucleophile?

Which is the electrophile?

Predict:

Match

9. An ylide is a neutral molecule that contains a negative carbon atom adjacent to a positive heteroatom. Given the following reaction between a sulfurylide and cyclopentanone, which of the following is the likely intermediate?

A.

B.

C.

D.

10. What is the outcome of the reaction of acetone with methylmagnesium chloride followed by workup with acid?

A.   2-Chloro-2-propanol
B.   2-Chloro-2-methyl propane
C.   2-Methyl-2-propanol
D.   Methyl ethanoate

Directed Practice

- *Biological Sciences Review Notes*: Orgo. Chs. 8, 10
- *Topical Tests*: Amines Test 1 (Passage I)

Unit 2

CARBOXYLIC ACIDS

Nomenclature

When naming compounds, carboxylic acids usually carry the highest priority in naming. Therefore, when naming, a carboxylic group (-COOH) is indicated by the suffix "-oic acid".

Common Examples

2-hydroxy propanoic acid

$$CH_3CH - C \overset{O}{\underset{OH}{\big\|}}$$ (with OH on the CH)

2-methyl propenoic acid

$$H_2C = C \overset{O}{\underset{OH}{\big\|}}$$ (with CH_3 group)

Cyclohexane carboxylic acid

ethandioc di acid

$$HOOC - COOH$$

2-butyl-heptanoic acid

$$CH_3 - CH_2 - CH_2 - CH_2 - CH - C \overset{O}{\underset{OH}{\big\|}}$$ (with $CH_3(CH_2)_4$ group)

Unit 2

Physical properties

high bp b/c hydrogen bonding

Critical Thinking Exercise

Which class of compounds would have a higher boiling point, Acyl Chlorides or Carboxylic Acids? Why?   b/c   H-bonding

---

Directed Practice

- *Biological Sciences Review Notes*: Orgo. Ch. 9

Acidity

low pKₐ = low pH = acidic = high Kₐ [handwritten]

Carboxylic acids are fairly strong acids (stronger than alcohols). The pK_a range for carboxylic acids is 2–5.

b/c resonance [handwritten]

propanoic acid: $pK_a \approx 4.9$

benzoic acid: $pK_a \approx 4.9$

Critical Thinking Exercise

Which is more acidic, Cl_3CCOOH or $ClCH_2COOH$?   *b/c EWG's* [handwritten]

Which is more acidic, FCH_2COOH or CH_3OCH_2COOH?   *b/c F more electronegative* [handwritten]

Which is more acidic, FCH_2CH_2COOH or $CH_3CHFCOOH$?   *b/c closer* [handwritten]

Synthesis

Oxidation of 1° alcohols and aldehydes

Carboxylic acids may be synthesized by the oxidation of 1° alcohols and aldehydes.

$$RCH_2OH \xrightarrow{\text{PCC}} RCHO \xrightarrow[\text{reagent}]{\text{Tollens'}} RCO_2H$$

$$KMnO_4 \text{ or } H^+/Cr_2O_7^{2-}{}_{(aq)} \text{ or } H^+/CrO_{3(aq)}$$

Carboxylation of Grignard reagents

The carboxylation of Grignard reagents is similar to the nucleophilic addition reactions of aldehydes and ketones.

carboxylate   carboxylic acid

Unit 2

Oxidative cleavage of alkenes

The oxidative cleavage of alkenes also produces carboxylic acids.

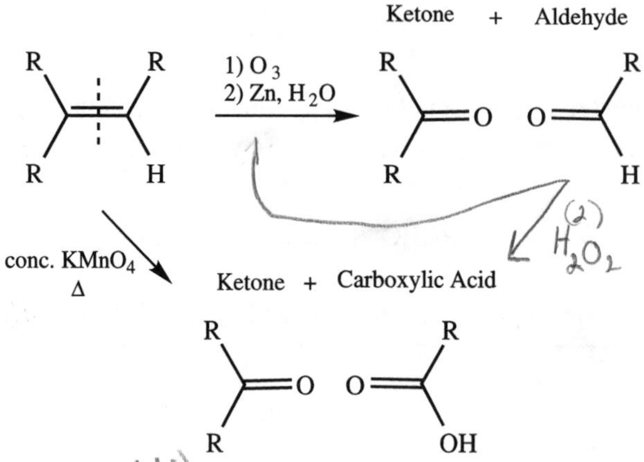

Decarboxylation   (1,3-dicarboxylic acids)

β-keto carboxylic acids will undergo decarboxylation. The mechanism of decarboxylation involves one carbonyl group assisting the loss of the other.

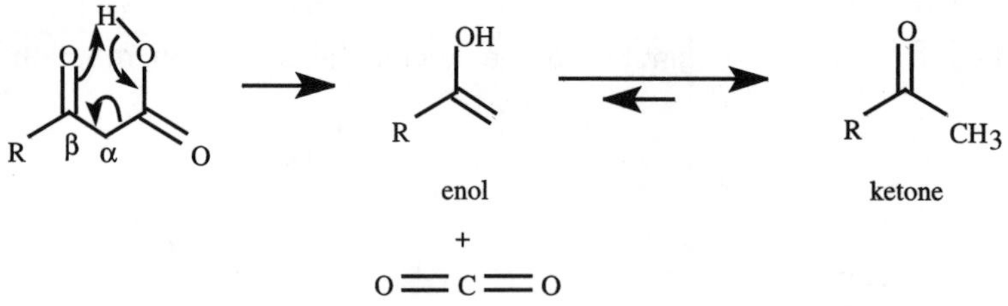

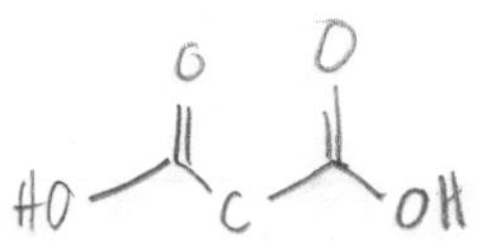

Critical Thinking Exercise

How many ketone groups are found in the product of the following reaction?

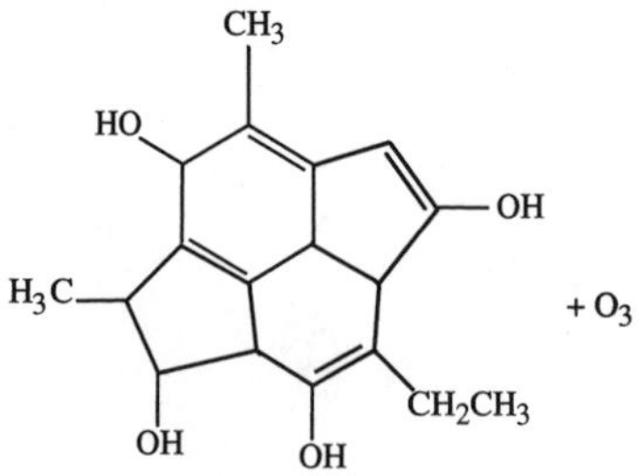

$+ O_3$ $+ Zn/H_2O$ $= 4$

Directed Practice

- *Biological Sciences Review Notes*: Orgo. Ch. 9

CARBOXYLIC ACID DERIVATIVES

Nomenclature

The acyl portion forms the "root" carboxylic acid from which the derivative is made, and this portion determines the root of the name. The "non-acyl" portion is treated separately, since it acts as a leaving group which can be exchanged for other nucleophiles.

acyl group → came from carboxylic acid

Derivative	Structure	Name of Derivative
Acid chloride		box → ethanoic acid ↓ ethanoyl chlorid
Acid anhydride		benzoic acid ↓ benzoic anhydride
Ester		Propanoic acid ↓ isopropyl propanoate
Amide		ethanoic acid ↓ N- benzyl ethanamide

Directed Practice

• *Biological Sciences Review Notes*: Orgo. Ch. 10

Unit 2

Synthesis and Reactions

The carbonyl carbon of carboxylic acids is susceptible to nucleophilic attack, just as in aldehydes and ketones.

Nucleophilic acyl substitution

Many of the same kinds of nucleophiles that add to aldehyde and ketone carbonyls will attack the carbonyl of an acid (acyl) derivative, like an acid chloride, to yield substitution products.

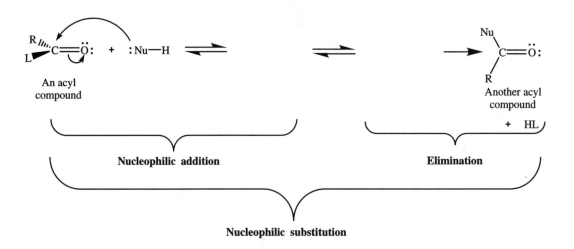

When the acyl compound is a carboxylic acid, the L group is an –OH group.

Order of Reactivity

The reactivity of carboxylic acid derivatives towards nucleophilic acyl substitution depends upon leaving group ability.

The better the leaving group, ___more reactive___

Rank the following carboxylic acid derivatives in order of reactivity.

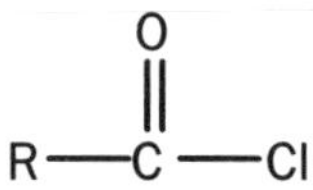

acyl halide 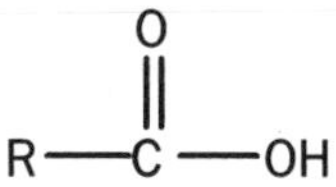   carboxylic acid 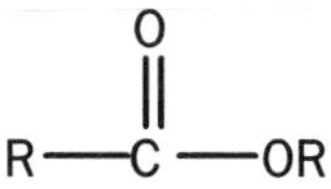   ester

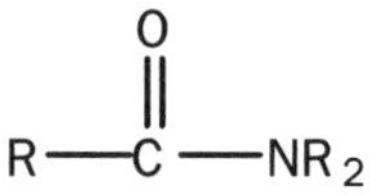

amide 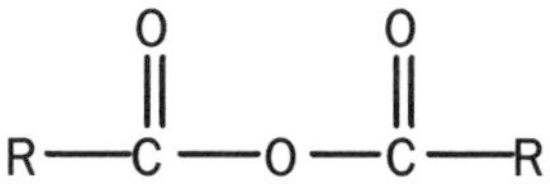   acid anhydride

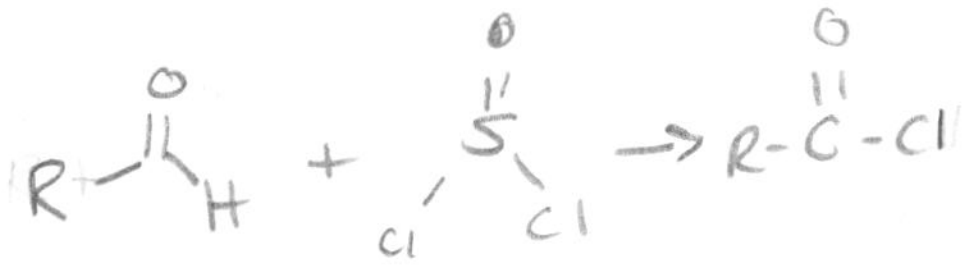

most reactive

___acyl halide___

___acid anhydride___

___Carboxylic acid___   ___ester___

___amide___

least reactive

Critical Thinking Exercise

Predict the product(s) for the following reactions.

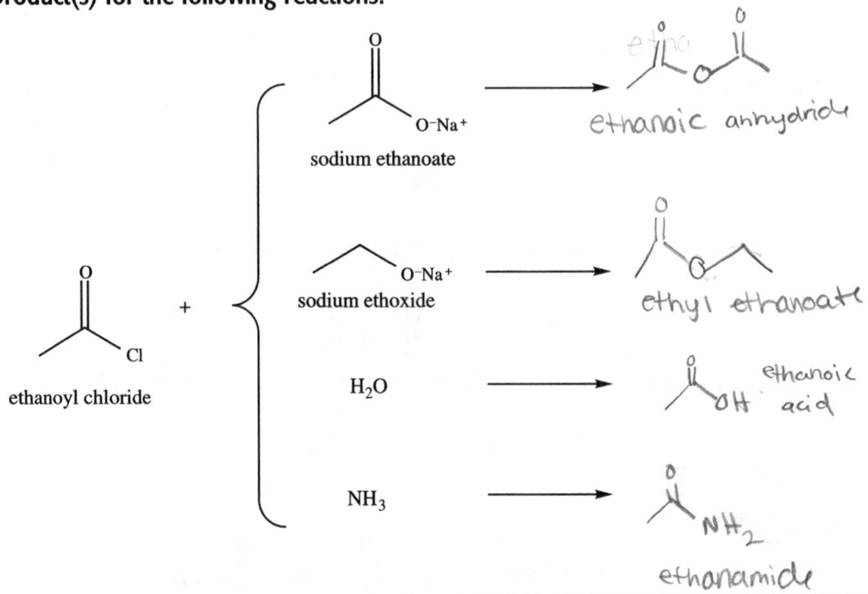

ethanoic anhydride

ethyl ethanoate

ethanoic acid

ethanamide

sodium ethanoate

sodium ethoxide

H_2O

NH_3

ethanoyl chloride

$R'OH + R\overset{O}{C}OH \underset{\rightleftharpoons}{\overset{H^+}{\longrightarrow}} R\overset{O}{C}OR' + H_2O$ (can go back ↳hydrolize)

can not go backwards w/ base

Unit 2

The Lesson Continues
on the Next Page
$\longrightarrow$

Passage III (Questions 11–16)

Esters are carboxylic acid derivatives that have a variety of industrial uses. Since they have pleasant odors, they are used in fruit drinks, soaps, and perfumes. They are also used as solvents and softeners in the polymer industry.

Esters can be synthesized by a process known as esterification, wherein a carboxylic acid and an alcohol are reacted with a catalytic amount of a mineral acid. The reaction is slow, and the ester is produced in equilibrium concentrations. Formation of the ester can be favored by using an excess of one of the reactants, as shown in Reaction 1.

One way to avoid the rate and equilibrium problems of esterification is by reacting an acyl chloride with an alcohol. Ethanoyl chloride is synthesized by the reaction of acetic acid and thionyl chloride, as shown in Reaction 2. Ethanoyl chloride is then reacted with ethanol in the presence of pyridine according to Reaction 3 to produce ethyl acetate. HCl is a by-product of this reaction.

$$+ H_2O$$

Reaction 1

Reaction 2

Reaction 3

Scratch Paper

11. Which of the following correctly represents the intermediate of the esterification after nucleophilic attack by the alcohol?

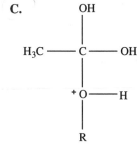

12. What is the role of pyridine in Reaction 3?

    A.   To neutralize the inorganic acid product preventing catalysis of ester hydrolysis upon aqueous workup.

    B.   To neutralize the inorganic acid product thereby preventing the formation of the ester product.

    C.   To neutralize the organic acid product preventing catalysis of ester hydrolysis upon aqueous workup.

    D.   To neutralize the organic acid product preventing catalysis of the reverse reaction.

Unit 2

Scratch Paper

Stop:

Think:

Predict:

Match

Stop:

Think:

Predict:

Match

13. Why should esterification reactions not be carried out in water?

   A.   Acetic acid is insoluble in water.
   B.   The polar nature of water overshadows the polar nature of the carboxyl group.
   C.   The extensive hydrogen bonding of water interferes with the S_N2 reaction mechanism.
   D.   Water molecules would hydrolyze useful products back to the parent carboxylic acid.

14. Which of the following represents an increasing order of acidity in organic compounds?
   A. CH_3OCH_3, CH_3CHO, CH_3COOH, CH_3CH_2OH
   B. CH_3OCH_3, CH_3CHO, CH_3CH_2OH, CH_3COOH
   C. CH_3CHO, CH_3OCH_3, CH_3COOH, CH_3CH_2OH
   D. CH_3CHO, CH_3OCH_3, CH_3CH_2OH, CH_3COOH

Directed Practice

   • *Biological Sciences Review Notes*: Orgo. Ch. 10

Scratch Paper

Stop:

Think:

Predict:

Match

Stop:

Think:

Predict:

Match

15. The first compound is more acidic than the second because:

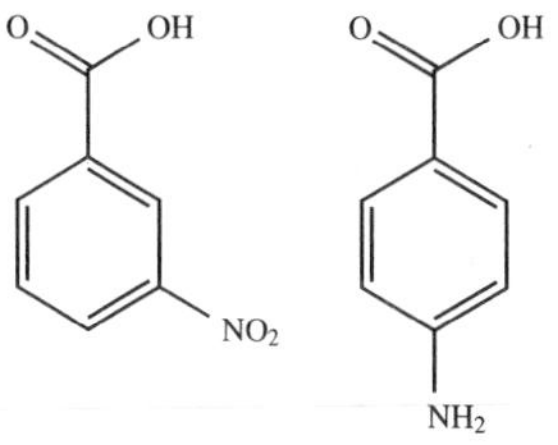

A. NO_2 is an activating group.
B. NH_2 is a deactivating group.
C. NO_2 is an electron-withdrawing group.
D. NH_2 is an electron-withdrawing group.

16. What are Compounds I and II in the following reaction?

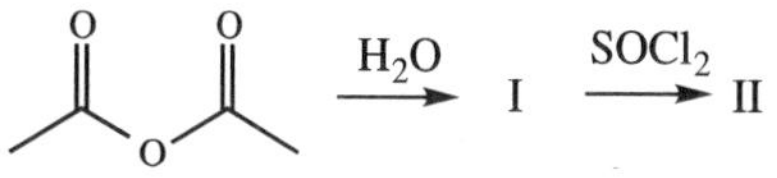

A.

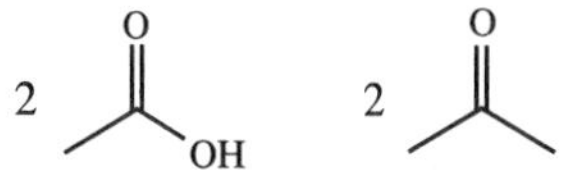

B.

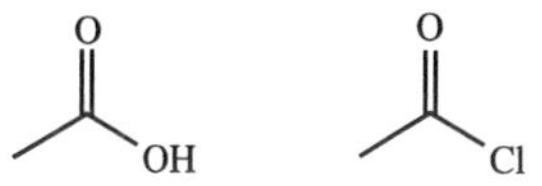

C.

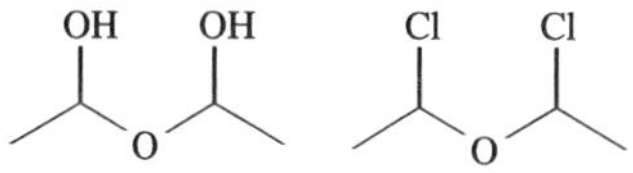

D.

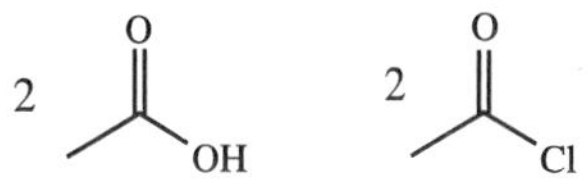

Unit 2

Directed Practice

- *Topical Tests*: Molecular Structure of Organic Compounds Test 1 (Passage II)

HOMEWORK

Review for Organic Chemistry 2

Topical Tests	❏ Molecular Spectroscopy Test 1 ❏ Oxygen-Containing Compounds Test 1
Subject Tests	❏ Test 4 (Optional, DD3083) ❏ Test 5 (Optional, DD3084)

Preview for Biology 2

Biology Review Notes	❏ *Chapters 6, 7, 9 and 12
Foundation Review	❏ Unit 2 (Optional, MM3260A)
Online Workshops	❏ *The Skeletal System and the Immune System

Unit 2

QUESTIONS AND ANSWERS

Biology 2

QUESTIONS AND ANSWERS: SYNTHESIS

- Digestive System
- Circulatory System
- Musculo-skeletal System
- Nervous System

THE KAPLAN QUESTION STRATEGY

STOP

> **Characterize the answer choices**

THINK

> **What is the question really asking**

> **What topic is being tested**

> **What relevant information do you need**

PREDICT

> **Formulate a framework or prediction for your answer**

MATCH

> **Which answer truly meets the requirements of the prediction**

Unit 2

Passage I (Questions 1–4)

Autoimmune diseases are caused by self-reactive lymphocytes that attack various parts of the body as if they were foreign pathogens. The tissues and target organs attacked vary from disease to disease, and include the large joints in lyme arthritis, peripheral nerves in Guillan-Barre syndrome, the corneal stroma in herpetic stromal keratitis (HSK) and myelin in multiple sclerosis. A number of hypotheses exist to explain what causes autoimmunity.

In a person with a normally functioning immune system, lymphocytes are selected based on their ability to ignore self so that they only react against foreign pathogens. Self-tolerance is a process by which a B or T cell which is found to be too reactive to self-antigens is either killed or allowed to remain in circulation only in a non-reactive state called anergy. However, in autoimmunity an activating step allows lymphocytes to attack the host.

Hypothesis I

According to the molecular mimicry hypothesis, autoimmunity is a result of a normal immune response to a microbial infection gone awry. This may occur if a viral antigen cross-stimulates a self-reactive T cell in addition to the viral-reactive T cell. For example, if a protein on the virus coat is structurally similar to a protein made by the host, then that antigen from the virus could activate the usually silent T cells that will recognize the similar self-protein. Once the self-reactive T cell is activated, it will attack the self-antigen it targets and destroy it.

There are a number of examples of viral infection correlating with autoimmunity. For example, in HSK, herpes simplex virus 1 (HSV-1) infection can lead to a chronic inflammation of the eye which peaks after it is no longer possible to detect virus in the eye, suggesting that HSV-1 infection has cross-stimulated self-reactive T cells that are now attacking the cornea.

Scratch Paper

Hypothesis II

A second theory is that the initiation of autoimmunity is antigen-nonspecific, which is also known as a bystander effect. According to this hypothesis, the immune system's response to a pathogen causes a non-specific activation of the entire immune system, which allows the activation and proliferation of non-specific T cells including auto-reactive T cells. In animal models of HSK it is necessary to both infect the mice with HSV-1 and give a corneal injury in order to get the chronic eye inflammation that characterizes HSK. The injury of the cornea may allow T cells of all specificities to enter the corneal stroma, an area to which they do not usually have access. The presence of these T cells combined with the pro-inflammatory environment of the corneal injury facilitates the activation of self-reactive cells. This would make the autoimmunity a result of the physical damage to the eye rather than cross-reactivity between a viral antigen and a self-protein.

Unit 2

Scratch Paper

Scratch Paper

Stop:

Think:

What is the molecular mimicry hypothesis?

Where does the passage discuss the molecular mimicry hypothesis?

Predict:

Match

Stop:

Think:

How do the bystander effect hypothesis and the molecular mimicry hypothesis differ?

Is this situation similar to either hypothesis?

Predict:

Match

1. Which of the following, if true, would strengthen the molecular mimicry hypothesis?

   A. It is not possible to prove that a patient with autoimmunity had a triggering viral infection.
   B. Of patients with viral infections prior to developing autoimmunity, viral DNA could still be detected in their blood.
   C. A mouse model of HSK was generated that did not require a corneal injury, and developed HSK simply due to the HSV-1 infection.
   D. Animals kept in germ-free environments are proven to be equally likely to develop autoimmunity.

2. T cells free of viral DNA or other infectious material are taken from a mouse with an autoimmune condition and transferred to a normal mouse of the same strain. If the previously normal mouse developed the same autoimmune condition, which hypothesis would be strengthened?

   A. Both hypotheses would be strengthened
   B. Neither hypothesis would be strengthened
   C. Only the bystander effect hypothesis would be strengthened
   D. Only the molecular mimicry hypothesis would be strengthened

Stop:

Think:

What is the molecular mimicry hypothesis?

What are the functions of the pancreas?

Predict:

Match

Stop:

Think:

What are the body's non-specific immune response mechanisms?

Predict:

Match

3. A strain of mouse is generated that expresses a viral protein in the pancreas. If this strain of mouse is infected with a virus that expresses the same viral protein, which of the following conditions may result according to the molecular mimicry hypothesis?

   A. The mice develop a type 1 diabetes-like disease
   B. The mice develop an arthritis like-disease
   C. The mice become unable to detoxify their blood
   D. The mice develop intestinal cancer

4. Which of the following is not involved in nonspecific immune defense?

   A. Skin
   B. Lysozyme
   C. Interferons
   D. B cells

Unit 2

DIGESTIVE SYSTEM: EXTRACELLULAR BREAKDOWN OF FOOD

Digestive tract

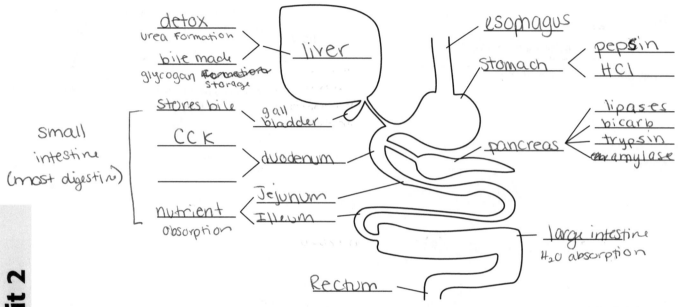

Components of the digestive tract

Mouth

In the mouth, salivary amylase digests starch.

Esophagus

Food moves down the esophagus via peristalsis (smooth muscle contraction).

Stomach

Gastric glands produce hydrochloric acid which makes the pH of the stomach very acidic.

Small intestine

The small intestine is the site of both ___digestion___ and _____.

Segment	Function
duodenum	proteins, carbs, fats
Jujenum	} absorption of
Illeum	nutrients

Large intestine

The large intestine is the site of _____.

Segment	Function
Cecum	blind outpacketing
Colon	H_2O absorption & ions
Rectum	Storage of feces

ecoli → digest plant matter

Accessory organs

Liver

The functions of the liver are:

- enzymes → detox (drugs, alcohol, blood)
- forms urea
- stores glycogan and break dow
- produces bile

Gall bladder

The gall bladder stores ___bile___.

Pancreas

The pancreas secretes pancreatic juices into the ___Small intestine___.

exocrin → close
endocrine → far away (insulin in blood)

Directed Practice

- *Topical Tests*: Digestive and Excretory System Test I (Passage II, Discrete Questions 11–13, 15).

Unit 2

Enzymes

Enzymes	Production Site	Activity Site	Function
Amylase	mouth / Pancreas	mouth / duodenum	Polysacharides → dextins
Pepsin	stomach/chief cells	stomach	Proteins digestion
Trypsin	Pancreas / acinar cells	duodenum	digests proteins
Maltase	pancreas / acinar cells	duodenum	maltase to glucose (break down)
Lipase	intestinal mucosa	duodenum	fat digestion
Carboxypeptidase	Pancreas / acinar cell	duodenum	protein digestion
Aminopeptidase	Pancreas / acinar cell	duodenum	protein digestion
Enterokinase	intestinal mucosa cells	duodenum	activates trypsin
Bile salts	liver	duodenum	fat emulsification
CCK	small intestine mucosa	Pancreas	stimulates pancreas and gall bladder

N ← C

N → C

Unit 2

Absorption

Amino acids → small intestine

Hydrolyzed fats → small intestine

Water → large intestine

Monosaccharides → small Intestine

Vitamins → some in large, some in small

Critical Thinking Exercise

Scratch Paper
Stop:
Think:
Predict:
Match

5. A certain individual lacks the enzyme maltase which breaks the disaccharide maltose into glucose monosaccharides. Which of the following is most likely to occur?

   A. Maltose will be digested by functional lactase enzymes in the small intestine.
   B. Maltose will not be absorbed by active transport but will passively diffuse into cells of the intestinal epithelium.
   C. Maltose will be digested by bacteria in the large intestine.
   D. The individual will be susceptible to malnutrition due to an inability to absorb glucose.

Directed Practice

- *Topical Tests*: Digestive and Excretory System Test I (Question 16)
- *Biological Sciences Review Notes*: Biology Ch. 7

CIRCULATORY SYSTEM: TRANSPORT OF NUTRIENTS, O_2, CO_2, HORMONES, ANTIBODIES

Heart

Circulatory pathway

Superior and Inferior Vena Cava → <u>right atrium</u> → <u>right ventrical</u> → <u>pulmanary arteries</u> → <u>lungs</u> → <u>pulmary viens</u> → <u>left atrium</u> → <u>Left ventrical</u> → <u>aorta</u> → Body

Blood vessels

Vessel	Function	Walls	Valves
Arteries	blood away from heart	thick	NO (except pulmary arteries
Veins	blood back to heart	thin	yes
Capillaries	exchange gases and nutrients	very thin	NO

Fetal Circulation

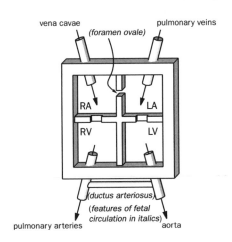

Structure	Connects	Purpose
ductus venosus	umbilical vein to inferior vena cava	by passes liver
foramen ovale	right atrium to left atrium	by pass blood from lungs
ductus arteriosus	pulmonary arteries to aorta	by pass blood from lungs

Unit 2

Critical Thinking Exercise

What initiates the coordinated contraction of the heart? Where does the signal travel?

SA to AV

Directed Practice

- *Topical Tests*: Circulatory and Lymphatic Systems Test 1 (Passage II)
- *Biological Sciences Review Notes*: Biology Ch. 9

Blood

Blood is composed of __plasma__ and __cells__ .

Red blood cells → hemoglobin

White blood cells → nuclocytes (immunity cells)

Platelets → fragments of large cell (clotting)

Blood groups/antigens

Blood Type	RBC Antigen	Rh Factor?	Antibodies	Receives From	Donates To
AB⁺	A B	yes	No	everyone	AB⁺
O⁻	None	NO	A, B, RH	O⁻	everyone

Critical Thinking Exercise

Why do red blood cells lack mitochondria? maximize oxygen

Scratch Paper
Stop:
Think:
Predict:
Match

6. A person with B⁻ type blood is given a blood transfusion and hemolysis occurs. Which answer choice contains blood type(s) that will cause this reaction?

    A.   AB⁺, B⁻, A⁺
    B.   AB⁺, A⁻, O⁺
    C.   B⁺, O⁻, A⁺
    D.   O⁺, B⁻, AB⁻

Directed Practice

- *Biological Sciences Review Notes*: Biology Ch. 9

O$_2$ dissociation curve

The O$_2$ dissociation curve shows hemoglobin's (Hb) binding of O$_2$ as a function of P$_{O_2}$.

99% Oxygen is bond to hemoglobin

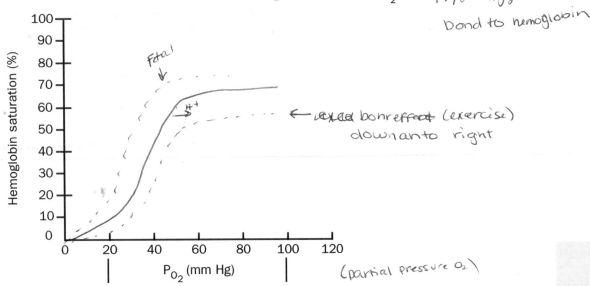

Fetal

H$^+$

← *lexled bohreffect (exercise) down an to right*

P$_{O_2}$ in active muscle (21 mm Hg)   P$_{O_2}$ in alveoli (104 mm Hg)

(partial pressure O$_2$)

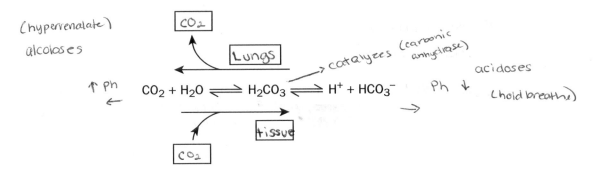

(hyperrenalate) alcoloses

↑ ph ←

CO$_2$

Lungs

catalyzes (carbonic anhydrase)

CO$_2$ + H$_2$0 ⇌ H$_2$CO$_3$ ⇌ H$^+$ + HCO$_3^-$ *Ph ↓* *acidoses* *(hold breathe)* →

tissue

CO$_2$

Critical Thinking Exercise

If the body in need of oxygen lowers oxygen affinity in response, how does the oxygen initially load?

What kind of tissues need a particularly large supply of oxygen? *muscles*

How would the dissociation curve look for fetal hemoglobin? Why? *left*

How does the curve look for myoglobin? Why?

↳ *¼ hemogloban (only carries 1*

Directed Practice

- *Biological Sciences Review Notes*: Biology Ch. 9

Passage II (Questions 7–10)

Red blood cells (RBCs) are the O_2-transporting cells of mammals. During maturation, RBCs lose their nuclei, as well as all other membrane-bound organelles. Besides O_2 transport, the other important function of RBCs is the transport of CO_2 to the lungs for expulsion. CO_2, which is the waste product of cell respiration, diffuses from the cells and into the capillaries. Approximately 70% of the CO_2 is transported in the blood as bicarbonate ion (HCO_3^-); the remaining 30% is either dissolved in the plasma or is bound to the amino group of hemoglobin (Hb) molecules.

In the RBCs of systemic capillaries, where the partial pressure of CO_2 is high and the partial pressure of O_2 is low, the CO_2 combines with water to form carbonic acid (H_2CO_3), which then dissociates into HCO_3^- and H^+. This reaction is catalyzed by the enzyme carbonic anhydrase and occurs while the Hb molecules release their O_2. The release of the O_2 induces a conformational change in the Hb that allows it to bind the H^+. By binding the H^+, the Hb serves as a buffer system for the blood, preventing fluctuations in blood pH. Meanwhile, the HCO_3^- is transported out of the RBC in exchange for a Cl^-. A transmembrane protein known as Band 3 is responsible for this exchange.

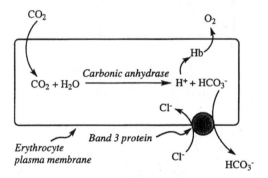

Figure 1

In pulmonary capillaries, where the partial pressure of CO_2 is low and the partial pressure of O_2 is high, the overall direction of the process is reversed. The re-formed gaseous CO_2 diffuses out of the RBC and is eventually expelled via the lungs.

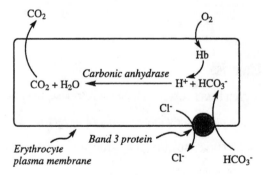

Figure 2

Scratch Paper

Stop:

Think:

Where does the passage discuss Band 3?

What is the sodium-potassium pump?

Predict:

Match

Stop:

Think:

What are the characteristics of RBCs?

Predict:

Match

7. The ion exchange facilitated by the Band 3 of an erythrocyte is similar to that of the sodium-potassium pump of a neuron in that both systems:

   A. cause electric potentials to form on the plasma membrane.
   B. import as many ions as they export.
   C. move ions against their concentration gradients.
   D. rely on plasma membrane proteins for ion exchange.

8. A researcher wanting to study aerobic respiration in mammalian cells would NOT chose RBCs for her protocols because:

   A. RBCs have a life span of only 120 days.
   B. Aerobic respiration occurs only in the cells of alveoli.
   C. RBCs lack mitochondria and therefore attain their ATP anaerobically.
   D. RBCs consume O_2 at a faster rate than other cells.

Scratch Paper

Stop:

Think:

What mechanism is the most likely to alter the volume of red blood cells?

Predict:

Match

Stop:

Think:

Refer to Figure 1.

What happens as $[CO_2]$ increases?

Predict:

Match

9. It has been observed that the volume of a red blood cell in venous circulation is normally 3% greater than that of a red blood cell in arterial circulation. The most likely reason for this volume discrepancy is that:

A. the partial pressure of O_2 is greater in venous blood than in arterial blood.
B. venous circulation contains three times as much blood volume as arterial circulation.
C. there are more red blood cells in venous blood than in arterial blood.
D. there is a higher concentration of Cl^- in the red blood cells of venous blood than in those of arterial blood.

10. The graph below represents CO_2 dissociation curves for deoxygenated blood and oxygenated blood. Which of the four points on the graph corresponds to the lowest HCO_3^- plasma concentration?

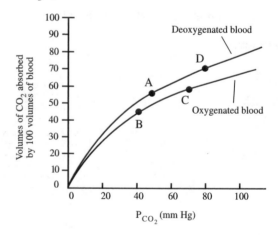

A. A
B. B
C. C
D. D

MUSCLE SYSTEM: CONTRACTILE TISSUE THAT GENERATES MOVEMENT

Skeletal muscle

Skeletal muscle is striated; the contraction of skeletal muscle is under voluntary control.

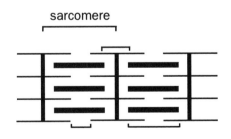

Sarcomere

The sarcomere is the functional unit of muscle; it is composed of thin filaments (actin) and thick filaments (myosin).

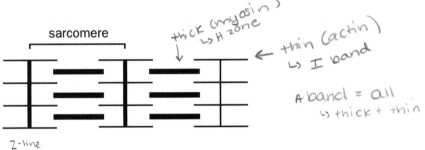

sarcomere

thick (myosin) ↳ H zone

← thin (actin) ↳ I band

A band = all ↳ thick + thin

Z-line

Contraction

sarcomere

Critical Thinking Exercise

How do you make a muscle lengthen?   need opposite muscle

Unit 2

Smooth muscle

Smooth muscle is _nonstriated_; the contraction of smooth muscle is _involuntary_.

  ↳ autonomic
   ↳ 1 nuclei
    ↳ digestive
     ↳ myogenic → does not need impulse

Cardiac muscle

Cardiac muscle is _striated_; the contraction of cardiac muscle is _involuntary_.

Muscle Type	Striated?	Nuclei	Vol/Invol
skeletal	yes	multiple	vol
smooth	NO	1	invol
cardiac	yes	1	invol

Critical Thinking Exercise

What is rigor mortis and what causes it?

  ATP not produced ;

Directed Practice

- *Biological Sciences Review Notes*: Biology Ch. 6

Unit 2

NERVOUS SYSTEM: ELECTRICAL/CHEMICAL COMMUNICATION

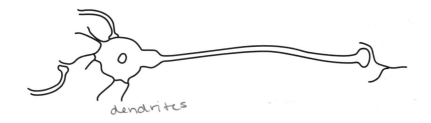

dendrites

Neuron

Dendrite → extensions — recieve stimulus (convert to electricity)

Synaptic knob → site of neuron transmitter release
    (1 nerve, 1 neuro transmitter)

Axon → transport action potential

Myelin → dielectric ; insulates (makes faster) — jumps
    ↳ Schaw and PNS
    ↳ oligodend : CNS

Synaptic Cleft

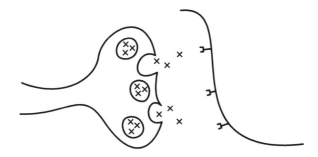

↳ Calcium release (releases neuro transmitor to bind to
        receptor)

Action potential

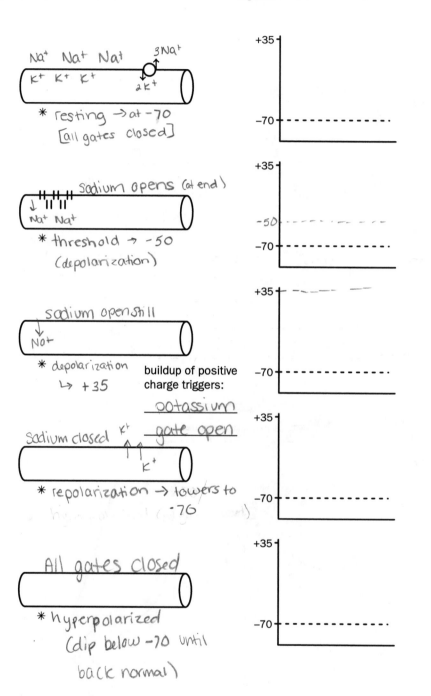

(−) inside w/out sodium
(becomes positive w/Na⁺)

Na⁺ Na⁺ Na⁺   3Na⁺
K⁺ K⁺ K⁺   2K⁺

* resting → at −70
[all gates closed]

Sodium opens (at end)
Na⁺ Na⁺

* threshold → −50
(depolarization)

Sodium open still
Na⁺

* depolarization
↳ +35

buildup of positive
charge triggers:

potassium
gate open

Sodium closed   K⁺
K⁺

* repolarization → lowers to
−70

All gates closed

* hyperpolarized
(dip below −70 until
back normal)

Unit 2

Vertebrate nervous system

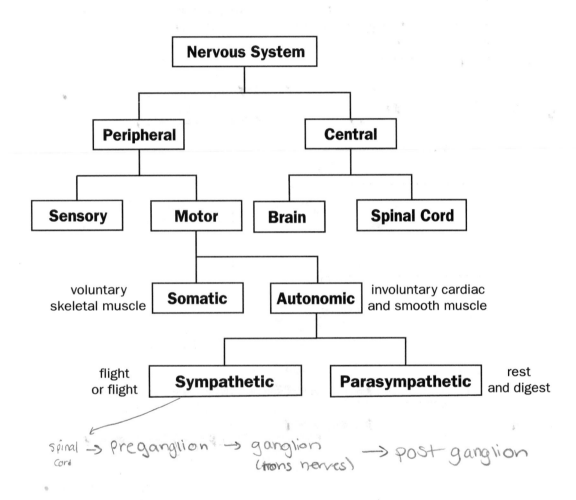

spinal → Preganglion → ganglion → post ganglion
Cord   (trons nerves)

Directed Practice

- *Biological Sciences Review Notes*: Biology Ch. 12

Passage III (Questions 11–14)

The simple nervous system of the sea snail Aplysia has been used as a model system to explore the processes of short-term memory. When the mollusk's siphon is touched, sensory neurons stimulate motor neurons causing the animal's gill to withdraw. However, with repeated touching of the siphon the animal becomes habituated to stimulus and no longer withdraws its gill in response. Electric shock resensitizes the snail and following a shock, it will once again withdraw its gill in response to a touch on the siphon. This resensitization can last for days and is a simple form of short-term memory.

The cause of habituation has been traced to a reduction in the amount of neurotransmitter released by the sensory neurons in response to repeated touching of the siphon. This leads to a decrease in the post-synaptic potential and a consequent decrease in contraction of the gill muscles.

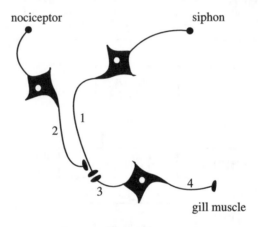

Figure 1

In sensitization, electric shock stimulates nociceptors which respond to pain stimuli. These neurons synapse on the presynaptic axon terminal of the siphon touch sense neurons, as shown in Figure 1. The nociceptor terminals release serotonin which binds to cell surface receptors on the sensory presynaptic terminal and leads to the production of cAMP within the cell. cAMP activates a protein kinase which phosphorylates voltage-gated K^+ channels on the membrane and causes them to remain shut. When action potentials arrive at the axon terminal, K^+ channels do not open and K^+ cannot flow out of the cell. Voltage-gated Ca^{++} channels remain open longer, allowing more Ca^{++} to flow into the cell. This leads to a larger release of neurotransmitter and a larger excited post-synaptic potential in the siphon motor neurons.

Scratch Paper

11. According to the information presented in the passage, which of the following is true regarding the membrane potential of the siphon axon terminal following sensitization?

    A. The axon terminal is hyperpolarized.
    B. The axon terminal is depolarized.
    C. The axon terminal remains polarized longer following action potential.
    D. The axon terminal remains depolarized longer following action potential.

12. A researcher gently brushes the *Aplysia* siphon and monitors action potentials in the mollusk nervous system. The researcher then presses the siphon more forcefully, leading to:

    A. larger action potentials at point 1.
    B. depolarization at point 2.
    C. more frequent action potentials at point 1.
    D. fewer action potentials at point 4.

Unit 2

Scratch Paper

Stop:

Think:

Predict:

Match

Stop:

Think:

Predict:

Match

13. Which of the following effects of repeated stimulation of the siphon provides a possible explanation for the habituation mechanism?

   A. Repeated stimulation leads to closure of calcium channels in the terminal membrane.
   B. Repeated stimulation leads to a decrease in the number of serotonin receptors in the terminal membrane.
   C. Repeated stimulation leads to a decrease in concentration of neurotransmitter degrading enzymes in the siphon/gill muscle nerve synapse.
   D. Repeated stimulation causes neurotransmitter vesicles to fuse with the terminal membrane in response to lower excitatory potentials.

14. Which of the following points indicated in Figure 1 are neuron axons?

   A. 1 and 2 only
   B. 1 and 3 only
   C. 2, 3, and 4 only
   D. 1, 2, and 4 only

The Lesson Continues
on the Next Page
→

HOMEWORK

Review for Biology 2

Topical Tests	❑ Circulatory and Lymphatic Systems Test 1
Subject Tests	❑ Test 4 (Optional, MM3214) ❑ Test 5 (Optional, MM3215)

Preview for MSCT 2

Section Tests	❑ Physical Sciences Test 1 ❑ Bring to class scratch paper used during Full-Length 1

Unit 2

MCAT Strategy & Critical Thinking 2

- Kaplan Pacing and Triaging Strategies
- Kaplan CBT Strategy
- Stress Reduction
- Sample Writing Sample Prompts and Databases
- Full-Length 1 Test Review

KAPLAN PACING STRATEGY

The MCAT CBT Interface Clock

The clock on the computer screen counts down. It indicates the official time for each section of the test. This clock should be used for pacing, as personal timing devices are not allowed in the testing room.

The Countdown

Section	Passage Pair	Time Left
Physical Sciences	Discretes	57 (13 mins)
	1st Pair	41 (16 mins)
	2nd Pair	25 (16 mins)
	3rd Pair	9 (16 mins)
	Last Passage	1 min
Verbal Reasoning	1st Pair	43 (17 mins)
	2nd Pair	26 (17 mins)
	3rd Pair	9 (17 mins)
	Last Passage	0.5 mins
Biological Sciences	Discretes	57 (13 mins)
	1st Pair	41 (16 mins)
	2nd Pair	25 (16 mins)
	3rd Pair	9 (16 mins)
	Last Passage	1 min

Unit 2

Crisis Prevention Tips

How did you use the clock on your last Full-Length?

Did you finish each section?

KAPLAN TRIAGING STRATEGY

Take Control of the Test: Triage

P:1   2   3   4   5   5   6   d   7
Q:1   6   13   17   d2t   2u   d33   32   42   47

Passage Triaging Criteria

· look for shortest
· on topic like
· do discretes first

Question Triaging Criteria

· length
· math
· within passage
· what good at

KAPLAN COMPUTER-BASED TEST STRATEGY

Scratch Work Strategy

PI; Q1

TP1: Pendulum - acts as accelerometer to meas. horiz. accel. of obj.

TP2: damping → suspend pend. in liquid

T: accelerometer

S: Simple pendulum as

PIV; Q21

TP1: Photosynthesis → chem. energy fr. light + CO_2

Rxn1: Photosyn. rxn → $CO_2 + O_2 + light →$ glucose + H_2O

TP2: Photon, carbon fixation → Sugar

Table: ΔH_f of prod. & react.

T: Photosyn.

S: Products/Reactants of

PVI; Q35

TP1: X-ray production descr.

TP2: e's accel. fr. cathode → anode by E field

TP3: 1st mech. for X-ray prod. w/ in metal - bremsstr.

TP4: 2nd mech → inner e's displaced by ΔE e$^-$

TP5: Amt X-rays abs'd. ∝ density

T: X-rays, S: 2 mechanism for X-ray prod.

PIII; Q17

TP1: Hear sensitiv. varies w/ freq

TP2: $I = \frac{P}{A}$

TP3: Eg. 1: Eq. for B → log scale

Fig. 1: Thresholds of pain & hearing

T: hearing

S: Sensitivity of human ear

PII; Q7

TP1: gas rxn meas. @ STP → closed vessel

Rxn1: $2A(g) + B(g) → 2C(s) + D(g)$

Fig. 1: PE diag. of Rxn 1

TP2: 2nd order rxn, 1st step slowest, gas ideal

T: Gases

S: Ideal gas rxn.

PV; Q30

TP1: Rxn rate deps. on RDS

Rxn1: 3 step mechan. of rxn; step1
↓ RDS

TP2: Rate of rxn = $K_i[A]$

TP3: Descr. pseudo 1st order rxns
- used at enzyme measurs.

TP4: Rxn rate dep. on intermediate
- RDS not 1st step

TP5: Redox rxns → use Nernst equ.
→ Kog relates to V

T: Rxn Kinetics

S: RDSs & rate laws

P VII; Q42

TP1: Toule-Thomson exp. apparatus
- adiabatic process; each chamber
own constant temp.

Fig. 1: JT apparatus

TP2: ideal gases don't change temp →
real gases do

TP3: Exp. inversion temp.

Equ. 1: Inversion temp ∝ a; b

TP4: Inv. temp w/ van der Waals constant.

Equ. 2: van der waals eq.

Table 1: van der Waals constants for some gases

T: JT exp S: studies real gas behavior

Unit 2

Benefiting from Test Day Computer Functionalities

Computer Function	How does it work?	How should I utilize it?
Highlighting	Place cursor over word chosen to highlight; use left mouse button	Key words (few words)
Strike through answer choices	Click on answer choice using left mouse button	
Tag questions as marked	Click on box labeled as "Guess"	occassionally

What should I do after finishing a section with time remaining?

1st task _make sure none omitted_

2nd task _review marked_

3rd task _Click Submitt_

Unit 2

TESTING INTERFACE: ITEM REVIEW

KAPLAN TEST PREP AND ADMISSIONS

◀ HOME

≻ GO TO ANALYSIS

Title	# of Items	Score	Seconds Used	View
Section 1: Physical Sciences	52	74%	3518	View

Q#	Answer Selected	Correct	Correct Answer	Previous Answer	Seconds Used	Q.Id	Explanation
Question Set					410	h020255	GO ⓘ
1	B	✗	D	D		h020255.01	
2	A	✔	A			h020255.02	
3	D	✔	D			h020255.03	
4	C	✔	C			h020255.04	
5	A	✗	B			h020255.05	
6	A	✔	A	B		h020255.06	
Question Set					433	h020256	GO ⓘ
7	A	✔	A			h020256.01	
8	D	✔	D			h020256.02	
9	C	✗	D			h020256.03	
10	C	✔	C	D		h020256.04	
11	A	✔	A	C		h020256.05	
Question Set					405	h020257	GO ⓘ
12	C	✔	C			h020257.01	
13	B	✗	A			h020257.02	
14	A	✔	A			h020257.03	
15	B	✔	B	D		h020257.04	
16	A	✔	A			h020257.05	
17	C	✔	C			h020257.06	
18	D	✔	D			h020257.07	
Question Set					421	h020258	GO ⓘ
19	B	✗	C			h020258.01	
20	B	✗	A	A		h020258.02	
21	B	✔	B			h020258.03	
22	B	✔	B			h020258.04	
23	D	✔	D			h020258.05	
24	C	✗	D			h020258.06	

Unit 2

Question	Q Type	Why missed

Question	Topic	Why missed

STRESS REDUCTION

Stress reduction is:

A. mini-naps at random times during the test.

B. biting fingernails and/or whistling during the test.

C. during the test, announcing that you can't take it anymore and leaving in a huff.

D. quick, practiced methods to keep the mind sharp and focused.

How to do it

- breathe
- stretch
- focus positively

When to do it

- between passages

CRISIS PREVENTION TROUBLESHOOTING

Symptoms and Solutions

Excessive Stress:
- Relaxation

Nervous Energy
- In-Seat Stretching

Loss of Focus
- In section breaks: using the Kaplan Section Strategy (Passage Pairs)

Fatigue
- Nutrition, rest and experience

Obsession with score, and "stupid answer" syndrome
- Post-Phrasing → *going back knowing right answer (why wrong) wrong*

Obsessive Reading
- Optimization Exercise

Worries about Test Day
- Concentration, imaging, visualization

Plateau in scores
- Moving the Comfort Zone with index cards and QuickSheets

Unit 2

MCAT WRITING SAMPLE: SAMPLE PROMPTS AND DATABASES

Advertising / Media

The media creates, rather than reflects, new trends

Business

In business, competition is superior to cooperation

Education

Students should be required to take courses in many fields rather than concentrate on one area

Government

Citizens who enjoy a country's benefits during peacetime have a responsibility to support their nation during times of war

History

History is all about the conflict of ideologies

International Politics

Countries should not interfere in the internal affairs of other nations.

National Politics

Political change is more effective than political stability

Law

Citizens must obey the laws of a nation

Science/Technology

Pure research is less valuable than applied research

Sociology

The healthiest societies are multicultural

Crisis Prevention Tip

Were there any prompts for which your databases did not apply?

Full-Length 1
Test Review

Full-Length 1 Physical Sciences Passage III (Questions 14–20)

Many nutrients required by plants exist in soil as basic cations: Mg^{2+}, Mn^{2+}, and Ca^{2+}. A soil's *cation-exchange capacity* is a measure of its ability to adsorb these basic cations as well as exchangeable hydrogen and aluminum ions. The cation-exchange capacity of soil is derived from two sources: small clay particles called micelles consisting of alternating layers of alumina and silica crystals, and organic colloids.

Replacement of Al^{3+} and Si^{4+} by other cations of lower valence creates a net negative charge within the inner layers of the micelles. This is called the soil's *permanent charge*. For example, replacement of an atom of aluminum by calcium within a section where the net charge was previously zero, as shown below, produces a net charge of –1, to which other cations can become adsorbed.

$$\boxed{O^{2-}Al^{3+}OH^-} \rightarrow \boxed{O^{2-}CA^{2+}OH^-}$$

Figure 1

A *pH-dependent charge* develops when hydrogen dissociates from hydroxyl moieties on the outer surfaces of the clay micelles. This leaves negatively-charged oxygen atoms to which basic cations may adsorb. Likewise, a large pH-dependent charge develops when hydrogen dissociates from carboxylic acids and phenols in organic matter.

In most clays, permanent charges brought about by substitution account for anywhere from half to nearly all of the total cation-exchange capacity. Soils very high in organic matter contain primarily pH-dependent charges.

In a research study, three samples of soil were leached with a 1 N solution of neutral KCl, and the displaced Al^{3+} and basic cations measured. The sample was then leached again with a buffered solution of $BaCl_2$ and triethanolamine at pH 8.2, and the displaced H^+ measured. Table 1 gives results for three soils tested by this method.

Table 1

	(meq/100 g)				Total Cation Exchange Capacity
	pH	Al^{3+}	Basic Cations	H^+	
Sample I	4.5	11.7	1.9	34.0	47.6
Sample II	5.3	1.6	16.3	19.5	37.4
Sample III	6.0	0.5	9.8	7.8	18.1

Unit 2

Due to the buffering effect of the soil's cation-exchange capacity, just measuring the soil solution's pH will not indicate how much base is needed to change the soil pH. In another experiment, measured amounts of acid and base were added to 10-gram samples of well-mixed soil that had been collected from various locations in a field. The volumes of the samples were equalized by adding water. The results were recorded in Figure 2.

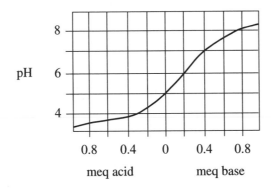

Figure 2

Unit 2

14. Which column(s) in Table 1 represent(s) the permanent charge of the soil micelles?

    A. Al^{3+}

    B. H^+

    C. Al^{3+} and Basic Cations

    D. Al^{3+} and H^+

15. What percentage of the cation exchange capacity of Sample I is base-saturated?

    A.   4%

    B.   6%

    C.   29%

    D.   40%

16. Which soil from Table 1 most likely has the highest percentage of organic matter?

    A.   I

    B.   II

    C.   III

    D.   Cannot be determined

17. What would be the effect of leaching the three soil samples in Table 1 with a buffered $BaCl_2$ solution at pH 9.5 instead of 8.3?

    A.   The measured permanent charge would be greater.

    B.   The measured pH-dependent charge would be greater.

    C.   The measured permanent charge would be smaller.

    D.   The measured pH-dependent charge would be smaller.

Unit 2

18. The amount of soil on a particular one-acre field down to a depth of one furrow slice weighs 9×10^5 kilograms. Based on Figure 2, how many kilograms of $CaCO_3$ would have to be added to this field to raise the pH from 5 to 6?

    A. 900 kg
    B. 1800 kg
    C. 9×10^5 kg
    D. 1.8×10^6 kg

19. Which of the following would probably NOT displace Al^{3+} in soil micelles?

    A. Na^+
    B. Mg^{2+}
    C. Si^{4+}
    D. Cr^{2+}

20. Anaerobic organisms are able to denitrify wet soils by the following metabolic pathway.

    $$HNO_3 \rightarrow HNO_2 \rightarrow H_2N_2O_2 \rightarrow N_2O(g) \rightarrow N_2(g)$$

    If all the oxygen in the nitric acid is converted to water, how many additional equivalents of acid will be consumed during the production of 5 *M* of nitrogen?

    A. 20
    B. 30
    C. 40
    D. 50

Unit 2

Full-Length 1 Physical Sciences Passage V (Questions 30–35)

Every atomic orbital contains plus and minus regions, defined by the value of the quantum mechanical function for electron density. When orbitals from different atoms overlap to form bonds, an equal number of new molecular orbitals results. These are of two types: σ or π bonding orbitals, formed by overlap between orbital regions with the same sign, and antibonding σ^* or π^* orbitals, formed by overlap between regions with opposite signs. Bonding orbitals have lower energy than their component atomic orbitals, and antibonding orbitals have higher energy. The electron pairs reside in the lower-energy bonding orbitals; the higher-energy, less stable orbitals remain empty when the molecule is in its ground state.

A benzene ring has six unhybridized p_z orbitals (one from each carbon atom), which together from six molecular π orbitals, each one delocalized over the entire ring. Of the possible π orbital structures for benzene, the one with the lowest energy has the plus region of all six p orbital functions on one side of the ring. The six electrons occupying the orbitals fill the three most stable molecular orbitals, leaving the other three empty.

Molecular orbitals are filled from the lowest to the highest energy level. The number of bonds between atoms is determined by the number of filled bonding orbitals minus the number of filled antibonding orbitals; each antibonding orbital cancels out a filled bonding orbital. For a diatomic molecule, orbitals in the $n = 2$ energy level are filled as follows: σ_{2s}, σ^*_{2s}, σ_{2p_z}, π_{2p_x} and π_{2p_y} (equal in energy), $\pi^*_{2p_x}$ and $\pi^*_{2p_y}$ (equal in energy), $\sigma^*_{2p_z}$. (The designation of the three p orbitals as p_x, p_y, and p_z are interchangeable.)

Absorption of a photon can raise an electron to a higher-energy molecular orbital. The excited electron does not immediately change its spin, which is opposite to that of the electron with which it was previously paired. This singlet state is relatively unstable: the molecule may interact with another molecule, or fluoresce and return to its ground state. Alternatively, there may be a change in spin direction somewhere in the system; the molecule then enters the so-called triplet state, which generally has lower energy. The molecule now cannot return quickly to its ground state, since the excited electron no longer has a partner of opposite spin with which to pair. It also cannot return to the singlet state, because the singlet has greater energy. Consequently, the triplet state, which has two unpaired electrons in separate orbitals, is long-lived by atomic standards, with a lifetime that may be 10 seconds or more. During this period, the molecule is highly reactive.

30. Which of the following four depictions of molecular π orbitals represents the highest energy state for a 6-carbon polyene molecule? (The signs given are the signs for the mathematical functions defining the *p* orbitals on one side of the molecule.)

    A.   – – – – – –
    B.   + + + – – –
    C.   + + – – + +
    D.   + – + – + –

31. Among conjugated polyenes (molecules with alternating carbon-carbon double and single bonds) why are those that are longer able to absorb longer wavelengths of light?

    A.   Larger molecular orbitals have a lower ground state.
    B.   A longer wavelength is better able to interact with a longer molecular orbital.
    C.   The larger number of molecular orbitals allows for smaller energy transitions.
    D.   Larger molecular orbitals can absorb more energy.

32. Given the order in which orbitals are filled, which molecule is a triplet in its ground state?

    A. H_2
    B. O_2
    C. N_2
    D. F_2

Unit 2

33. Molecular orbitals in hydrocarbons are formed between the 1s atomic orbital of hydrogen and the *sp*, *sp*^{2}, or *sp*^{3} hybrid atomic orbitals of carbon. Which choice correctly lists the energy level of the C-H bonds, from lowest to highest?

A. C_6H_6, HC≡CH, CH_4
B. H_2C=CH_2, CH_4, C_6H_6
C. C_6H_6, CH_4, H_2C=CH_2
D. HC≡CH, C_6H_6, CH_4

34. Which of the following figures describes the shape of $\sigma^*_{2p_z}$ molecular orbital?

A.

B.

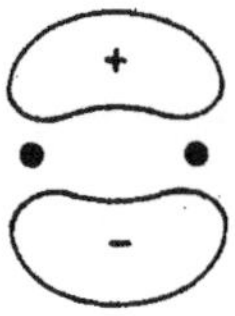

C.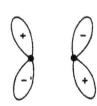

D.

35. The quantum number that distinguishes the p_x orbital from the p_y orbital is called the:

A. azimuthal quantum number.
B. magnetic quantum number.
C. principal quantum number.
D. spin quantum number.

**The Lesson Continues
on the Next Page**

Unit 2

Full-Length 1 Physical Sciences Passage VII (Questions 42–47)

The simple harmonic motion of a mass suspended from vertical springs is investigated in two experiments. The springs used in both experiments have a spring constant k and a natural length L_0. The material used to make the springs has a Young's modulus of 2×10^{11} Pa.

In the first experiment, a mass m is suspended from a spring. The mass stretches the spring to a new length L, called the equilibrium length.

In the second experiment, the mass m is suspended from two identical springs as shown in Figure 2 below. When the mass m is in equilibrium, each spring is stretched from its natural length by the same amount x_e.

In both experiments, the masses of the springs are negligible, and the elastic limits of the springs are never exceeded.

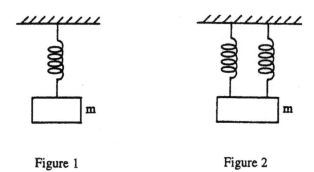

Figure 1   Figure 2

Unit 2

42. In the first experiment, what is the mass of the object hanging from the spring?

    A. kL/g

    B. kL_0/g

    C. $k(L - L_0)/g$

    D. k/g

43. The mass in the first experiment is pulled down a distance A from its equilibrium position and then released from rest. The mass will then oscillate with simple harmonic motion. As the mass moves up and down, energy is dissipated due to factors such as air resistance and internal heating of the spring. The mass will no longer oscillate when the total energy dissipated equals:

    A. $kL^2/2$.

    B. $kA^2/2$.

    C. $k(L + A)^2/2$.

    D. $kL_0^2/2$.

44. In the first experiment the mass is pulled down and set into motion. The position of greatest speed is:

    A.   at the equilibrium position.

    B.   at the position where the spring's length is its natural length.

    C.   at the lowest point in its motion.

    D.   at the highest point in its motion.

45. In the first experiment, when a 5-kg mass is oscillating, the frequency of oscillation is 2 Hz. What is the value of the spring constant?

    A. $5/\pi^2$ N/m

    B.   20 N/m

    C. $40\pi^2$ N/m

    D. $80\pi^2$ N/m

Unit 2

46. The two springs in Experiment 2 are replaced by a single spring having a spring constant k' such that the equilibrium length x_e does not change. What is the ratio of k' to k?

    A.   1/2
    B.   1
    C. $\sqrt{2}$
    D.   2

47. If the spring in Experiment 1 were suspended from the ceiling of an elevator accelerating with acceleration a, how would the equilibrium length of the spring compare to the equilibrium length of the spring when the elevator is stationary?

    A.   The equilibrium length of the spring would be greater when the elevator is accelerating upward.
    B.   The equilibrium length of the spring would be greater when the elevator is stationary.
    C.   The equilibrium length of the spring would be greater when the elevator is accelerating downward with acceleration smaller than the acceleration due to gravity.
    D.   The equilibrium length of the spring doesn't depend on the acceleration of the elevator.

Unit 2

The Lesson Continues
on the Next Page

Unit 2

Full-Length 1 Verbal Reasoning Passage I (Questions 1–5)

The notion of realism in literature is based largely on the implicit belief that writers can accurately transform common objects or ideas from life into words on a page while maintaining an accurate representation of the object or idea. If an author writes a novel which seems believable, meaning that a reader can imagine events in the novel actually happening, then that book is often considered a "realistic" work of literature. The problem with this term is that "realism" does not maintain a stable definition across geographic and temporal boundaries. So how can we use an ambiguous term to categorize certain works of literature? If the meaning of "realism" continues to change, is it possible to agree on a general working definition of the term?

One of the first critics to tackle this subject was Erich Auerbach in his 1953 book, *Mimesis: The Representation of Reality in Western Literature.* By analyzing certain scenes in classic literary works, Auerbach shows that authors in different time periods have employed varying styles and literary techniques in order to structure their systems of mimesis and present realistic views of life in their centuries. Subsequent theorists have criticized Auerbach for positing the idea that realistic works are tightly linked to historical events and attitudes, and that certain novels cannot be properly comprehended and appreciated if a reader is ignorant of the socio-historical context in which the writer was living and working. A problematic implication of Auerbach's theory is that it renders most novels obsolete, since later readers cannot completely comprehend the historical context of an older novel. Yet, Auerbach contradicts himself when discussing certain realist authors, including Balzac, by claiming that they share certain world views in common with their readers, which consequently renders their novels realistic and verisimilar for any reader in any era. But how could a twentieth-century reader share a similar view of the world with a nineteenth-century author?

For contemporary theorists, realism has come to imply a coherent structural semiotic system, created by an author, maintained throughout a novel, and based on the author's observations of the world. Twentieth-century literary critics were especially interested in how words acquire meaning and can transmit that meaning in a comprehensible manner. Julia Kristeva is one well-known theorist who explored semiotic systems for this reason, developing an important theory relating *signs* (words) to *signifiers* (images) to *signifieds* (objects). Consequences of this system include the recognition that words are arbitrary constructs of human society that are not inherently linked to their objects, and may constitute their own closed system within the text of a novel. This is why a school can also be called une école or una escuela—different languages use different combinations of letters to refer to the same ideas or objects.

In some ways, the study of semiotics reflects Auerbach's contention that Balzac shares a common world view with his readers, since the link from *signs* to *signifiers* to *signifieds* depends on a common understanding shared by members of a society, which thus renders effective and logical communication possible. Otherwise, the link between signs and signified becomes arbitrary and incomprehensible. A contemporary example of how new verbal signs acquire a meaning can be illustrated by considering the word email: just a few decades ago, this combination of letters was not considered an accepted word with an associated meaning, whereas now the word has fully entered into the active vocabulary of the English language. For this reason, if an author uses unfamiliar terms in a novel, a reader will not consider the work "realistic" since it doesn't correspond to the reader's established understanding of the world.

Realism thus depends on several disparate factors: socio-cultural and historical context, an author's style, an accepted common semiotic system shared by author and reader, and an essential complicit understanding between author and reader which provides a successful conduit for the transmission of ideas between a novel's creator and its recipient. In the final analysis, however, we must admit that novels can never accurately and fully represent reality, since words describing an object are not, in actuality, the object itself.

1. The author of this passage would most likely agree that:

   A. contemporary theories of realism ignore Auerbach's theories.
   B. determining a satisfactory and fixed definition of realism remains an illusory goal.
   C. words remain meaningful despite cultural and historical changes.
   D. any reader can correctly interpret realistic novels.

2. The author's attitude towards Auerbach's study of mimesis can best be described as:

   A. appreciative of the scope of Auerbach's work but skeptical of its wide applicability due to an emphasis on the importance of historical context.
   B. laudatory of Auerbach's research and impressed that Auerbach's conclusions remain valid today.
   C. critical of Auerbach's premise that authors can construct systems of mimesis and wary that Auerbach's study is too limited.
   D. impressed with Auerbach's analyses of classic literature but doubtful that Auerbach's work has relevance to other literary genres.

Unit 2

3. In order to classify a novel as "realistic," which of the following factors would be LEAST important?

   A. Familiarity with the attitudes and standards of the time periods of both the author and the reader.

   B. Analysis of the author's style as it compares with that of his contemporaries.

   C. Understanding of the author's intent at the time he wrote the novel.

   D. Establishment of a common semiotic system shared by both the author and the reader.

4. The author mentions Julia Kristeva's semiotic theory and its relation to the novel in order to:

   A. disprove a previous theory of realism which has become obsolete.

   B. prove that mimesis can be reinforced by establishing a clear semiotic system.

   C. show how language is a semiotic system whose qualities affect the mimesis of a novel.

   D. argue that a text cannot be a closed system and must always be related to exterior influences.

5. With which of the following statements about mimesis would the author most likely agree?

   A. Examination of the literary techniques used by an author is the only effective way to evaluate a novel's mimetic system.

   B. The classification of a novel as "realistic" is independent of its mimetic and semiotic systems and the coherence thereof.

   C. The mimetic system of a particular author can never accurately reflect the author's observations of his time period.

   D. A coherent system of mimesis, established by the author and recognized by the reader, reinforces the realism of a novel.

Unit 2

The Lesson Continues
on the Next Page

Unit 2

Full-Length 1 Verbal Reasoning Passage V (Questions 24–28)

In 1993, Frances Rauscher and colleagues published a letter in the journal *Nature* showing that listening to Mozart's sonata for two pianos in D major produced a small, short-term improvement on college student's spatial skills. These skills typically include the ability to correctly construct objects, to navigate, and to manipulate visual images. From this humble beginning, others have sought to sell parents sets of Mozart CDs by promising to improve their children's IQs and nearly every other quality parents find desirable. Since most parents want to raise bright, healthy children, they tend to be prey for those hawking products that seem to offer some scientific way to improve their children's intelligence. Based on this research, the state of Georgia provides Mozart CDs for all newborns in the state. We need to ask whether Georgia's actions are justified, and whether parents should play Mozart in the house and insist their caregivers play Mozart as well.

Since 1993, when the first report of the "Mozart Effect" was published, the Mozart Effect has been replicated with mixed success. Some researchers have found an effect, while others have been unable to do so. Researchers have since determined that the effect is not specific to Mozart's music, music is not necessary for the effect, and only a small set of tasks are influenced. Even when researchers have found an effect, it has always been small, brief, and, usually, limited to spatial-temporal tasks. In other words, no study has ever shown a lasting improvement on any population's general intelligence scores. A recent review of studies drives home this point: at most the Mozart Effect would alter IQ scores by about 1.4 points—much less than the variability expected when the same subject takes the test a second time.

Although passively listening to Mozart's music has not been shown to have a long lasting effect on intellectual development, active music training has been shown to have a lasting effect. Several researchers have shown that music training has an effect on and can improve children's spatial-temporal skills.

Although the Mozart Effect is small, it does raise issues that parents and researchers need to address. The first one concerns the nature of intelligence. How much is one's intellectual level innate and how much can it be influenced by one's environment? Is intelligence best considered as a unitary phenomenon measured by a single number, or is it composed of many different abilities? It appears that heritability can explain about 50% of the variability in intelligence scores. Identical twins show a high correlation in their intelligence scores: around 80%. In fact, even when reared apart, identical twins are more similar in intelligence than siblings reared together. At present, most researchers believe that there are many different types of intelligence specific to different tasks.

One popular proposal is Howard Gardner's. He proposed that there are at least seven separate intelligences: linguistic, mathematical-logical, spatial, musical, bodily-kinesthetic, interpersonal, and intrapersonal.

Second, the Mozart Effect debate raises questions about what the goals of preschool instruction should be. Should parents attempt to raise their children's intelligence via intense instruction when the children are young? Children who start receiving academic instruction earlier might have a leg up on other children. While the idea seems to make sense, some studies have shown that early intense instruction actually has a detrimental effect on children's interest in school and later school functioning.

The bottom line is that the Mozart Effect is a small, 10-minute improvement on spatial-temporal skills. If parents and their infants enjoy Mozart, or nearly any other type of music, then they should by all means play it. However, they should not expect that purchasing a special boxed set of classical composers will improve their baby's intelligence. Parents who want to use music to aid in their children's intellectual development would do better to teach them to play an instrument.

24. According to the passage, the "Mozart Effect" is:
    A. an improvement in intelligence scores after listening to Mozart's music.
    B. a meteorological phenomenon.
    C. a type of intelligence.
    D. the amount of intelligence explained by heredity.

25. According to the author, most psychologists would agree with which of the following statements about intelligence?
    A. Intelligence is best measured by a single number.
    B. Intelligence can be improved by listening to music.
    C. The concept of intelligence is useless and should be dropped.
    D. What we call intelligence is probably composed of multiple abilities.

26. Based on the information in the passage, the author does not consider the occurrence of IQ improvement after listening to Mozart's music significant because:
    A. the writer prefers another classical composer.
    B. although it is a huge improvement, it only lasts a short time.
    C. it is a small, short-term improvement.
    D. although it is a long-term improvement, it is small.

27. Although many people believed that listening to Mozart improved one's general intelligence, on what skills did people actually show an improvement?

    A. remembering dates in history
    B. verbal ability
    C. mathematical reasoning
    D. manipulating visual images

28. According to the passage, the studies of twins were important in order to:

    A. show the influence of heredity.
    B. show that twins are more susceptible to the Mozart Effect.
    C. show that there are many kinds of intelligence.
    D. emphasize that one should learn to play an instrument.

WHAT IS TO COME

Preview of Unit 3: Integrated Practice

- Incorporate Kaplan's Section, Passage, Question and Answer Strategies and Pacing Strategy into a unified test-taking tactic.

- Focus on Section Tests and Full-Length Exams.

- Practice using Test Day computer functions.

- Build endurance and stamina.

Unit 2

HOMEWORK

Review for MSCT 2

Online Workshops	❏ Stress Management Workshop

Preview for Physics 3

Physics Review Notes	❏ *Chapters 5, 10–12
Section Tests	❏ Physical Sciences Test 2 ❏ Physical Sciences Test 3
Foundation Review	❏ Unit 3 (Optional, (MM3259A)
Online Workshops	❏ *Atomic and Nuclear Phenomena

Unit 2

UNIT THREE
INTEGRATED PRACTICE

Physics 3

INTEGRATED PRACTICE: FOUNDATION

- Fluids and Solids
- Light and Optics
- Mini MCAT

THE KAPLAN MCAT TRAINING PROGRAM

Unit 3

Diag	MSCT 1

Unit 1: Critical Reading

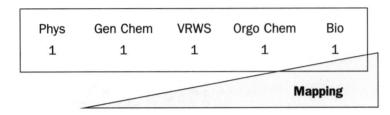

Phys 1	Gen Chem 1	VRWS 1	Orgo Chem 1	Bio 1

Mapping

Unit 2: Attacking Questions

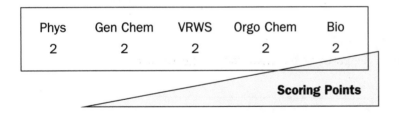

Phys 2	Gen Chem 2	VRWS 2	Orgo Chem 2	Bio 2

Scoring Points

FL#1	MSCT 2

✳ Unit 3: Integrated Practice

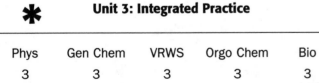

Phys 3	Gen Chem 3	VRWS 3	Orgo Chem 3	Bio 3

Pacing & Focus

Unit 4: Test Day Simulation

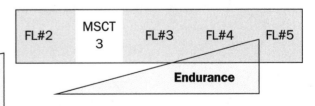

FL#2	MSCT 3	FL#3	FL#4	FL#5

Endurance

✳ YOU ARE HERE

FLUIDS AND SOLIDS

Density

$\rho = \dfrac{m}{V}$

Pressure

$P = \dfrac{F}{A}$

pascals $= 10^5$ atmospheres

Gauge pressure

The gauge pressure of a fluid is the pressure above atmospheric pressure.

Pascal's principle

Applied pressure is transmitted undiminished to all parts of the fluid and to the walls of container.

$$P = \frac{F_1}{A_1} = \frac{F_2}{A_2}$$

$$V = Ad \longrightarrow W = Fd$$

Hydrostatic pressure

$P = P_0 + \rho g z$

Critical Thinking Exercise

Scratch Paper

1. How would the plot of hydrostatic pressure versus depth change for a vessel filled with liquid and exposed to the environment if it were transported to the moon?

A.
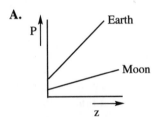

B.
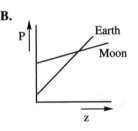

C.
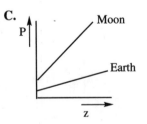

D.
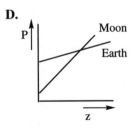

Unit 3

Buoyancy

Buoyant force

$F_b = \rho_{fluid} g V_{submerged}$

weight displaced fluid = buoyancy

Density rule

Critical Thinking Exercise

Scratch Paper

2. A cube of solid ice is floating in a glass of water. After the ice melts, the height of the water in the glass:

   A. is higher.
   B. is lower.
   C. remains the same.
   D. cannot be determined with the information provided.

Fluid dynamics — *moving fluids*

Continuity equation

$A_1 v_1 = A_2 v_2$

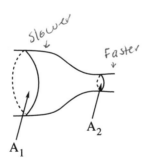

slower

Faster

A_2

A_1

Bernoulli's equation

$P_1 + \dfrac{1}{2}\rho v_1^2 + \rho g h_1 = P_2 + \dfrac{1}{2}\rho v_2^2 + \rho g h_2$

$V \uparrow \quad P \downarrow$

conservation energy

Directed Practice

- *Physical Sciences Review Notes*: Physics Ch. 5

Unit 3

Elasticity of Solids

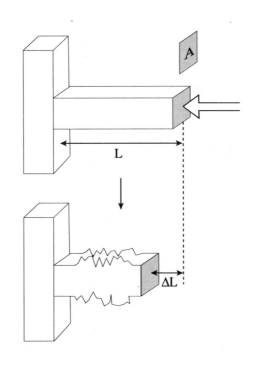

Stress

$$P = \frac{F}{A}$$

Stress is the force applied divided by the cross-sectional area over which the force is applied.

Strain

Strain is change in length of an object under stress as a fraction of its original length.

$$\frac{\Delta L}{L}$$

Young's modulus → measure stiffness

$$Y = \frac{F/A}{\Delta L/L}$$

Critical Thinking Exercise

What would have a greater Young's modulus, steel or silly putty? Steel (stiffer)

Shear modulus (lateral)

$$S = \frac{F/A}{x/h}$$

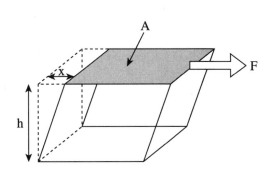

Directed Practice

- *Topical Tests*: Fluids and Solids Test 1 (Passage II)
- *Physical Sciences Review Notes*: Physics Ch. 5

Unit 3

Passage I (Questions 3–6)

An experiment is performed to measure the density of a large sample of sea water. By observing the acceleration of an object falling freely in the sea water, the buoyant force due to the water can be measured. This is equal to the weight of the water that is displaced by the object. By using objects of different shape and surface area, the effects of the viscosity of the sea water can also be studied.

In order to get an accurate measurement, three samples made from different materials are prepared. Sample A is a cube 0.1 m in length on each edge. Sample B is a cylindrical rod 1 m long with a cross-sectional area of 0.01 m^2. Sample C is a sphere of volume 4.9×10^{-5} m^3. In the first test, the acceleration of each sample is measured both in fresh water and in sea water at a temperature of 25°C.

Further tests were performed to determine the effects of pressure on the samples. The Young's modulus of each sample, which equals the stress over the strain, was determined experimentally by measuring the strain of each sample at various applied stresses. The results for all the tests performed are listed in Table 1 along with the corresponding mass and density of each sample. (The density of fresh water is 1,000 kg/m^3, and the acceleration due to gravity is g = 9.8 m/s^2.)

Sample	Density (kg/m³)	Mass (kg)	Acceleration in sea water (m/s²)	Acceleration in fresh water (m/s²)	Young's Modulus (Pa)
A	2,200	2.2	5.2	5.3	7×10^{10}
B	11,000	110	8.9	8.9	1.6×10^{10}
C	1,015	0.05	0	0.14	3×10^{9}

Table 1

Scratch Paper

Unit 3

3. When completely submerged in fresh water, sample A experiences a force along its bottom surface of 9.8 N. What is the pressure due to this force?

    A. 0 Pa
    B. 0.1 Pa
    C. 490 Pa
    D. 980 Pa

4. In Table 1, the acceleration in sea water listed for sample C is zero. Which of the following can be deduced from this fact?

    A. The temperature of the sea water was greater than 25°C when the experiment was performed.
    B. The viscosity of sea water is greater than that of fresh water.
    C. The density of sea water is greater than or equal to 1,015 kg/m^3.
    D. The specific gravity of sea water is less than 1.0.

5. Two of the samples are found to experience different gauge pressures when submerged in fresh water. This can best be explained by the fact that:

    A. they have different surface areas.
    B. they have different densities.
    C. they are at different depths.
    D. they have different Young's moduli.

6. If an equal pressure is applied to each sample, which one would experience the least strain?

    A. Sample A
    B. Sample B
    C. Sample C
    D. All the samples would experience the same strain.

Unit 3

LIGHT AND OPTICS

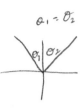

$\theta_1 = \theta_2$

Reflection

Law: _Same angle to normal_

////////////////////////////

Refraction

Index of refraction $\rightarrow$ two different surfaces

$$n = \frac{c}{v} = \frac{\text{speed light}}{\text{speed median}}$$

$n_{air} = 1$

$n_{water} = 1.33$

air

n_1

n_2

water

$n_2 > n_1$

$\theta_2 < \theta_1$

* bends to normal

θ_1

* equal
doesn't bend

$n_2 < n_1$
$\theta_2 > \theta_1$
* bends away

n_1

n_2

θ

Directed Practice

- *Topical Tests*: Light and Geometrical Optics Test 1 (Passage II)
- *Physical Sciences Review Notes*: Physics Ch. 10

Unit 3

Behaviors of Light: Particle vs. Wave

Particle		Wave
	Young's double slit experiment	✓
✓	The photon	
✓	(light) $c = 3.0 \times 10^8$ m/sec	✓
	Polarization (electromagnetic field ⊥ direction)	✓
	$c = \lambda f$	✓
✓	The photoelectric effect (shine light energy → excite photon)	
	Diffraction (spreading light)	✓
✓	$E = hf$ (energy photon)	
	Refraction	✓

Unit 3

Snell's law

$$n_1 \sin \theta_1 = n_2 \sin \theta_2$$

At a Boundary

	Air (lower *n*) to Glass (higher *n*)
Frequency	doesn't
Wavelength	↓
Speed	↓ (S = wavelength · frequency)

Critical Thinking Exercise

A diver under water looks straight up. What does he see? What does he see when he looks outward at a large enough angle?

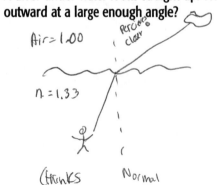

a. Air = 1.00   Perceives clear

n = 1.33

(thinks closer)   Normal

b. ocean floor

*total reflected light (reflected back)
*never leaves (can't go out)

$n_1 \sin \theta_{critical} = n_2 \sin (90)$

$\frac{1}{f} = \frac{1}{o} + \frac{1}{i}$ (o = object , i = image) → virtual → otherside

$m = -\frac{i}{o}$ (magnification)   ↳ positive = real (in front) → same side

↳ m = (-) = inverted

$f = \frac{1}{2} r$ (for spherical mirrors only)

fo[al] lengh th

Lenses and mirrors (thin lenses)

Converging mirrors:

(concave → goes in)

f < 0 < r

r = 4 , f = 2   0 = 3

$\frac{1}{2} - \frac{1}{3} = \frac{1}{i} \rightarrow i = 6$

$m = -\frac{6}{3} = -2$

$i = \infty$

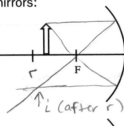

↑ i (after r)

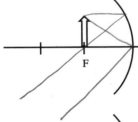

F

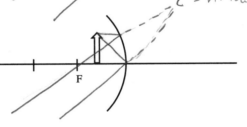

i = virtual (upright)

F

Diverging mirrors: (convex)

0 < f

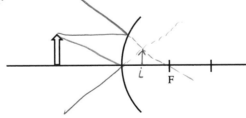

i   F

Converging lenses:

drawing
1. parallel
2. Folcal
3. through
    center

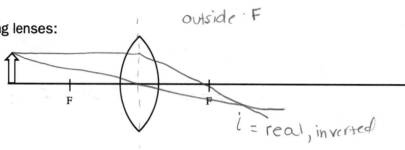

outside F

i = real, inverted

on F

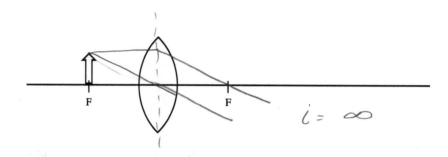

$i = \infty$

inside F

virtual = i

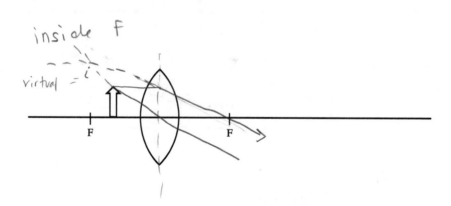

Diverging lenses:

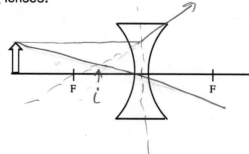

i

	Positive	**Negative**
f	converging	diverging
i	real	virtual
o	same side light	opposite side light
m	up right	inverted
	m>1=larger	m<1=smaller

	Converging	**Diverging**
Concave	mirror	lense
Convex	lense	mirror

Unit 3

Combinations of lenses

Image produced by one lense is
object for next lense

Aberrations → imperfection projection of light

	Cause	Applies to
Chromatic	dispersion (w/ color)	lenses
Spherical	different focusing of light (not perfect)	mirrors

Parabala perfect

Directed Practice

- *Topical Tests*: Light and Geometrical Optics Test 1 (Passage I)
- *Physical Sciences Review Notes*: Physics Ch. 10

Kaplan's Pacing Strategy—Sciences

13 discrete questions in 13 minutes

7 Passages in 57 minutes

Minutes per **passage pair**: _____

Passage 1

Passage 2

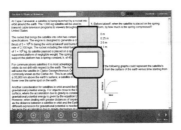

Passage 3

Passage 4

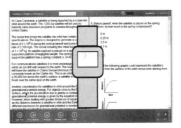

Passage 5

Passage 6

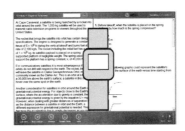

Passage 7

Unit 3

DO NOT TURN THIS PAGE UNTIL YOU ARE INSTRUCTED TO DO SO

Physics
Mini MCAT

Time: 19 minutes
Questions: 1–12

Passage I (Questions 1–4)

In household wiring, a balance must be set between the convenience of the users and their safety. The residents of a house would like to be able to use an unlimited number of appliances at any one time. However, the more appliances used by a household, the larger the current that is drawn into the house. Eventually, the current may exceed the capacity of the wires to carry it. The wires may then overheat, possibly resulting in an electrical fire.

Fuses or circuit breakers are placed to ensure that the current demand in the house never exceeds the safety limit. They are designed to disrupt the current to the appliances completely if the current is greater than a certain threshold value: a fuse rated at 8 A, for example, would "blow" and break the circuit if the current through it exceeds 8 A. The voltage across a fuse is negligible when a current is running through it.

Figure 1 shows a possible wiring diagram for a two-room shack. Appliances within rooms are connected in parallel. The electrical power is delivered by a 120-V_{rms}, 60-Hz AC source.

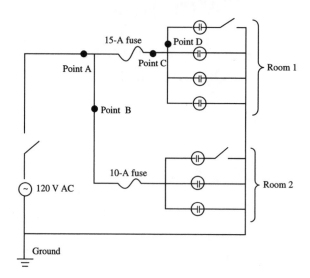

Figure 1

1. A coffee maker and a lamp are both operating in the same room. If a toaster oven in the other room is then turned on, which of the following would be true?

    A. The voltage across the coffee maker would decrease.
    B. The current through the coffee maker would remain the same.
    C. The power consumed by the toaster oven would decrease.
    D. The voltage across the 10-A fuse would decrease.

2. If we would like to monitor the current through the 15-A fuse, at which point would we connect an ammeter?

    A. Point A
    B. Point B
    C. Point C
    D. Point D

3. A 0.5-A current flows through a 2 kΩ-resistor. If the television operates with 216 W of power, how long must the current flow to dissipate the same amount of energy that is consumed by the television in one hour?

    A. $\dfrac{(0.5)^2 \times 2000}{216 \times 3600}$ s

    B. $\dfrac{216 \times 3600}{(0.5)^2 \times 2000}$ s

    C. $\dfrac{216 \times 3600}{0.5 \times 2000}$ s

    D. $\dfrac{216}{(0.5)^2 \times 3600 \times 2000}$ s

4. Ignoring the fuses and the switches, which of the following is equivalent to the circuit in Figure 1?

A.

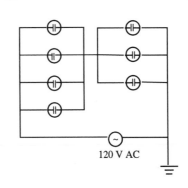

C.

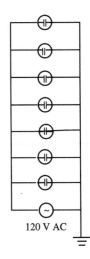

B.

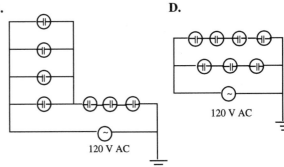

D.

120 V AC

Questions 5 through 7 are NOT based on a descriptive passage.

5. Which of the following will produce a magnetic field?

   I.   A current-carrying wire
   II. Moving a wire through a field-free region
   III. Electrons orbiting a nucleus

   A. I only
   B. II only
   C. I and III only
   D. I, II, and III

6. When a 5-kg mass is attached to a vertical spring it stretches 40 cm. What is the force constant of the spring?

   A. 0.01 N/m
   B. 8 N/m
   C. 49 N/m
   D. 123 N/m

7. A light ray traveling in air is incident at an angle of 45° on a glass block with an index of refraction of 1.5. Which of the following diagrams best represents what happens to the ray?

   A.

   C.

   B.

   D.

The Lesson Continues
on the Next Page

Unit 3

Passage II (Questions 8–12)

Lightning is one of the unharnessed sources of electricity. A typical bolt of lightning transfers a charge of 16 C in 0.02 seconds with a power output on the order of 10^9 W. Lightning occurs when the electric field in a cloud becomes stronger than the dielectric strength of the atmosphere. Most scientists believe that the electric fields in clouds are created naturally as a result of the circulation and distribution of charge via convection and/or precipitation in the atmosphere. Lightning is the transfer of charge across the potential difference between two clouds or a cloud and the ground.

In addition to occurring naturally, lightning can be induced by large explosions on the Earth's surface that send fireballs up into the atmosphere. The intense rush of high energy photons from the fireball collide with electrons in the air molecules. In these elastic collisions, enough energy is transferred to the electrons so that they can separate from the air molecules. The separation of ionized air molecules and surrounding free electrons create electric fields strong enough to produce lightning. The change in wavelength of a photon scattered by an electron is given by:

$$\Delta\lambda = \lambda_2 - \lambda_1 = (h/mc)(1 - \cos\theta),$$

where λ_1 is the wavelength of the incident photon, λ_2 is the wavelength of the photon after the collision, $h = 4.1 \times 10^{-15}$ eV • s is Planck's constant, m is the mass of the electron $= 9.1 \times 10^{-31}$ kg, c is the speed of light, and θ is the scattering angle for the photon. (Note: For a long straight wire, $B = \mu_0 I/2\pi r$, where B is the magnitude of the magnetic field, $\mu_0 = 4\pi \times 10^{-7}$ N/A^2, I is the current, and r is the distance from the wire.)

8. A 1-km long metal lightning rod is struck by a typical lightning bolt. What is the instantaneous magnetic field induced by the current 10 m to the side of the rod?

   A. 1.6×10^{-7} T
   B. 8.0×10^{-6} T
   C. 1.6×10^{-5} T
   D. 3.2×10^{-5} T

9. The Earth's surface and the bottom surface of a typical thunder cloud may be thought of as a parallel plate capacitor. The potential difference between the cloud and the ground: (Note: Assume that the charge on the cloud remains constant.)

   A. increases as the cloud moves closer to the ground.
   B. decreases as the cloud moves closer to the ground.
   C. remains the same as the cloud moves closer to the ground.
   D. increases as the area of the bottom of the cloud increases.

10. Which of the following will increase the power delivered when electric charge is transferred in the form of lightning?

   I. Increasing the time over which the charge is transferred.
   II. Increasing the amount of charge transferred.
   III. Increasing the potential difference over which the charge is transferred.

   A. II only
   B. I and II only
   C. I and III only
   D. II and III only

11. Which of the following is true of the collision between the photon and the electron that leads to fireball induced lightning?

   A. The collision is inelastic, and the frequency of the photon decreases.
   B. The collision is elastic, and the frequency of the photon decreases.
   C. The collision is inelastic, and the frequency of the photon increases.
   D. The collision is elastic, and the frequency of the photon increases.

12. What is the maximum increase in wavelength that a photon can experience as a result of a collision with an electron?

   A. h/2mc
   B. h/mc
   C. 2h/mc
   D. no maximum

Unit 3

HOMEWORK

Review for Physics 3

Topical Tests

- ❏ Light and Geometrical Optics Test 1
- ❏ Atomic and Nuclear Structure Test 1
- ❏ Fluids and Solids Test 1
- ❏ Physics Discretes Test 1
- ❏ Physics Discretes Test 2
- ❏ Physics Strategic Supplemental (MM3230)

Section Tests

- ❏ Physical Sciences Test 4
- ❏ Physical Sciences Test 5

Preview for General Chemistry 3

General Chemistry Review Notes

- ❏ *Chapters 8–11

Foundation Review

- ❏ Unit 3 (Optional, (MM3258A)

Online Workshops

- ❏ *Properties of Solutions

General
Chemistry 3

INTEGRATED PRACTICE: COMPREHENSION

- Acids and Bases
- Titrations
- Oxidation Reduction Reactions
- Mini MCAT

ACIDS AND BASES

Definitions

Arrhenius

An acid is a ___proton___ donor; a base is a _____ donor.

The Arrhenius definition for acids and bases is limited only to aqueous solutions.

Acids: _____

Bases: _____

Brønsted-Lowry

An acid is a proton (H^+) ___donor___; a base is a proton (H^+) ___acceptor___.

Acids: ___H_2O, HNO_3, HCl (anything w/ H)___

Bases: ___H_2O, NH_3___

Lewis

An acid is an ___electron acceptor___; a base is an ___electron donor___.

Lewis bases are also called ligands. Lewis acid-base reactions are also called complexation reactions.

Amphoteric species

Amphoteric species can act as either an acid or a base.

H_2O

Directed Practice

- *Physical Sciences Review Notes*: Gen. Chem. Ch. 10

Unit 3

Conjugate acids and bases

$$HA \rightleftharpoons \underset{cA}{H^+} \; A^-$$

$$CH_3COOH + H_2O \rightleftharpoons CH_3COO^- + H_3O^+$$

Strong acid = weak conj. base

Acid and base strength

K_a is the equilibrium constant for acid ionization.

$$HA \rightarrow H^+ + A^-$$

* depends on temperature

$$K_a = \frac{[H^+][A^-]}{[HA]}$$

K_b is the equilibrium constant for base ionization.

For Brønsted-Lowry Bases:

$$B + H_2O \rightarrow HB^+ + OH^-, \; K_b = \frac{[HB^+][OH^-]}{[B]}$$

$$pH = 14 - pOH$$

$$K_w = [H^+][OH^-]$$

$$B^- + H_2O \rightarrow HB + OH^-, \; K_b = \frac{[HB][OH^-]}{[B^-]}$$

K_w is the equilibrium constant for the autoionization reaction of water. At 25°C, it has a value of 1×10^{-14}.

↳ acid and base w/in water

$$H_2O(l) \rightleftharpoons H^+ (aq) + OH^- (aq)$$

Directed Practice

- *Topical Tests*: Acids and Bases Test 1 (Passage II)
- *Physical Sciences Review Notes*: Gen. Chem. Ch. 10

Unit 3

Strong Acids	Weak Acids	Strong Bases	Weak Bases
HCl	CH_3COOH	NaOH	NH_3
H_2SO_4	HF	KOH	H_2O
HNO_3	H_2O	H^-	F^-
HBr	HCN	NH_2^-	CN^-
$HClO_4$	$NH_4^{\oplus}$	Na_2O	CH_3COO^-
HI		CaO	
		$Ca(OH)_2$	

p(Anything)

p(Anything) = –log [Anything]

$Ph \uparrow = [\ ] \downarrow$

$11 = -\log_{10}[10^{-11}]$

Examples

$pK_a = -\log [K_a]$

$pK_b = -\log [K_b]$

Critical Thinking Exercise

What is the pH of a solution whose hydronium ion concentration is 6.4×10^{-3}?

$-\log[n \times 10^{-m}] \rightarrow -\log[6.4 \times 10^{-3}] = 3 - \log(6.4)$

$\downarrow$

$m - \log n$

≈ 2.2

Directed Practice

• *Physical Sciences Review Notes*: Gen. Chem. Ch. 10

Critical Thinking Exercise

What is the pH of a solution when 1×10^{-10} mol of HCl is added to one liter of pure water?

[handwritten] ✳ need to add autoionization to HCl concentration

[handwritten]
$$1000 \times 10^{-10} + 1 \times 10^{-10} = 1.001 \times 10^{-7}$$
water   HCl
⟿ pH = 7

The water autoionization reaction is endothermic. If the temperature is increased, what happens to the pH of the solution?

[handwritten]
Δ = goes to right but both go up
so stays same
Kw would change

Scratch Paper

1. The dielectric constant of a solvent is a measure of its polarity. The higher its value, the better the solvent is at solvating ions. Below is a list of the dielectric constants of certain solvents at 20°C:

Solvent	Dielectric constant
Benzene	2.3
Chloroform	5.1
Diethyl ether	4.3
Hexane	1.9

If the same amount of nitric acid is added to 0.5 L of each solvent, which solvent would result in a solution with the highest pH?

A. Benzene
B. Chloroform
C. Diethyl ether
D. Hexane

Titrations

Titrations are the addition of a solution of known concentration and volume to another solution to determine its unknown concentration.

Equivalence point $\rightarrow$ mols acid = mols base

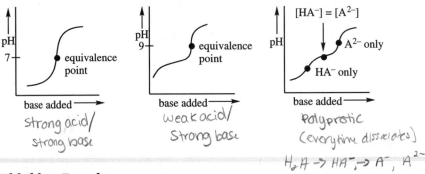

strong acid/
strong base

weak acid/
strong base

polyprotic
(everytime dissociates)

$H_2A \rightarrow HA^- \rightarrow A^-, A^{2-}$

Critical Thinking Exercise

Scratch Paper

2. One liter of an aqueous ammonia ($K_b = 1.8 \times 10^{-5}$) solution is titrated with 1.1 N HCl(aq). If 50.0 mL of the acidic solution is required to reach the equivalence point, what was the pH of the ammonia solution before the titration was begun?

   A.   5.00
   B.   5.24
   C.   10.26
   D.   11.00

Directed Practice

- *Topical Tests*: Acids and Bases Test 1 (Passage I)
- *Physical Sciences Review Notes*: Gen. Chem. Ch. 10

Buffers

Buffers resist changes in pH.

Henderson-Hasselbach equation ✳

$$pH = pK_a + \log \frac{[\text{conjugate base}]}{[\text{weak acid}]}$$

$$pOH = pK_b + \log \frac{[\text{conjugate acid}]}{[\text{weak base}]}$$

Example of Buffers

$$CH_3COOH + H_2O \rightleftharpoons H_3O^+ + CH_3COO^-$$

$$K_a = \frac{[H_3O^+][CH_3COO^-]}{[CH_3COOH]} \qquad [H_3O^+] = \frac{K_a[CH_3COOH]}{[CH_3COO^-]}$$

Indicator

An indicator changes color at a particular pH. Indicators are used to monitor titrations.

Methyl Red Buffer System

red   yellow

Critical Thinking Exercise

The pK_a of methyl red is 5.2. Describe the relative concentrations of the colored forms of a 1 M solution of methyl red at pH 4.2, 5.2, and 6.2. *yellow color change → when pKa = pH*
red *pH < pKa → red, pH = pKa = orange, pH > pKa = yellow*

Directed Practice

- *Physical Sciences Review Notes*: Gen. Chem. Ch. 10

Passage I (Questions 3–7)

In order for a titration to yield concentration data with an acceptable level of accuracy, standardized solutions with precisely known normalities must be prepared. This is no small accomplishment, as most commonly-used titrants are difficult to handle in the pure state. Sodium hydroxide, for example, is a common basic standard; it is hygroscopic as a solid and thus absorbs water from the atmosphere. Hydrogen chloride, a common acidic standard, is a gas at ambient temperatures and pressures; saturated aqueous solutions can be prepared simply by bubbling the gas through deionized water, but temperature effects on solubility and volatility generally limit the significance of concentration calculations to the nearest 0.1 M.

To overcome the difficulties inherent in the preparation of standard solutions, one usually resorts to the use of a primary standard such as sodium carbonate, Na_2CO_3, or potassium hydrogen phthalate (KHP). The primary standard is used to determine the concentration of a newly prepared solution, whose concentration can then be adjusted via dilution. The fundamental criteria for the selection of a primary standard are listed below:

1. It must be stable in light, in air, and in the solution to be titrated.
2. It must be free of any significant quantity of impurities.
3. It must be sufficiently soluble in the solution to be titrated.
4. It must react with the substance to be titrated by a single, known pathway.
5. Its reaction with the titrated substance must be rapid.
6. It should be nontoxic, and present few disposal problems.
7. It should be readily available and relatively inexpensive.

A student preparing to perform a series of titrations on a group of vitamin samples produced a secondary standard of 0.01000 N NaOH(aq) by first making a more concentrated solution. She dissolved approximately 2.5 mg of NaOH(s) in enough water to make 250.0 mL of solution. This solution was then standardized against KHP according to the reaction:

KHP
(204.2 g/mol)

+ NaOH $\longrightarrow$ + H_2O

The student placed 385.43 mg of KHP into a clean flask, added 50 mL of deionized water and two drops of phenolphthalein solution, and then titrated with the freshly prepared NaOH solution. The endpoint was reached upon addition of 25.10 mL of the basic solution. From this titration data the student calculated the concentration of the NaOH solution as 0.07520 N then, using a pipette and a volumetric flask, diluted the NaOH solution, as needed, to a final concentration of 0.01000 N.

Scratch Paper

Unit 3

3. Commercially available KHP must be prepared in a "dry box," usually under an argon atmosphere. One likely reason for this necessity is that:

   A. freshly prepared KHP is hygroscopic, and thus must be kept in an inert atmosphere.
   B. the phthalic acid from which it is made is extremely volatile, and thus must be used in the absence of oxygen.
   C. the KOH used in the preparation is hygroscopic and thus must be weighed in an anhydrous environment.
   D. very pure KHP is extremely toxic, and thus requires careful handling.

4. During the standardization described in the passage, the student began by dissolving the KHP in 50 mL of water. If the actual volume of water added were slightly larger than the measured volume, what effect would this have had on the final determination of the concentration?

   A. The calculated concentration of NaOH would have been higher than the actual concentration.
   B. The calculated concentration of NaOH would have been lower than the actual concentration.
   C. The calculated concentration of NaOH would have been the same as the actual concentration.
   D. The concentration of NaOH could not have been calculated.

5. Sodium carbonate is the preferred primary standard for acidic solutions. What is the mass of sodium carbonate required to neutralize 25.10 mL of 0.07520 N HCl(*aq*)? (The molecular weight of sodium carbonate is 106.0 amu.)

   A. 50.00 mg
   B. 100.0 mg
   C. 200.0 mg
   D. 1.000×10^5 mg

6. According to the information contained in the passage, which of the following reactions would be the best choice for the standardization of an aqueous nitric acid solution?

A. $Al_2O_3(s) + 6HNO_3(aq) \rightarrow 2Al(NO_3)_3(aq) + 3H_2O(l)$
B. $ZnCl_2(aq) + 2HNO_3(aq) \rightarrow Zn(NO_3)_2(aq) + 2\,HCl(aq)$
C. $2Cu(s) + 6HNO_3(aq) \rightarrow 2Cu(NO_3)_2(aq) + NO(g) + NO_2(g) + 3H_2O(l)$
D. $NaOH(s) + HNO_3(aq) \rightarrow NaNO_3(aq) + H_2O(l)$

7. While analyzing samples for vitamin B content, the student found it necessary to titrate for niacin, the structure of which is shown below. If a 5.00 mL sample containing no other acidic compounds required the addition of 3.75 mL of 0.01000 N NaOH solution to reach the equivalence point, then how many moles of niacin would be found in one liter of the sample solution?

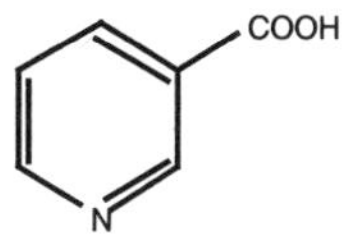

A. 18.75
B. 0.75
C. 1.3×10^{-2}
D. 7.5×10^{-3}

REDOX CHEMISTRY

Oxidation state

To keep track of the movement of electrons, assign oxidation numbers to each element. Oxidation occurs when an atom or ion loses electrons. Reduction occurs when an atom or ion gains electrons.

Oxidizing Agent/Reducing Agent → oilrig

↳ get reduced   ↳ get oxidized

Critical Thinking Exercise

Identify the oxidizing agent and the reducing agent in the reaction below:

$AgNO_3(aq) + CuNO_3(aq) \rightarrow Ag(s) + Cu(NO_3)_2(aq)$

OA   ↳RA

	starts	ends
NO_3	-1	-1
Ag	+1	0 → reduced
Cu	+1	+2 — oxidized

Directed Practice

- *Physical Sciences Review Notes*: Gen. Chem. Ch. 11

Unit 3

Critical Thinking Exercise

8. Ascorbic acid (vitamin C) is believed to function as an antioxidant in biochemical systems, oxidizing according to the simplified equation:

$$C_6H_8O_6 \rightarrow C_6H_6O_6 + H_2$$

Which of the following is a likely half-reaction relevant to the redox titration of ascorbic acid with a suitable oxidizing agent?

A. $C_6H_8O_6 \rightarrow C_6H_6O_6 + 2H^+ + 2e^-$

B. $C_6H_8O_6 + 2e^- \rightarrow C_6H_6O_6 + H_2$

C. $C_6H_8O_6 \rightarrow C_6H_6O_6 + H_2 + 2e^-$

D. $C_6H_8O_6 + 4e^- \rightarrow C_6H_6O_6 + 2H_2O$

Directed Practice

- *Physical Sciences Review Notes*: Gen. Chem. Ch. 11

ELECTROCHEMISTRY

Electrochemical cells

Electrodes → connected

Oxidation occurs at the anode, and reduction occurs at the cathode.

Galvanic/Voltaic (battery)

Spontaneous reactions occur in galvanic cells.

ex.

$$Cu^{+2} + Zn(s) \rightarrow Zn^{+2} + Cu(s)$$

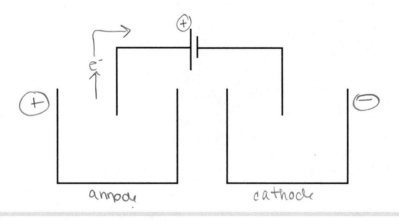

annode

cathode

$$Zn(s) \rightarrow Zn^{+2} + 2e^- \quad (half\ reaction)$$

$$Cu^{+2} + 2e^- \rightarrow Cu(s)$$

Electrolytic

Electrolytic cells require energy to drive the nonspontaneous reaction.

annpde

cathode

Directed Practice

• *Physical Sciences Review Notes*: Gen. Chem. Ch. 11

Emf(E)

$$E^\circ_{cell} = E^\circ_{cathode} - E^\circ_{anode} \quad \rightarrow reduction$$
$$\quad\quad\quad\quad \oplus \quad\quad\quad (-)$$

oxidation potentials
(just change sign)

$$Co^{3+}(aq) + e^- \longrightarrow Co^{2+}(aq) \quad E^\circ = 1.82 \, V$$
$$Na^+(aq) + e^- \longrightarrow Na(s) \quad\quad E^\circ = -2.71 \, V$$
$$E' = 4.53$$

$E^\circ > 0$ for galvanic
$E^\circ < 0$ for electrolytic

mols electrons transferred

$$\Delta G^\circ = - nFE^\circ_{cell} \quad \rightarrow F = 10^5 \, J/mol$$

$$nFE^\circ_{cell} = RT \ln K_{eq}$$

Quantitative electrolysis - Faraday's Laws

Total charge transferred can be calculated using the following equation.

$$I \times t = n \times F$$

where I is the current, t is the time in seconds, n is the number of moles of electrons transferred, and F is Faraday's constant.

Directed Practice

- *Topical Tests*: Electrochemistry Test I
- *Physical Sciences Review Notes*: Gen. Chem. Ch. 11

Unit 3

The Nernst equation *different concentrations*

The Nernst equation relates a cell's emf to the concentration of the species involved. Use it to determine the emf as the reaction progresses, or when concentrations deviate from the standard state (1 M).

$$E = E° - \frac{0.0592}{n} \log \left(\frac{[C]^c [D]^d}{[A]^a [B]^b} \right) \text{ for } aA + bB \rightleftharpoons cC + dD$$

$K_{eq} = Q \rightarrow E = 0$

Do work (cells)
   1. potential
   2. concentration

Concentration cells

Concentration cells are made of half-cells that are identical except for the concentrations of ions. The emf of the cell can be determined from the Nernst equation.

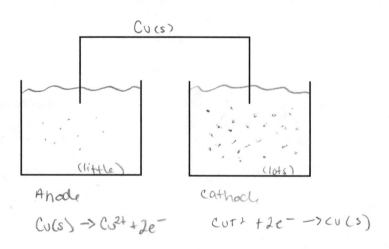

Cu (s)

(little)   (lots)

Anode   Cathode

$Cu(s) \rightarrow Cu^{2+} + 2e^-$ $Cu^{2+} + 2e^- \rightarrow Cu(s)$

Unit 3

DO NOT TURN THIS PAGE UNTIL YOU ARE INSTRUCTED TO DO SO

General Chemistry
Mini MCAT

Time: 19 minutes
Questions: 1–12

Passage I (Questions 1–5)

The solubilities of ionic compounds vary by species. Salts of Group IA elements are considered soluble in water, whereas carbonates, except carbonates of Group IA elements, are usually insoluble. Another class of ionic compounds, sparingly soluble salts, dissolves somewhat in water. Two scientists developed hypotheses to determine if one sparingly soluble salt was more or less soluble than the other.

Scientist 1

Water, a polar solvent, is better at solvating species with higher, rather than lower, polarity. The difference in the electronegativities of the ions that compose an ionic compound gives a measure of the polarity of the compound. Comparing ZnF_2 and $PbBr_2$, fluoride is more electronegative than bromide, and the lead(II) ion is more electronegative than the zinc(II) ion. The polarity of ZnF_2 is greater than the polarity of $PbBr_2$; therefore, ZnF_2 is more soluble than $PbBr_2$.

Table of Selected Electronegativities

Element	Electronegativity
Zn	1.6
Pb	1.9
I	2.5
Br	2.8
F	4.0

Scientist 2

Upon dissolution, sparingly soluble salts are partially converted to ions. These ions vary in their ionic radii. Water forms hydrogen bonds with other water molecules. When ions with a smaller ionic radius are solvated, they do not significantly disrupt the hydrogen-bonding network of water. Larger ions, though, disrupt the intermolecular forces of water, and thus are less soluble. The relative sizes of the ions of the sparingly soluble salts ZnF_2 and $PbBr_2$ are: $Br^- > F^- > Pb^{2+} > Zn^{2+}$. The ions of ZnF_2 are smaller than those of $PbBr_2$; therefore, ZnF_2 is more soluble than $PbBr_2$.

1. What would Scientist 2 predict about the relative solubilities of PbF_2 and ZnF_2?

   A. PbF_2 is more soluble than ZnF_2 because the electronegativity-difference of the ions that compose PbF_2 is smaller.
   B. PbF_2 is more soluble than ZnF_2 because the ions that compose PbF_2 are larger.
   C. PbF_2 is less soluble than ZnF_2 because the electronegativity-difference of the ions that compose PbF_2 is smaller.
   D. PbF_2 is less soluble than ZnF_2 because the ions that compose PbF_2 are larger.

2. The solubility of ZnF_2 is 2.03 g/100 mL at 25°C. What is the K_{sp} value for ZnF_2?

   A. 8.32×10^{-3}
   B. 3.04×10^{-2}
   C. 4.11×10^{-2}
   D. 8.21×10^{-2}

3. How does the addition of a small amount of ZnF_2 to a saturated solution of PbF_2 affect this solution?

   A. ZnF_2 does not dissolve and PbF_2 remains in solution.
   B. ZnF_2 dissolves and PbF_2 precipitates.
   C. ZnF_2 dissolves and PbF_2 remains in solution.
   D. ZnF_2 does not dissolve and PbF_2 precipitates.

4. If PbF_2 were more soluble than $PbBr_2$, how would this affect the hypotheses?

   A. Only Scientist 1's hypothesis would be supported.
   B. Only Scientist 2's hypothesis would be supported.
   C. Both Scientist 1 and 2 would be supported.
   D. Neither Scientist 1 nor 2 would be supported.

5. Which of the following is the correct order for the boiling points of the listed solutions and water? (The K_b of water is 0.51 °C·kg/mol.)

   I. Saturated solution of ZnF_2 in water
   II. Saturated solution of $PbBr_2$ in water
   III. Pure water

   A. III < II < I
   B. III < I < II
   C. I < II < III
   D. II < I < III

Unit 3

Passage II (Questions 6–9)

A student constructs an electrochemical cell consisting of two half-cells. The left-hand cell consists of a 1.0 M copper(II) sulfate solution with a solid strip of copper immersed in it, and the right-hand cell consists of a 1.0 M zinc sulfate solution containing a strip of zinc. The two solid electrodes are connected by a wire and a voltmeter, and the solutions are connected by a porous salt bridge containing KCl. The apparatus is maintained at 25°C. A list of standard reduction potentials for several oxidation-reduction reactions is given in Table 1.

Reaction	E° (V)
$ZnS\ (s) + 2\ e^- \rightarrow Zn\ (s) + S^{2-}\ (aq)$	–1.440
$Zn^{2+}\ (aq) + 2\ e^- \rightarrow Zn\ (s)$	–0.763
$2\ H^+ + 2\ e^- \rightarrow H_2\ (g)$	+0.000
$SO_4^{2-}\ (aq) + 4\ H^+ + 2\ e^- \rightarrow H_2SO_3 + H_2O$	+0.170
$Cu^{2+}\ (aq) + 2\ e^- \rightarrow Cu\ (s)$	+0.337
$Ag^+\ (aq) + e^- \rightarrow Ag\ (s)$	+0.799
$NO_3^- + 4\ H^+ + 3\ e^- \rightarrow NO\ (g) + 2\ H_2O$	+0.960
$Pd^{2+} + 2\ e^- \rightarrow Pd\ (s)$	+0.987

Table 1

(Note: Faraday's constant, *F*, equals 96,485 coulombs per mole of electrons.)

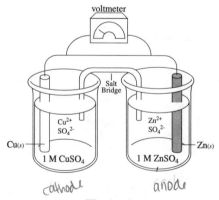

Figure 1

6. Which of the following will occur once the cell begins to operate?

    I.   The copper electrode will gain weight and the concentration of Cu^{2+} in the surrounding solution will decrease.

    II.   The zinc electrode will gain weight and the concentration of Zn^{2+} in the surrounding solution will decrease.

    III.   The copper electrode will lose weight and the concentration of Cu^{2+} in the surrounding solution will increase.

    IV.   The zinc electrode will lose weight and the concentration of Zn^{2+} in the surrounding solution will increase.

    A.   I and III only
    B.   I and IV only
    C.   II and III only
    D.   III and IV only

7. What is the standard cell potential of the cell in Figure 1?

    A.   −1.10 V
    B.   −0.43 V
    C.   +0.43 V
    D.   +1.10 V

8. This cell is an example of a(n):

    A.   galvanic cell with a zinc cathode and a copper anode.
    B.   electrolytic cell with a zinc cathode and a copper anode.
    C.   galvanic cell with a zinc anode and a copper cathode.
    D.   electrolytic cell with a zinc anode and a copper cathode.

9. What is the standard cell potential for an electrochemical cell in which the following reaction takes place?

$$Cl_2\ (g) + 2Br^- \rightarrow Br_2 + 2Cl^-$$

$$\Delta G^\circ = -52.5 \text{ kJ/mol}$$

    A.   −0.544 V
    B.   −0.272 V
    C.   +0.272 V
    D.   +0.544 V

Unit 3

Questions 10 through 12 are NOT based on a descriptive passage.

10. For a diprotic acid H_2A, $K_{a_1} = 1.0 \times 10^{-3}$ and $K_{a_2} = 1.0 \times 10^{-6}$. The pH range for which HA^- is the dominant species is:

    A. −6 to −3.
    B. 0 to 3.
    C. 4 to 5.
    D. any pH greater than 6.

The following half-reactions are relevant for questions 11 and 12.

$$CO^{3+} (aq) + e^- \rightarrow CO^{2+} (aq) \quad E° = 1.82 \text{ V}$$

$$Na^+ (aq) + e^- \rightarrow Na (s) \qquad E° = -2.71 \text{ V}$$

11. Given the reduction potentials above, which of the following is the equilibrium constant for the reaction

    $$Co^{3+} (aq) + Na (s) \rightarrow Co^{2+} (aq) + Na^+ (aq)$$

    at a temperature T?

    A. $e^{\frac{4.53 \text{ F}}{RT}}$

    B. $e^{\frac{-4.53 \text{ F}}{RT}}$

    C. $\dfrac{4.53 \text{ F}}{RT}$

    D. $-\dfrac{4.53 \text{ F}}{RT}$

12. If the reaction

    $$CO^{3+} (aq) + Na (s) \rightarrow CO^{2+} (aq) + Na^+ (aq)$$

    produces a curent of 3A for 2 sec, how many moles of Na (s) are consumed?

    A. 6×10^{-5} moles
    B. 6 moles
    C. 12 moles
    D. 18 moles

The Lesson Continues
on the Next Page
→

Unit 3

HOMEWORK

Review for General Chemistry 3

Topical Tests	❑ Acids and Bases Test 1
	❑ Electrochemistry Test 1
	❑ General Chemistry Discretes Test 1
	❑ General Chemistry Discretes Test 2
	❑ General Chemistry Strategic Supplemental
Section Tests	❑ Physical Sciences Test 6
	❑ Physical Sciences Test 7

Preview for Verbal Reasoning & Writing Sample 3

Verbal Reasoning Strategy and Practice	❑ Tests 4 and 5
Writing Sample section in Verbal Reasoning Strategy and Practice	❑ *Chapter 5, Part 2
Foundation Review	❑ Unit 3 (Optional, MM3261A)
Online Workshops	❑ *Critical Reading Challenge
	❑ *Argument Dissection Challenge
Section Test	❑ Test 5

Unit 3

Verbal Reasoning and Writing Sample 3

INTEGRATED PRACTICE: APPLYING THE PROCESS

- Troubleshooting the Writing Sample
- Dissecting Arguments
- Five Minutes Left
- Mini MCAT

THE KAPLAN 5-STEP METHOD FOR THE WRITING SAMPLE

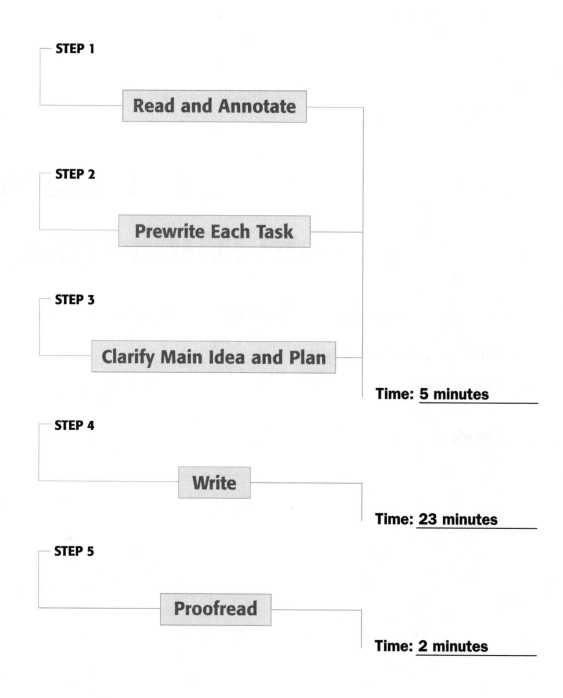

STEP 1

Read and Annotate

STEP 2

Prewrite Each Task

STEP 3

Clarify Main Idea and Plan

Time: **5 minutes**

STEP 4

Write

Time: **23 minutes**

STEP 5

Proofread

Time: **2 minutes**

Unit 3

TROUBLESHOOTING THE ESSAY

Task 1: explain and example

There are two ways to respond to a person's actions, one is praise and the other is criticism. "Praise is more effective than criticism." In reality, both work well if they're used properly. For instance, when a child does something wrong, he has to learn what he/she did wrong and how to correct it. Criticism makes her understand the problem quickly and know she did something wrong. There's no place here for praise, because it won't correct the problem and may make the child think he's ok and do the wrong thing again and maybe even hurt himself. The job of a parent or other caretaker is to teach children right from wrong. This is a hard task and many parents/caretakers fail, but it has to be done.

Problems with Task 1:	**How to avoid Task 1 problems:**
1. restated prompt	1. rephrase
2. not example	2. more specific (state meaning)
3. opinion	3. be objective (know tasks)
4. not unified	4. Solid prewrite

Task 2: Counterexample

A counterexample of when criticism doesn't work well is if a child is really trying his best but doesn't succeed. He already feels bad about not succeeding and criticism just makes him feel worse and possibly give up altogether. Praise would be better here because it will encourage the young person to keep trying. "If at first you don't succeed, try, try again" is a good rule to follow.

Problems with Task 2:	**How to avoid Task 2 problems:**
1. Cleshay	1.
2.	2.

Task 3: when correct

No one, child or adult, likes to be criticized all the time. In many cases it's even counter-productive. Sometimes, however, one methods works better than another. It's all a question of what the goal is. So praise is better than criticism when you want someone to keep trying and not give up. On a bad school paper, the teacher who writes "Good try, but incomplete" will get a better response from the student than if she just wrote: "F."

Problems with Task 3:	**How to avoid Task 3 problems:**
1. New example	1.
2.	2.
3.	3.

Unit 3

STEP 5

Proofread

Tips on Proofreading

Which word processing functions are available?

Copy /paste

Which are not?

No grammar or spelling

Should you make substantial changes?

No , stick to prewrite

Crisis Prevention Tip

How can I practice essays?

DISSECTING ARGUMENTS

An **argument** is:

a **conclusion** (what someone wants to convince the reader)

plus

its supporting **evidence** (or the reasons why).

Critical Thinking Exercise

What are the two ways to identify evidence and conclusion in a passage?

1. Key words
2. analyze content

SIMPLIFYING ARGUMENTS

The author believes [the conclusion] because of [the evidence].

> During the second and third centuries CE, Mithraism was the dominant religion of Rome, and spread to every corner of that empire. Several reasons have been cited for the success of Mithraism among the Romans. Rome's traditional state religion had lost much of its <u>power to inspire reverence</u>; Mithraism, along with several other eastern cults, had the appeal of <u>antiquity and exoticism</u>. In addition, Mithra was a special <u>patron of soldiers</u>, and his cult brought <u>stability</u> to the lives of the many imperial soldiers serving far from their native lands. Also, since Mithraism was consistent with absolute <u>loyalty to the emperor</u>, many of the emperors encouraged Mithra worship.

believes → Mithraism was dominant

because → traditional weak, antiquity + exotic, soldiers (stable), emperors liked

---

Critical Thinking Exercise

Can you briefly restate the author's argument about what caused Mithraism to become dominant?

IDENTIFYING IMPLIED PARTS OF ARGUMENTS

All humans are mammals, and my brother is human, so my brother is a mammal.

There are four possible parts to any argument:

Stated conclusions	**Explicit:** Found directly in the passage
Stated evidence	
Inferences (implied conclusions)	**Implicit:** Requires deduction from what is stated in the passage
Assumptions (implied evidence)	

All humans are mammals, and my brother is human (therefore we can infer ...)

Since all humans are mammals, my brother must be a mammal (assuming that ...)

Poison is harmful. Chemical X is a poison.

Since poison is harmful, chemical X must be harmful.

Unit 3

Arguments Quiz

In some circles, Mendelssohn's reputation diminished rapidly after his death in 1847. By 1852, he was already regarded by many as "the object of pitying disparagement." European musical audiences, newly enamored with the expansiveness of Wagner's Tristan and Isolde, soon found Mendelssohn's music too restrained and academic.

As time progressed, post-Wagnerian anti-Romanticism did little to salvage the composer's standing. Proponents of Schoenberg and his twelve-tone serialism regarded Mendelssohn as a quaint, conservative composer who crafted superficial, "tenderly sentimental" music.

Such "arbiters" as these have moved far too illiberally to certain conclusions. The atmospheric melodic beauty of the Overture to A Midsummer Night's Dream shows the imprint of an original mind, anticipating the orchestral achievement of Rimsky-Korsakov. At the time of its composition, the Octet displayed unexampled lightness and rhythmic effect; the impressionistic Hebrides Overture inspired the painting of Turner. And Mendelssohn's greatest pictorial works, the Scottish and Italian symphonies, constantly reveal new vistas. The work of one of the first, great nineteenth-century Nature composers, Mendelssohn's music simply endures; critics would do well to ask why.

Scratch Paper

1. The author apparently regards both present and historical critics of Mendelssohn as:

    A. ignorant and ill bred.
    B. shortsighted and ungenerous.
    C. brilliantly perceptive.
    D. ambitious and insincere.

2. The author refers to the proponents of Wagner and Schoenberg primarily in order to:

    A. describe the differences between those composers' musical innovations.
    B. show that Mendelssohn's critics also failed to appreciate other great composers.
    C. prove that music critics in every period have lacked sensitivity toward earlier composers.
    D. illustrate how some people have unjustly ignored Mendelssohn's musical achievements.

3. On the basis of the information provided in the passage, we can assume the author would be likely to agree that Mendelssohn's music:

    I. was constrained by traditional forms and styles.
    II. was innovative and influential.
    III. should be judged on its own terms, not according to the standards of later taste.

    A. I only
    B. II only
    C. III only
    D. II and III only

4. The author's argument in favor of Mendelssohn is primarily developed by:

    A. appealing to the authority of post-Wagnerian and anti-Romantic critics.
    B. citing examples that demonstrate Mendelssohn's originality and skill.
    C. arguing the superiority of Mendelssohn's achievements to those of other admired composers.
    D. pointing out that Mendelssohn's critics have focused on unrepresentative aspects of his work.

Unit 3

ARGUMENTS IN PASSAGES

Sensing that government defined by the Articles of Confederation did not meet the needs of the newly born United States, the Congress of the Articles of Confederation authorized commissioners to "devise such further provisions as shall appear to them necessary to render the Constitution of the federal government adequate to the exigencies of the Union." These provisions were to be reported to Congress and confirmed by every state. The recommendatory acts also state that this change, to be done through alterations of the Articles of Confederation, is the most probable means of establishing a strong national government.

Having given these instructions, Congress was quite surprised by the terms of the Constitution as submitted. In fact, it was claimed that the commissioners did not have the legal authority to submit such a revolutionary constitution. In *The Federalist Papers*, James Madison defends the commissioners by returning to the terms of their mandate.

Given the goals expressed in the recommendatory acts, and the principle that conflicts ought to be resolved in favor of more important goals, Madison argued that the degree to which the Constitution departs from the Articles couldn't make the Constitution illegal. Where the goal of amending the Articles conflicts with the goal of creating good government, the Articles must yield, since the goal of "good government" is an overriding consideration.

Although Madison argued fairly convincingly that the degree of change present in the Constitution cannot be grounds for declaring it illegal, this same argument does not apply to the commissioners' decision to allow the Constitution to be ratified by only three-quarters of the states. Even though unanimous approval appears last in Madison's list of the goals of the convention, it was a fundamental aspect of national government under the Articles. Requiring non-ratifying states to be bound by the new Constitution was thus a powerful diminishment of their sovereignty.

The new constitution, once adopted, changed the national government from a weak union of independent states to a strong union in which the interests of the many states could outweigh the protests of the few. Although history has validated the wisdom of the change, the question of whether the change was legal is another matter. In our time, it is easy to forget that the first states of the Union considered themselves to be independent entities.

In authorizing the commissioners, the individual states requested a proposal for the alteration of the national government in order. They did not intend to waive their veto power. So even if Madison is correct, and the commissioners could have proposed anything they deemed likely to fulfill the goal of good government, it does not follow that their proclamations should affect the legal rights of the several states.

Does this imply that the constitution ratified by the states has no moral authority? Not necessarily. No government ought to have the power to entrench itself against amendment, and so the fact that the government under the Articles of Confederation did not consent to the alteration of the ratification process does not establish the moral illegitimacy of the Constitution.

The case for rebelling against the government under the Articles is further strengthened by the fact that the government itself admitted its unfitness for the exigencies of the Union. Indeed, the ratification process altered by the new Constitution is representative of the procedures that initially led Congress to seek reform. In addressing the relevance of opposing the government of the Articles of Confederation, we should also consider the position of the framers. They had already rebelled against England, one of the great powers of the time, and thus had demonstrated an unwillingness to tolerate bad government. Defying the government of the Articles must have seemed easy by comparison.

Argument 1: __Author__   Argument 2: __James Madison__   Argument 3: __Congress__

Conclusion: __Moral not legal__   Conclusion: __radical change__   Conclusion: _new_ __Constitution not legal__

Evidence: __unable to exept__   Evidence: __good gov. superior__   Evidence: __deviates, ratification,__
          __bad gov.__   __took states power__

Scratch Paper

P: morally but not legally
    justified

5. It can be inferred that Congress's surprise over the radical nature of the Constitution submitted by the commissioners could be attributed in part to the fact that its members did not foresee:

    A. the eventuality that the constitution it requested would be adopted without the unanimous ratification of the states.

    B. the possibility that the constitution it requested would contain provisions that jeopardized the government's moral authority.

    C. a conflict between the modification of the Articles of Confederation and the creation of a constitution adequate to the needs of the nation.

    D. the possibility that the constitution it requested would differ from the Articles of Confederation.

6. Which of the following views can most reasonably be attributed to Madison?

    A. In the case of conflicting interests, priority should be given to the course of action that best promotes peace in the nation.

    B. Applications of conflict resolution principles can be used to determine the legality of an action.

    C. Unanimous approval is the most important objective in drafting a new constitution.

    D. The constitution drafted by the commissioners corresponded precisely to the expectations of the Congress of the Articles of Confederation.

Unit 3

7. Suppose that a government decrees that it is illegal to make any changes to the structure or practices of the state, and that a group within the state attempts to violate the decree. The author would most likely view the group:

   A. with skepticism regarding its motivations.

   B. with admiration since any law passed by such a government has no moral authority.

   C. with approval regarding its moral right to disobey the decree.

   D. with disdain for its violation of the orders of the state.

8. Which of the following, if true, would most seriously *weaken* the argument put forth in defense of the legality of the constitution submitted by the commissioners?

   A. Non-unanimous ratification of such a new constitution is incompatible with the goal of creating a good government.

   B. Extensive debate among statesmen is necessary in order to create a fair and legal constitution.

   C. It is nearly impossible to create an effective constitution out of the pieces of a previous constitution.

   D. No legal constitution can include provisions to safeguard the power of the ruling elite that commissioned the document.

9. The author mentions England at the end of the final paragraph primarily in order to:

   A. suggest that the United States Constitution would help the new nation to take its place among the great powers in the world.

   B. illustrate the depth of the commissioners' devotion to fighting for a political cause.

   C. downplay the relative importance in American history of the creation of the Constitution.

   D. rebut the notion that the creation of the United States Constitution was an uncomplicated task.

Scratch Paper

10. According to the passage, which of the following provided justification for the revolutionary nature of the new constitution?

    A. The current government's admission of its inadequacy in national affairs
    B. The right of any given state to refuse to ratify the new constitution
    C. The moral right of a new government to entrench itself against amendment
    D. The recommendation that the new constitution be created from alterations of the current Articles of Confederation

11. The author implies which of the following relationships between legal and moral authority?

    A. The morality of a constitution is the primary determinant of its legality.
    B. A principle lacking moral authority can still be legally binding.
    C. The morality of an action can never be determined irrespective of the legality of that action.
    D. A document lacking legal authority can still carry moral weight.

ARGUMENTS IN DIFFICULT PASSAGES

If one always ought to act so as to produce the best possible circumstances, then morality is extremely demanding. No one could plausibly claim to have met the requirements of this "simple principle." It would seem strange to punish those intending to do good by sentencing them to an impossible task. Also, if the standards of right conduct are as extreme as they seem, then they will preclude the personal projects that humans find most fulfilling.

From an analytic perspective, the potential extreme demands of morality are not a "problem." A theory of morality is no less valid simply because it asks great sacrifices. In fact, it is difficult to imagine what kind of constraints could be put on our ethical projects. Shouldn't we reflect on our base prejudices, and not allow them to provide boundaries for our moral reasoning? Thus, it is tempting to simply dismiss the objections to the simple principle. However, in *Demands of Morality*, Liam Murphy takes these objections seriously for at least two distinct reasons.

First, discussion of the simple principle provides an excellent vehicle for a discussion of morality in general. Perhaps, in a way, this is Murphy's attempt at doing philosophy "from the inside out." Second, Murphy's starting point tells us about the nature of his project. Murphy must take seriously the collisions between moral philosophy and our intuitive sense of right and wrong. He [must do so] because his work is best interpreted as intended to forge moral principles from our firm beliefs, and not to proscribe beliefs given a set of moral principles.

Murphy argues from our considered judgments rather than to them. For example, Murphy cites our "simple but firmly held" beliefs as supporting the potency of the over-demandingness objection, and nowhere in the work can one find a source of moral values divorced from human preferences.

Murphy does not tell us what set of "firm beliefs" we ought to have. Rather, he speaks to an audience of well-intentioned but unorganized moral realists, and tries to give them principles that represent their considered moral judgments. Murphy starts with this base sense of right and wrong, but recognizes that it needs to be supplemented by reason where our intuitions are confused or conflicting. Perhaps Murphy is looking for the best interpretation of our convictions, the same way certain legal scholars try to find the best interpretation of our Constitution.

This approach has disadvantages. Primarily, Murphy's arguments, even if successful, do not provide the kind of motivating force for which moral philosophy has traditionally searched. His work assumes and argues in terms of an inner sense of morality, and his project seeks to deepen that sense. Of course, it is quite possible that the moral viewpoints of humans will not converge, and some humans have no moral sense at all. Thus, it is very easy for the moral skeptic to point out a lack of justification and ignore the entire work.

On the other hand, Murphy's choice of a starting point avoids many of the problems of moral philosophy. Justifying the content of moral principles and granting a motivating force to those principles is an extraordinary task. It would be unrealistic to expect all discussions of moral philosophy to derive such justifications. Projects that attempt such a derivation have value, but they are hard pressed to produce logical consequences for everyday life. In the end, Murphy's strategy may have more practical effect than its first-principle counterparts, which do not seem any more likely to convince those that would reject Murphy's premises.

Scratch Paper

12. According to Murphy, the application of reason is necessary for forming moral principles when:

    A. the beliefs of one group supersede the beliefs of another.

    B. people's firmly held beliefs are conflicting or confused.

    C. the belief system of a group conflicts with an overriding ethical principle.

    D. individuals have no moral sense at all.

13. The author suggests that the application of Murphy's philosophy to the situations of two different groups:

    A. would help to solve the problems of one group but not of the other.

    B. could result in the derivation of two radically different moral principles.

    C. would be contingent on the two groups sharing the same fundamental beliefs.

    D. could reconcile any differences between the two groups.

14. The passage implies that a moral principle derived from applying Murphy's philosophy to a particular group would be applicable to another group if:

    A. the first group recommended the principle to the second group.

    B. the moral viewpoints of the two groups do not converge.

    C. the members of the second group have no firmly held beliefs.

    D. the second group shares the same fundamental beliefs as the first group.

15. Which of the following can be inferred about "doing philosophy from the inside out?"

    A. Murphy was the first philosopher to employ such an approach.

    B. It allows no place for rational argument in the formation of ethical principles.

    C. It is fundamentally different from the practice of first-principle philosophy.

    D. It is designed to dismiss objections to the "simple principle."

Unit 3

Scratch Paper

16. In the context of the passage, the Constitution serves as the basis of:

   A. a logical proof.
   B. the author's main point.
   C. an analogy.
   D. a rebuttal.

17. A school board is debating whether or not to institute a dress code for the school's students. According to Murphy, the best way to come to an ethical decision would be to:

   A. consult the fundamental beliefs of the board members.
   B. analyze the results of dress codes instituted at other schools.
   C. survey the students as to whether or not they would prefer a dress code.
   D. determine whether or not a dress code has ever been instituted in the school's history.

18. According to the passage, evidence of the existence of individuals who entirely lack a moral sense would:

   A. confirm the notion that moral principles should be derived from the considered judgments of individuals.
   B. substantiate a potential disadvantage of Murphy's philosophical approach.
   C. support Murphy's belief that reason is necessary when intuitions are conflicting or confused.
   D. prove that first-principle strategies of ethical theorizing are no more motivating than Murphy's approach.

19. Suppose an individual who firmly believes in keeping promises has promised to return a weapon to a person she knows to be extremely dangerous. According to Murphy, which of the following, if true, would constitute a reason why she should NOT return the weapon?

   A. She also firmly believes that it is morally wrong to assist in any way in a potentially violent act.
   B. She believes herself to be well intentioned in the matters of right and wrong.
   C. The belief that one should keep promises is shared by most members of her community.
   D. She derived her moral beliefs from first-principle ethical philosophy.

The Lesson Continues
on the Next Page

⟶

Unit 3

FIVE MINUTES LEFT

Help! I Have Five Minutes Left...

...and one entire passage to go

When running out of time, you could

1. read 1st paragraph
2. read 1st sentence
3. Scan questions

Nearly twenty years ago, former President Nixon signed the National Environmental Policy Act, this nation's first major federal environmental law. **Although** the nation has now witnessed almost twenty years of continuing debate about environmental law, a relatively new element has recently entered the **controversy**: the **use of risk assessment** procedures to determine levels of acceptable risk from threats of hazardous wastes.

Before the development of risk assessment as a decision-making tool, when a spill of a pollutant occurred, a government agency often simply told a responsible party to remove the pollutant. Blah blah blah blah. blah blah, blah blah blah. Blah blah blah blah. blah blah, blah blah blah. Blah blah blah blah. blah blah, blah blah blah. Blah blah blah blah. blah blah, blah blah blah. Blah blah blah blah. blah blah, blah blah blah. Blah blah blah blah. blah blah, blah blah blah. Blah blah blah blah. blah blah, blah blah blah. Blah blah blah blah. blah blah, blah blah blah. Blah blah blah blah. blah blah, blah blah blah. Blah blah blah blah. blah blah, blah blah blah.

But are risk assessments really neutral scientific procedures? Blah blah blah blah. blah blah, blah blah blah. Blah blah blah blah. blah blah, blah blah blah. Blah blah blah blah. blah blah, blah blah blah. Blah blah blah blah. blah blah, blah blah blah. Blah blah blah blah. blah blah, blah blah blah. Blah blah blah blah. blah blah, blah blah blah. Blah blah blah blah. blah blah, blah blah blah. Blah blah blah blah. blah blah, blah blah blah. Blah blah blah blah. blah blah, blah blah blah. Blah blah blah blah. blah blah, blah blah blah. Blah blah blah blah. blah blah, blah blah blah. Blah blah blah blah. blah blah, blah blah blah. Blah blah blah blah. blah blah, blah blah blah. Blah blah blah blah. blah blah, blah blah blah. Blah blah blah blah. blah blah, blah blah blah. Blah blah blah blah. blah blah, blah blah blah. Blah blah blah blah. blah blah, blah blah blah. Blah blah blah blah. blah blah, blah blah blah.

Environmental decisions based on **current risk assessment procedures** should therefore be viewed primarily as **ethical choices** rather than as technically dictated conclusions. Blah blah blah blah. blah blah, blah blah blah. Blah blah blah blah. blah blah, blah blah blah. Blah blah blah blah. blah blah, blah blah blah. Blah blah blah blah. blah blah, blah blah blah. Blah blah blah blah. blah blah, blah blah blah. Blah blah blah blah. blah blah, blah blah blah. Blah blah blah blah. blah blah, blah blah blah. Blah blah blah blah. blah blah, blah blah blah.

Unit 3

Would you work on this question?

Best guess answer:

34. Which one of the following best expresses the main point of the passage?

    A. Risk assessment is an improvement over past cleanup methods because it is based more on factual evidence than on intuition.

    B. Former President Nixon did more than his predecessors to protect the environment from pollutants by approving the use of risk assessment.

    (C.) Though perhaps more scientific than previous pollution control measures, the claim that risk assessment is a value-free process is not wholly credible.

    D. While the concept of risk assessment is enticing from a scientific viewpoint, this method is so expensive that its use is impractical on a large scale.

Would you work on this question?

Best guess answer:

35. Each of the following is explicitly mentioned in the passage as part of the risk assessment process EXCEPT:

    A. visual observation. → *guess*

    B. exposure assessment.

    C. hazard identification.

    D. risk characterization.

Would you work on this question?

Best guess answer:

36. The author most probably mentions confidence levels (paragraph 3) in order to:

    A. demonstrate that risk assessment is more scientific than past cleanup methods.

    B. question the accuracy of post-cleanup visual observations.

    C. suggest that government should eliminate ambiguities in its environmental cleanup agenda.

    (D.) show that nonscientific principles can affect the results of scientific processes.

Unit 3

Scratch Paper

Would you work on this question?

Best guess answer:

Would you work on this question?

Best guess answer:

Would you work on this question?

Best guess answer: NO

37. The author suggests which one of the following about pollution cleanup methods that predated the development of risk assessment?

   A. They are considered to be completely ineffective in protecting the environment.
   B. Many environmental professionals are not satisfied with the results produced by these methods.
   C. They are often difficult to apply because they depend on precise scientific measurements.
   D. The best features of these methods should be integrated into the risk assessment process.

38. Which one of the following words, as it appears in the passage, best supports the author's view of the role of nonscientific components in the risk assessment process?

   A. "improvement" (paragraph 2)
   B. "neutral" (paragraph 2)
   C. "adverse" (paragraph 3)
   D. "underlie" (paragraph 4)

39. The passage's reference to the factual and scientific basis of the risk assessment process in paragraph 2 serves which one of the following functions?

   A. It explains the government's unwillingness to choose between older pollution cleanup methods and risk assessment.
   B   It underscores the belief of environmentalists that risk assessment is a useful method for controlling pollution.
   C. It introduces pollution control policy choices for which there is no *a priori* assessment method.
   D. It highlights the attitude of environmentalists toward the National Environmental Policy Act.

40. The author of the passage is primarily concerned with:

    A. explaining why government should make explicit the ethical choices involved in environmental cleanup.

    B. highlighting government's inability to deal effectively with pollution cleanup.

    C. reviewing the evolution of pollution cleanup methods over the past two decades.

    D. proposing a new method for environmental cleanup that incorporates the best features of risk assessment.

Unit 3

Kaplan's Pacing Strategy—Verbal Reasoning

7 Passages in 60 minutes

Minutes per **passage pair**: _____

Passage 1

Passage 2

Passage 3

Passage 4

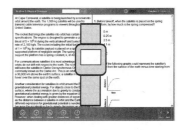

Passage 5

Passage 6

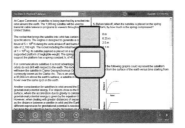

Passage 7

Unit 3

DO NOT TURN THIS PAGE UNTIL YOU ARE INSTRUCTED TO DO SO

Verbal Reasoning
Mini MCAT

Time: 17 minutes
Questions: 1–13

Unit 3

Passage I (Questions 1–7)

The Modern Girl makes only a brief appearance in our histories of pre-war Japan. She is a glittering, decadent, middle-class consumer who, through her clothing, smoking, and drinking, flaunts tradition in the urban playgrounds of the late 1920s. Arm in arm with her male equivalent, the Modern Boy (the *mobo*) and fleshed out in the Western flapper's garb of the roaring twenties, she engages in *ginbura* (Ginza-cruising). Yet by merely equating the Japanese Modern Girl with the flapper we do her a disservice, for the Modern Girl was not on a Western trajectory. Moreover, during the decade when this female, a creation of the mass media, excited her Japanese audience, she was not easily defined. Who was this "Modern Girl"? Why did she do what she did?

The Modern Girl is rescued from her depoliticized representation when her willful image is placed alongside the history of working, militant Japanese women. Then the depiction of the Modern Girl as apolitical (and later, as apolitical and non-working) begins to appear as a means of displacing the very real militancy of Japanese women (just as the real labor of the American woman during the 1920s was denied by trivializing the work of the glamorized flapper). But whereas the American woman worker by the mid-1920s had allowed herself to be depoliticized by a new consumerism, the modern Japanese woman of the 1920s was truly militant. Her militancy was articulated through the adoption of new fashions, through labor in new arenas, and through political activity that consciously challenged social, economic, and political structures and relationships. The Japanese state's response encompassed attempts to revise the Civil Code, consideration of universal suffrage, organization and expansion of groups such as the Women's Alliance (*Fujin Doshikai*) and the nationwide network of *shojokai* (associations of young girls), censorship, and imprisonment of leaders. The media responded by producing the Modern Girl.

Yet the Modern Girl must have represented even more, for the determination that talk about the Modern Girl displaced serious concern about the radical nature of women's activity does not fully address her multifaceted nature.

Why, in other words, was she Japanese and Western, intellectual and worker, deviant and admirable? An answer is suggested by Natalie Davis in "Women on Top," which argues that the "unruly woman" in early-modern Europe served both to reinforce social structure and to incite women to militant action in public and in private. The culturally constructed figure of the Japanese Modern Girl certainly meets these two requirements. Like the disorderly woman on top, the Modern Girl as multifaceted symbol questioned relations of order and subordination.

Finally, the Modern Girl, who was both Japanese and Western—or possibly neither—played with the principle of cultural or national difference. Seen in this way, she highlighted the controversy over adoption of non-Japanese customs in everyday life and called into question the essentialist attitude that subordinated the Japanese woman to the Japanese man.

This thesis was indeed offered by the feminist Kitamura, who claimed that "labor struggle, tenancy struggle, household struggle, struggle between man and woman" were inevitable and had recently been joined to a new battle: "a struggle over good conduct" that pitted Japanese against Western behavior and used the Modern Girl to work out the struggle.

This, then, is the significance of the Japanese Modern Girl in the broadest context of prewar Japanese history. The Modern Girl stood as the vital symbol of overwhelming "modern" or non-Japanese change instigated by both women and men during an era of economic crisis and social unrest. She stood for change at a time when state authority was attempting to reestablish authority and stability. The Modern Girl of the 1920s and early 1930s thus inverted the role of the Good Wife and Wise Mother. The ideal Meiji woman of the 1870s, 1880s, and 1890s had served as a "repository of the past," standing for tradition when men were encouraged to change their way of politics and culture in all ways.

1. According to the passage, the Modern Girl reflected tensions in all of the following issues EXCEPT:

    A. the influence of non-Japanese cultural traditions.

    B. the extent of women's participation in the workforce.

    C. whether, within Japanese families, women ought to be subordinate to men.

    D. whether the popular media should be accountable for the images they present.

2. Which of the following is a claim that the author would most likely endorse?

    A. In 1920s Japan, foreign influences were instigated by men, as well as by women.

    B. The influence of the Modern Girl is best understood through comparisons to the American flapper.

    C. The Modern Girl reflected the preservation of traditions personified by the Good Wife and Wise Mother.

    D. The Modern Girl was the first Japanese media figure to demonstrate non-Japanese mannerisms.

3. Which of the following, if true, would most *weaken* the author's claim about the significance of the Modern Girl?

    A. In the 1920s, most Japanese did not associate the Modern Girl's behavior with Western influences.

    B. The Modern Girl disappeared from most popular Japanese media at the onset of World War II.

    C. The social unrest experienced by Japan in the 1920s was less pronounced than that of other countries at the time.

    D. Since society is influenced by a wide variety of factors, social change can never be solely attributed to one cultural figure.

4. In the context of the passage, "truly militant" (paragraph 2) most nearly means:

    A. disciplined in matters of war.

    B. determined and resolute.

    C. inflexible and narrow-minded.

    D. contentious and aggressive.

5. The author most likely cites the example of the "unruly woman" (paragraph 4) in order to:

    A. illustrate the extent of radical political action in 1920s Japan.

    B. suggest that gender conflicts in 1920s Japan were inevitable.

    C. help explain the complicated nature of Modern Girl.

    D. compare the Modern Girl to her American counterpart.

6. Which of the following is a claim made by the author but NOT supported in the passage by evidence, explanation or example?

    A. Japanese women in the 1920s challenged conventional notions of gender roles.

    B. Female workers in America lost their political status due to a new consumerism.

    C. The Modern Girl stood in contrast to earlier cultural exemplars.

    D. The role of the Modern Girl was not limited to strictly political issues.

7. Implicit in the author's discussion of the Modern Girl is the assumption that:

    A. Japanese women of the 1920s viewed *ginbura* as incompatible with economic advancement.

    B. Western nations were not influenced by Japanese cultural traditions.

    C. the Modern Girl's influence contrasted with the influence of the *mobo*.

    D. political activities can be influenced by media portrayals.

Unit 3

Passage II (Questions 8–13)

The system of farming practiced in the United States today evolved during the 1950s, when the development of chemical pesticides, fertilizers, and high-yielding crop strains brought a mass shift towards specialization. Using agrochemicals, farmers found that they could grow a single crop on the same field year after year, without impairing the yield or incurring pest problems. Encouraged by government programs subsidizing the production of grains such as wheat and corn, most farmers consolidated to cultivate a limited number of crops and to invest in the equipment to mechanize labor-intensive farm processes. For the last forty years, this system has enabled American farmers to lead the world in efficiency and crop production. Today, however, rising costs and problems such as groundwater contamination, soil erosion, and declining productivity are forcing many farmers to question their dependence on agrochemicals and to investigate alternative systems.

Perhaps the most likely system to replace today's agriculture is a composite of nonconventional techniques defined as sustainable agriculture. Using a combination of organic, low-input methods that benefit the environment and preserve the integrity of the soil, many scientists believe that sustainable agriculture could reach productivity levels competitive with conventional systems. Farmers converting to sustainable systems would find themselves using the same machinery, certified seed, and feeding methods as before. But instead of enhancing productivity with purchased chemicals, sustainable farms would use as far as possible natural processes and local renewable resources. Returning to a system of crop rotation, where fields are used to grow a succession of different crops, would improve crop yields and bolster pest resistance. Using crop residues, manures, and other organic materials would help to restore soil quality in areas such as air circulation, moisture retention, and tilth, or soil structure. And systems such as integrated pest management (IPM) would combat pests by diversifying crops, regulating predators of pest species, and using pesticides intermittently when necessary.

In order to gain acceptance, however, sustainable agriculture must also be shown to be sufficiently productive and profitable to support farmers economically. Federal farm programs currently encourage monocropping by providing subsidies for only a limited number of crops. Extending price supports to a wide variety of crops would promote diversification and crop rotation, and perhaps make sustainable agriculture feasible on a national scale. Comparative studies suggest that under the present conditions, sustainable farms are capable of producing greater returns than conventional farms, due to lower production costs. And yet, the majority of today's farmers elect to use specialized, chemical-dependent systems on the basis of their short-term profitability. If efforts to establish an ecologically sustainable agriculture are to succeed, higher priority must not only be given to researching alternative technology. The fruits of such research must also be made available to farmers.

8. Which of the following best summarizes the main idea of the passage?

 A. Sustainable agriculture should be supported for a variety of reasons.

 B. Growing only a single crop in a given tract of land can make that crop more susceptible to pests.

 C. Sustainable agriculture does not provide a viable alternative to today's farming methods.

 D. Methods of farming must be altered to prevent further damage to the environment.

9. According to the passage, all of the following are advantages of sustainable agriculture EXCEPT:

 A. increased resistance to pests.

 B. decreased damage to the environment.

 C. more efficient feeding methods.

 D. decreased costs.

10. Which of the following does the author suggest was true of farming methods used in the U.S. prior to the 1950s?

 A. They caused less damage to the environment than sustainable agriculture techniques.

 B. They were not suited for monocropping.

 C. They had no adequate defenses against pest damage.

 D. They were more efficient than the methods used in other countries at the time.

11. Which of the following, if true, would most *weaken* the author's argument concerning the extension of price supports?

 A. Most of today's farmers consider economic issues to be more important than environmental concerns.

 B. Increasing the number of crops grown on a single farm would require expensive alterations to farming machinery.

 C. Damage caused by pests is a more pressing concern now than it was in the 1950s.

 D. The total number of functioning farms has declined steadily since the 1950s, even though the total number of acres farmed has been relatively constant.

12. Which of the following does the author suggest is a barrier to more widespread use of sustainable agriculture techniques?

 I. Uncertainty among U.S. farmers concerning its effects on productivity

 II. The economic attitudes of many U.S. farmers

 III. U.S. farmers' alarm over its potential to harm the environment

 A. I only

 B. II only

 C. I and II only

 D. I, II, and III

13. According to the passage, all of the following are elements of a sustainable system EXCEPT:

 A. rotating the crops grown in a single field.

 B. organic soil preservation methods.

 C. implementing natural techniques for improving crop yields.

 D. reducing the number of crops grown on a given farm.

HOMEWORK

Review for Verbal Reasoning & Writing Sample 3

Verbal Reasoning Strategy and Practice	❑ *Test 3 ❑ Tests 6–11
Writing Sample section in Verbal Reasoning Strategy and Practice	❑ *Chapter 5, Parts 3 and 4

Preview for Organic Chemistry 3

Review Notes	❑ *Chapters 11, 12, 14, 15
Foundation Review	❑ Unit 3 (Optional, MM3257A)

Organic
Chemistry 3

INTEGRATED PRACTICE: ANALYSIS

- Carbonyl Compounds as Nucleophiles
- Purification and Separation
- Biological Molecules
- Mini MCAT

CARBONYL COMPOUNDS AS NUCLEOPHILES

Acidity of α-hydrogen → very acidic b/c resonance

The carbanion resulting from the deprotonation is known as an **enolate ion**, which is resonance-stabilized.

Aldol condensation

The addition product of an aldol condensation reaction has both <u>Ketone</u> and <u>alcohol</u> functional groups.

$$H_3C-\overset{\overset{\displaystyle O}{\|}}{C}H \quad \xrightarrow{- H^+}$$

Crossed aldol condensation

An aldol reaction that starts with two different carbonyl compounds is called a **crossed aldol reaction**.

Directed Practice

- *Biological Sciences Review Notes*: Orgo. Ch. 8

The Claisen condensation reaction

2 esters

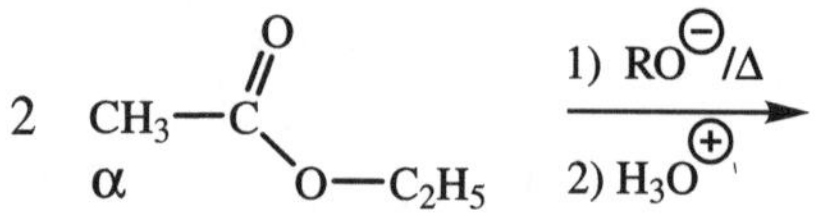

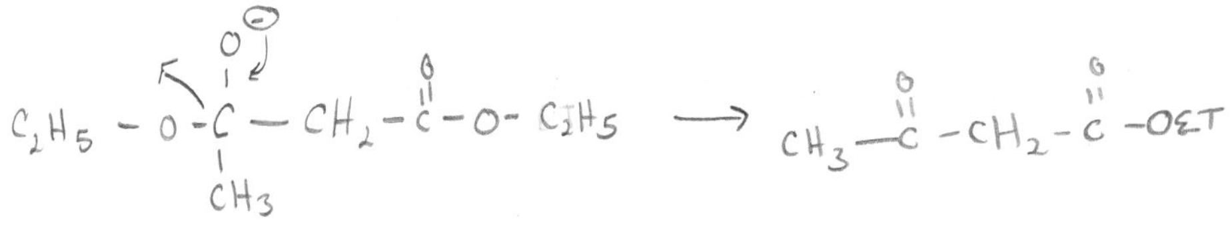

Critical Thinking Exercise

Physiological degradation of fatty acids occurs by a mechanism analagous to a reverse Claisen condensation, assisted by acetyl coenzyme A. What are the expected products of the degradation of myristic acid (intermediate shown)?

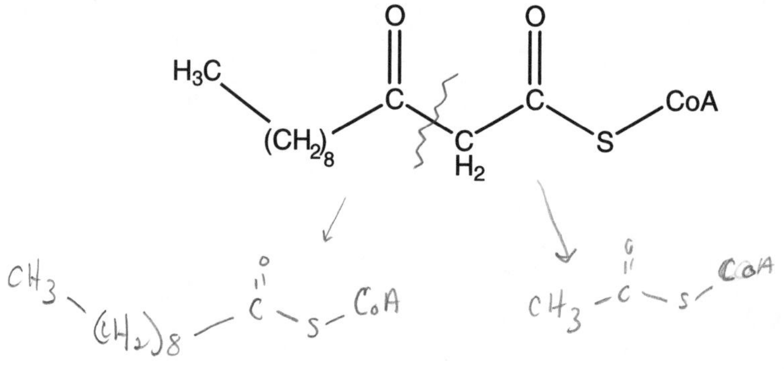

Unit 3

AMINES

Nomenclature

$H_3C-\overset{\overset{\displaystyle H}{|}}{N}-CH_2CH_3$

N-Methyl Ethylamine
or
ethyl methyl amine

$\overset{\overset{\displaystyle H}{|}}{N}-CH_3$ (on benzene ring)

N-methyl phenylamine

$H_2N(CH_2)_4OH$

4-amino -1-butanol

Physical properties

Primary and secondary amines can form hydrogen bonds, and have higher boiling points than their corresponding alkanes.

Tertiary amines have the lowest boiling and melting points because they can't form hydrogen bonds.

Critical Thinking Exercise

Between a tertiary amine and ammonia, which is more nucleophilic?   tertiary (has e⁻ donating groups)

Which conjugate acid has stronger intermolecular forces? ammonia .

Quaternary ammonium ions exist as salts which, as ionic compounds, have extremely high melting points and are water-soluble.

Unit 3

Synthesis

Reduction of other N-containing functional groups

Amines can be synthesized by reduction of other nitrogen-containing functional groups such as nitro compounds, amines, nitriles, and imines.

Nucleophilic substitution of alkyl halides → not ideal (many products)

Salts of primary amines can be prepared from ammonia and alkyl halides by nucleophilic substitution reactions. Subsequent treatment of the resulting ammonium salts with base gives primary amines.

Directed Practice

- *Biological Sciences Review Notes*: Orgo. Ch. 11

Unit 3

Key Reactions

Alkylation

Amines can act as S_N2 nucleophiles on alkyl halides.

$$\overset{..}{N}H_3 \; + \; R\!-\!X \longrightarrow R\!-\!\overset{\oplus}{N}H_3\; X^{\ominus} \xrightarrow{\;OH^{\ominus}\;} RNH_2$$

Salt formation

Neutral amines react with acids to form quaternary ammonium salts.

R-NH$_2$	+	HCl	→	R-NH$_3$$^+$ Cl$^-$
1° amine		Generic name		
		Solubility		soluble depending on R-group
		Phase		ionic → depends on R-group

Formation of amides

Amides are formed from amines *via* a nucleophilic acyl substitution reaction where an amine displaces a leaving group from an acid derivative.

$$\underset{\text{amine}}{R\!-\!\overset{\displaystyle R}{\underset{\displaystyle H}{N}}\!:} \; + \; \underset{\text{acyl halide}}{R\!-\!\overset{\displaystyle O}{\overset{\|}{C}}\!-\!Cl} \xrightarrow{\;HCl\;} \underset{\text{amide}}{\overset{\displaystyle R}{\underset{\displaystyle R'}{N}}\!-\!\overset{\displaystyle O}{\overset{\|}{C}}\!-\!R}$$

Directed Practice

- *Topical Tests*: Amines Test 1 (Passage I)

Passage I (Questions 1–5)

Two students attempted to oxidize 1-propanol to propionaldehyde (propanal) using chromic acid (H_2CrO_4), prepared *in situ* by mixing H_2SO_4 and $K_2Cr_2O_7$ (potassium dichromate). Because chromic acid is a strong oxidizing agent, both students decided to monitor the reaction by measuring the amount of chromic acid in the reaction mixture using UV-Vis spectroscopy. By recording the UV-Vis spectrum of the reaction mixture at intervals, the students hoped to prevent the 1-propanol from being oxidized beyond the aldehyde, propanal, to the carboxylic acid, propanoic acid. The equation for the oxidation of 1-propanol to propanal in the presence of chromic acid is shown below:

$$CH_3-CH_2-CH_2-OH \ + \ Cr_2O_7^{2-} \ + \ H^+$$

b.p. = 97.2 °C

$$CH_3-CH_2-\overset{\overset{\displaystyle O}{\|}}{C}-H \ + \ 2Cr^{3+} \ + \ 7H_2O$$

b.p. = 49.0 °C

Equation 1

Student A used the following procedure. He combined 0.1 moles of potassium dichromate (0.5M $K_2Cr_2O_7$ solution in 1M H_2SO_4) and 0.25 moles of 1-propanol in a round bottom flask. He then measured the UV-Vis absorption spectrum of the reaction mixture at 350 nm over 30-second intervals. When the peak at 350 nm disappeared, he distilled the reaction mixture under reduced pressure. In order to determine if he obtained the intended product, he recorded an IR spectrum of the distillate in CCl_4 (see Table 1).

Student B used a modification of Student A's procedure. She increased the amount of 1-propanol used to 0.40 moles and distilled the propionaldehyde off the reaction mixture as it was produced. Like Student A, she used the UV-Vis absorption spectrum of the reaction mixture at 350 nm to determine when the reaction was complete. The IR data obtained from Student B's distillate is listed in Table 1.

Table 1

Student	I.R. Data of Distillate (CCl_4) $\nu(cm^{-1})$*
A	3637(sh), 3333(br), 2963(mult), 1466(mult), 1383(mult), 1250(sh), 1090(sh)
B	2900 (mult), 1730 (sh), 1450(mult), 1370(mult), 1270(mult), 1106(sh)

*   sh = sharp
    br = broad
    mult = multiple peaks
    w = weak

Scratch Paper

Scratch Paper

1. The distillate obtained by Student A is likely to be:

    A.   propanal.
    B.   propanal and water.
    C.   propionic acid.
    D.   1-propanol.

2. The distillate obtained by Student B is likely to be:

    A.   propanal.
    B.   propanal and water.
    C.   propionic acid.
    D.   1-propanol.

3. Why is UV-Vis a useful tool for monitoring the oxidation of 1-propanol to propanal using chromic acid?

    I.   The oxidation state of chromium changes during the reaction.
    II.   All of the dichromate ion is consumed during the reaction.
    III. As 1-propanol is consumed, the absorption spectrum of the dichromate ion is shifted to another wavelength.
    IV.   The other compounds in the reaction mixture do not interfere with the absorption spectrum of dichromate.

    A.   I only
    B.   I and II only
    C.   III only
    D.   I, II and IV only

Scratch Paper

4. If the students had been using proton NMR to confirm the identity of their products, what unique peak would they be looking for to confirm the presence of an aldehyde?

    A.   A peak at 1.2-ppm
    B.   A peak at 9.8-ppm
    C.   A peak at 39.3-ppm
    D.   A peak at 200.2-ppm

5. In a second experiment, Student A follows the same procedure using 2-propanol instead of 1-propanol. He measures the IR spectrum of the distillate and records the following data:

$\nu(cm^{-1})$: 2970 (w, mult), 2950 (mult), 1750 (sh), 1430 (mult), 1230 (sh), 1080 (sh)

What product does he obtain?

    A.   2-propanol
    B.   propionic acid
    C.   2-propanone
    D.   propanal

Directed Practice

- *Biological Sciences Review Notes*: Orgo. Ch. 12

Unit 3

PURIFICATION TECHNIQUES

Extraction

When:

How:

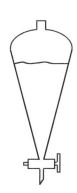

What to add: immiscible

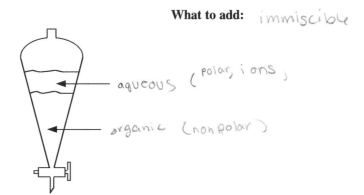

aqueous (polar, ions)

organic (nonpolar)

Critical Thinking Question

At the end of an experiment, a solution of benzoic acid is contaminated with cresol. A student attempts to isolate benzoic acid by carrying out two extraction experiments. Part of the cresol/benzoic acid mixture is extracted using NaOH, and part of the cresol/benzoic acid mixture is extracted using $NaHCO_3$. Spectroscopic data shows that the cresol/benzoic acid separation is most successful using $NaHCO_3$. Why are these results observed?

Why does $NaHCO_3$ work better? weaker base

Which compound is more acidic: cresol or benzoic acid?

Which base will deprotonate both acids? NaOH → aqueous (becomes salt)

In the NaOH separation, where does cresol end up? What about benzoic acid? same

In the $NaHCO_3$ separation, where does cresol end up? What about benzoic acid? C → organic ; B → aqueous (salt)

Directed Practice

- *Biological Sciences Review Notes*: Orgo. Ch. 10

Distillation

Distillation is used to separate _liquids_ according to differences in their _bp_ .
Compounds with lower boiling points will be boiled off first.

Simple :
  difference>25
  (temp, below 125°C)

When:

two miscible liquids w/

vaccum :
(really high bp

How:

heat and collect condensate

Critical Thinking Exercise

Can you separate two compounds with the same boiling point? Not distillation

What is an azeotropic mixture? appear same

Can you separate an azeotropic mixture under standard conditions? No

What if the boiling points are different but extremely high? use vaccum

Recrystallization

Recrystallization is a process in which impure crystals are dissolved in a minimum amount of
hot solvent. As the solvent is cooled, the crystals reform, leaving the impurities in solution.

Directed Practice

- *Biological Sciences Review Notes*: Orgo. Ch. 12

Unit 3

Chromatography

TLC

When:
Sampu in relation to know sampu

How:
stationary → silica
moble → solvent

$R_f:$ $\dfrac{\text{movement stationar}}{\text{movement mobiu}}$

Column

When: backed colums

How:

HPLC (high pressure)

When: have little product (small tube, capilary)

How:

GC

When:

How:

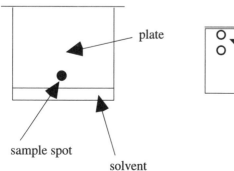

plate

sample spot

solvent

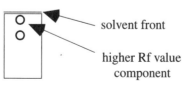

solvent front

higher Rf value component

Electrophoresis

Electrophoresis is used to separate proteins and/or nucleic acids based on their ___Size___ and ___Charge___ .

Agarose

SDS-Polyacrylamide – straightens protein and uniformly charged

Isoelectric focusing – Ph gradient = PI (columns for chromatography)

↓ Run on gel

cathode ⊖

1000 b.p. ⟶ ▬

100 b.p. ⟶ ▬

anode ⊕

agarose gel

Critical Thinking Exercise

Scratch Paper

6. Given the information in the following table, which technique would be the MOST effective in separating proteins A and B?

	Protein A	Protein B
mass (kD)	18.0	42.0
pI	8.4	8.4
mp (°C)	155.0	155.0
dipole moment (debye)	250.0	480.0
Specific rotation ($[\alpha]$D)	+13.5	−95.5

    A. gas chromatography
    B. isoelectric focusing
    C. sublimation
    D. centrifugation

Directed Practice

- *Topical Tests*: Separations and Purifications Test 1 (Passage II)

Unit 3

BIOLOGICAL MOLECULES—CARBOHYDRATES

The D/L Convention – *enantiomers*

In a Fischer projection with the aldehyde group at the very top of the drawing, the molecule will be an L-sugar if the hydroxyl group on the last chiral carbon is on the left. The molecule will be a D-sugar if the hydroxyl group is on the right.

D-glucose   L-glucose

All sugar names end with suffix –ose.

Sugars with aldehyde groups are aldoses; those with ketone groups are ketoses.

Critical Thinking Questions

What type of isomers are D and L glucose? *enantiomers*

Directed Practice

* *Biological Sciences Review Notes*: Orgo. Ch. 14, Monosaccharides, Stereochemistry

Unit 3

Sugars as Diastereomers

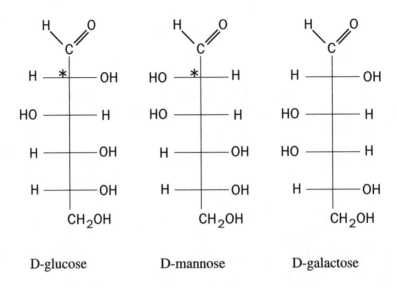

D-glucose   D-mannose   D-galactose

Two Epimers

Stereoisomers of one particular family (either D or L) that differ in the configuration at only one chiral carbon are called **epimers.**

C-2 epimers

D-ribose   D-arabinose

Sugar hemiacetals (pyranose/furanose)

Because aldoses and ketoses have both a carbonyl group and a hydroxyl group, they can undergo intramolecular reactions to form cyclic structures, usually a 5-membered ring _Furanose_ or a 6-membered ring _puranose_ .

α-D-glucopyranose   β-D-glucopyranose

If the sugar is an aldose it forms a cyclic _hemi- acetal_ . If the sugar is a ketose it forms a cyclic _hemi- ketal_ .

Rings thus formed can reopen and close to form two different anomers in a process called _mutarotation_ .

D-glucose

Directed Practice

- *Biological Sciences Review Notes*: Orgo. Ch. 14
- *Topical Tests*: Biological Molecules Test 1 (Passage I)

Glycosides (nonreducing, sugar acetals)

Besides the hemiacetal hydroxyl group in a cyclic pyranose or furanose, the other hydroxyl groups can react in the same manner as other alcohols (i.e., reacting with acetic anydride to make esters).

Critical Thinking Question

Scratch Paper

7. Aldoses can be reduced with lithium aluminum hydride to compounds known as alditols. What is the product of the reduction reaction of D-glucose?

CH2OH
O
HO
HO
OH
OH
LiAlH4
?

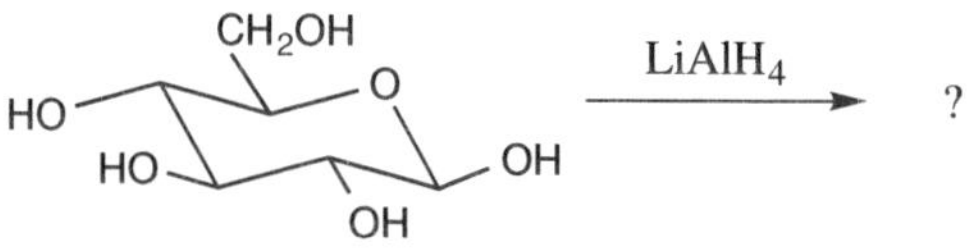

A.

COOH
H
OH
HO
H
H
OH
H
OH
CH2OH

C.

CH2OH
H
OH
HO
H
H
OH
H
OH
COOH

B.

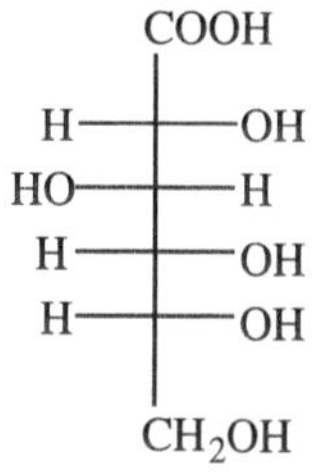

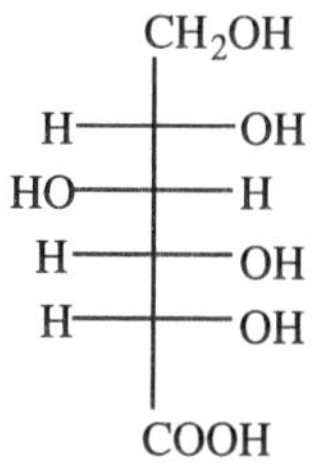

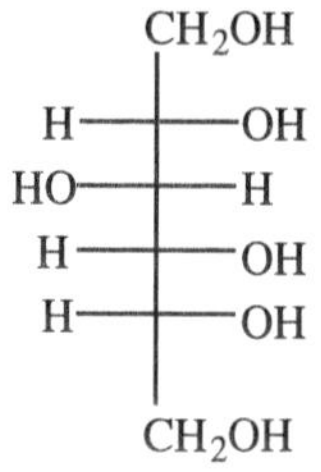

CH2OH
H
OH
HO
H
H
OH
H
OH
CH2OH

D.

COOH
H
OH
HO
H
H
OH
H
OH
COOH

reducing sugar

COOH → CH_2OH

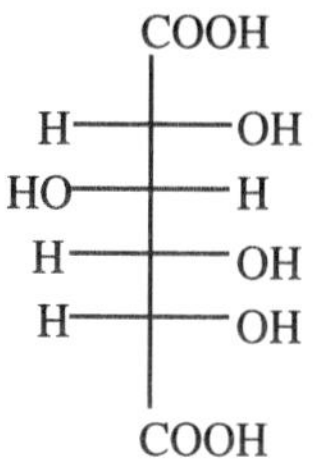

BIOLOGICAL MOLECULES—α-AMINO ACIDS/PEPTIDES

Three Different Forms of an Amino Acid

Amino acids (except glycine) are chiral. Natural amino acids have the S-configuration (L-amino acids).

The R group can be a neutral nonpolar group, neutral polar group, acidic, or basic.

| low pH | ~ neutral pH (zwitterionic) | high pH |

Zwitterion

A Zwitterion is a dipolar molecule in which the carboxyl group exists as a carboxylate ion and the amino group is protonated.

+ and –

pI vs. pK$_a$

two lowest pka's = PI
two highest PKA's = PI

Critical Thinking Question

If an amino acid were subjected to electrophoresis, to which electrode would each form of the amino acid migrate ?

Acidic Form: *+negative (cathode)*

Basic Form: *positive (anode)*

Zwitterion: *wouldn't move*

Directed Practice

- *Biological Sciences Review Notes*: Orgo. Ch. 15

Unit 3

Peptide Bonds (amide links)

The $\overset{\underset{\|}{O}}{-C}-\overset{H}{N}-$ (amide) linkage that forms between the amino acids is known as a **peptide bond** or **peptide linkage**.

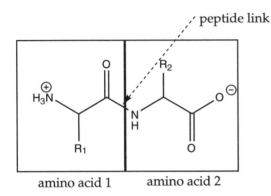

peptide link

amino acid 1   amino acid 2

Strong acid = Cleave

Protein Structure

Primary Structure

Primary structure refers to the linear sequence of amino acids in a protein.

Secondary Structure

The regular, recurring spatial arrangements of amino acids close to each other in the linear sequence is called the secondary structure of the protein.

Tertiary Structure

Tertiary structure refers to the overall spatial arrangement of amino acids.

Quaternary Structure

The arrangement of subunits in a multi-subunit protein is the quaternary structure.

Directed Practice

- *Biological Sciences Review Notes*: Orgo. Ch. 15

Unit 3

BIOLOGICAL MOLECULES—LIPIDS

Fatty Acids

Fatty acids contain a straight alkyl chain (hydrophobic) portion, and a terminal carboxylic acid (hydrophilic) group.

hard to break down
(straight, long)

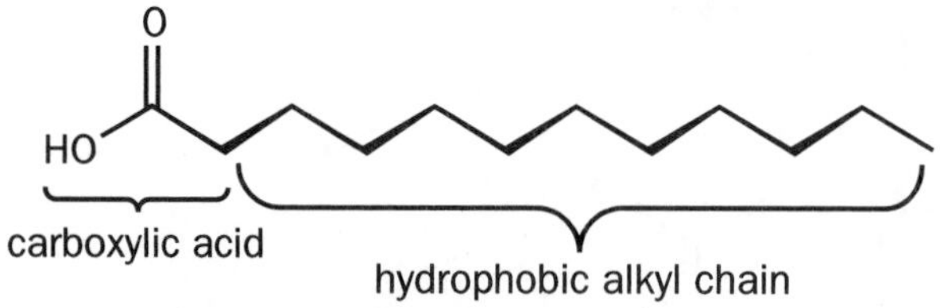

carboxylic acid

hydrophobic alkyl chain

saturated fatty acid

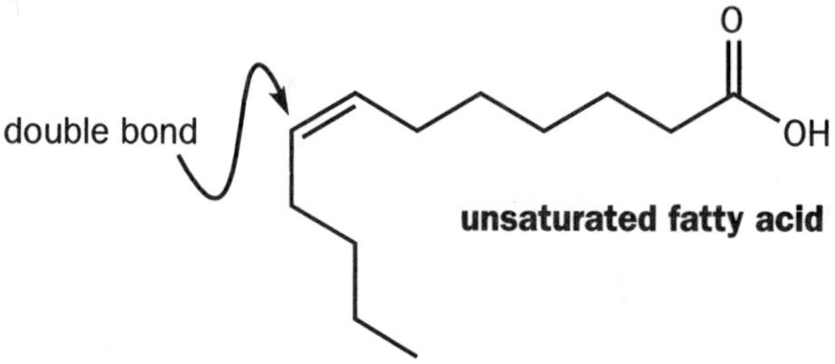

double bond

unsaturated fatty acid

Triacyl glycerols → *store fatty acids as chemical*

Triacyl glycerols are esters of glycerol.

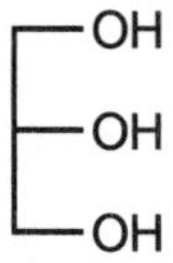

glycerol

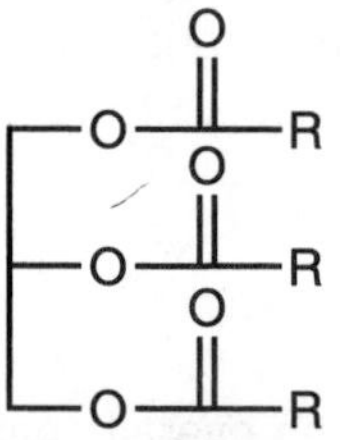

Triacyl glycerol
high energy

Critical Thinking Exercise

Why are fats solid at room temperature while oils are liquid?

Directed Practice

• *Biological Sciences Review Notes*: Orgo. Ch. 4

Unit 3

Formation of sodium salts

Alkaline hydrolysis (i.e., saponification) of triacylglycerols produces glycerol and a mixture of salts of long-chain carboxylic acids.

cross section of a micelle

fat + base = soap

Directed Practice

- *Biological Sciences Review Notes*: Orgo. Ch. 9

DO NOT TURN THIS PAGE UNTIL YOU ARE INSTRUCTED TO DO SO

Organic Chemistry Mini MCAT

Time: 19 minutes
Questions: 1–13

Passage I (Questions 1–4)

A chemist carried out the following procedure in order to identify the compounds in a waste bottle and so dispose of them safely.

The unknown solution was dissolved in dichloromethane and extracted with water. The extracted compound, Compound W, formed ethene when heated in the presence of sulfuric acid. Next, the dichloromethane solution was extracted with sodium bicarbonate yielding Compound X. When Compound X was acidified, it showed evidence of aromatic hydrogens on its ^{1}H NMR spectrum and IR peaks at 3300 and 1700 cm^{-1}. A third extraction of the dichloromethane solution was conducted with HCl to isolate Compound Y. Compound Y contained four separate peaks in its ^{1}H NMR spectrum, all lower than 4.0 ppm, totaling 15 hydrogens when integrated. Upon reaction with sodium nitrite in the presence of hydrochloric acid, Compound Y produced a mixture of alcohols and alkenes consistent with reaction through an unstable diazonium salt intermediate. (A diazonium cation has the general form R–N$_2$$^+$.) Nitrogen gas was a by-product of this reaction. Finally, the remaining dichloromethane solution was distilled to isolate Compound Z. The IR spectrum of Compound Z contained a prominent peak at 1700 cm^{-1}.

The separation and purification pathways are illustrated in Figure 1.

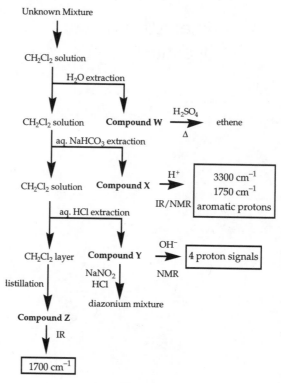

Figure 1

1. Compound W is most likely:

   A. an alkane.
   B. an alcohol.
   C. a carboxylic acid.
   D. a ketone.

2. The reason why a diazonium intermediate is unstable is that:

   A. the nitrogen-nitrogen bond is weak.
   B. it is a strong Lewis acid.
   C. it possesses a good leaving group.
   D. it is susceptible to attack by nucleophiles.

3. From the given data, compound X is most likely:

   A. an amine.
   B. a hydrocarbon.
   C. the sodium salt of a carboxylic acid.
   D. the sodium salt of an alcohol.

4. Compound Z dissolves and remains in the dichloromethane layer because of dipole-dipole interactions. What is compound Z most likely to be?

   A. Hexanenitrile
   B. 2-Hexyne
   C. Chlorocyclohexane
   D. Cyclohexanone

Directed Practice

   • *Biological Sciences Review Notes*: Orgo. Ch. 13

Passage II (Questions 5–10)

Proteins have several levels of structural complexity, each of which has important consequences in the proteins' physical, chemical, and biological properties. A protein's primary structure is the sequence of covalent peptide bonds connecting amino acid residues, generally expressed starting with the N-terminal residue and ending with the C-terminal residue. Secondary structure deals with the presence of three-dimensional structural elements such as α-helices or β-pleated sheets. These structures are formed by short sections of the primary structural sequence and are held together by hydrogen bonds between amino acid residues. Tertiary structure expresses the complete three-dimensional arrangement of the secondary structural elements across an entire peptide chain. For example, α-helices from different sections of the primary structural sequence may be spatially close together, thus defining a portion of the peptide's tertiary structure. Quaternary structure defines the spatial relationship between two or more polypeptides in a single protein or enzyme.

The geometry of the peptide bond, which is restricted to planar conformations, is an important factor in the formation of secondary and tertiary structure. The planar restriction leads to two possible conformations, called s-*cis* and s-*trans,* shown below:

s-*trans*   s-*cis*

Figure 1

In addition to the peptide bond linking each amino acid residue, disulfide links also play important roles in determining the relationships between amino acid residues defined by secondary, tertiary, and quaternary structure. Disruption of peptide conformations or disulfide links can result in denaturation of the protein.

5. Coplanar atoms in peptide links are often shown by defining the plane which they occupy. Which of the following correctly shows the coplanar atoms in the dipeptide Gly-Ala? (Glycine has a hydrogen atom as a side chain, while alanine has a methyl side chain.)

A.

B.

C.

D.

6. Disulfide links can be easily formed, as shown in the following reaction:

$$2 \, RCH_2SH + I_2 \rightarrow RCH_2S–SCH_2R + 2HI$$

In this reaction, the two cysteine residues undergo which type of reaction?

A. Nucleophilic substitution
B. Reduction
C. Nucleophilic addition
D. Oxidation

✗ lost Hydrogen

7. The presence of s-*cis* or s-*trans* peptide links can lead to vastly different structural features in a peptide chain. However, most peptide links in a chain are of the:

A. s-*cis* type because of its lack of nonbonded strain.
B. s-*cis* type because of its excess nonbonded strain.
C. s-*trans* type because of its lack of nonbonded strain.
D. s-*trans* type because of its excess nonbonded strain.

8. A protein is subjected to conditions that cleave all disulfide links. Molecular weight determinations performed on the molecule before and after cleavage yield results that are not significantly different. Which of the following can be concluded?

A. The protein has elements of quaternary structure.
B. The protein does not have elements of quaternary structure.
C. The protein has no quaternary structure elements that depend upon disulfide links.
D. The protein has quaternary structure elements that depend upon disulfide links.

9. Because of the peptide bond restriction to planar conformations, all of the following can be concluded about the atoms in the link EXCEPT:

A. the nitrogen lone pair has π-overlap with the carbonyl π-bond.
B. there is considerable positive-charge character on the nitrogen atom.
C. the nitrogen atom is sp^3 hybridized.
D. there is considerable negative-charge character on the carbonyl oxygen.

Unit 3

10. Which structure shown below most accurately represents a Cys-Cys dipeptide in its most stable conformation when the side chains are connected by a disulfide link? (Cysteine has a side chain of CH_2SH.)

A.

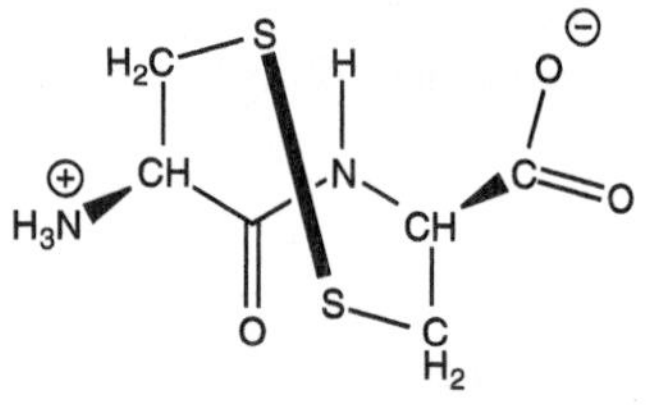

B.

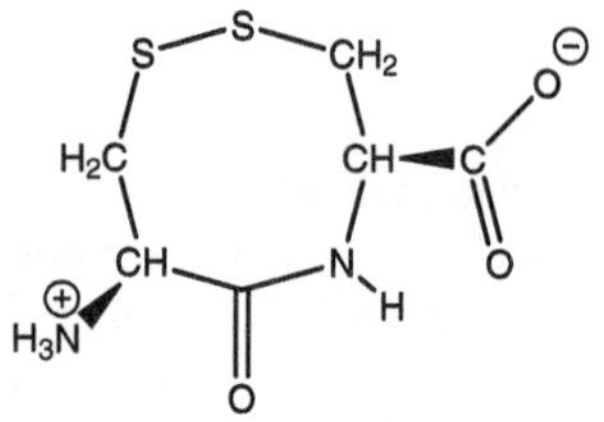

C.

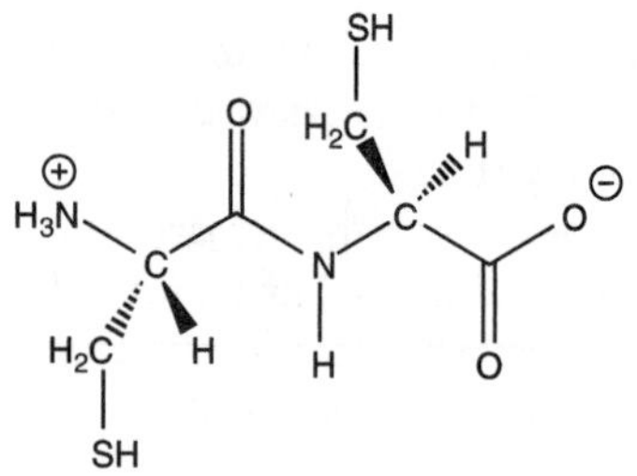

D.

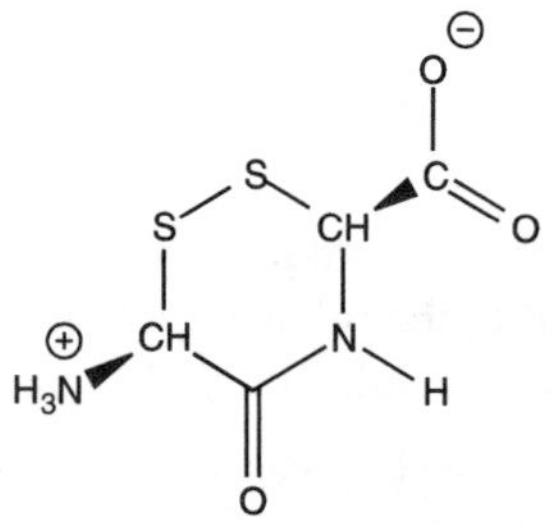

Questions 11 through 13 are NOT based on a descriptive passage.

11. If separated between equal volumes of carbon tetrachloride and water, which of the following would show the greatest preference for the carbon tetrachloride layer?

non polar

A. Ph–CH_3
B. $CH_3CH_2CH_2Cl$
C. CH_3CH_2COOH
D. OH—$CH_2CH_2CH_2$—OH

12. What is the product of the following reaction?

$$NaCN + CH_3–CH_2–SO_4H \rightarrow$$

A. $HCNCH_2CH_2SO_4H$
B. CH_2CHSO_4H
C. CH_3CH_2CN
D. $CH_3CH_2CN + CH_2CH_2$

13. What is the correct IUPAC name for the following compound?

$$CH_3CHCHCOOCHCl_2$$

A. chloromethyl-2-butenoate
B. dichloromethyl-2-butenoate
C. 2-butene-chloromethanoate
D. 2-butene-dicholoromethanoate

Directed Practice

• *Biological Sciences Review Notes*: Orgo. Ch. 15

The Lesson Continues
on the Next Page ⟶

Unit 3

HOMEWORK

Review for Organic Chemistry 3

Topical Tests	❏ Separations and Purifications Test 1
	❏ Biological Molecules Test 1
	❏ Organic Chemistry Discretes Test 1
	❏ Organic Chemistry Discretes Test 2
	❏ Organic Chemistry Strategic Supplemental (MM3229)
	❏ Amines Test 1
Section Tests	❏ Biological Sciences Test 3
	❏ Biological Sciences Test 4

Preview for Biology 3

Biology Review Notes	❏ *Chapters 8, 10, 11, 14 and 15
Foundation Review	❏ Unit 3 (Optional, MM3260A)
Online Workshops	❏ *The Lymphatic System and the Respiratory System
	❏ *Molecular Genetics

Unit 3

UNIT THREE

INTEGRATED PRACTICE

Biology 3

INTEGRATED PRACTICE: SYNTHESIS

- Homeostatis
- Endocrine System
- Molecular Genetics
- Evolution
- Mini MCAT

HOMEOSTASIS: MAINTENANCE OF A CONSTANT INTERNAL ENVIRONMENT

Osmoregulation — regulation of water

Kidneys

The kidneys regulate water and nutrient reabsorption from filtrate into blood.

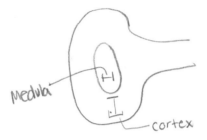

Medula
cortex

Aldosterone; ADH

Aldosterone and ADH act to maintain blood volume and determine urine concentration.

↳ more ions in, ↑blood volume, more water absorbed

ADH → anti-dieretic hormone (produced = hypothalumus)

Excretion

kidney → __bladder__ → _____ → __urine__

Angiotonsin I
↓ ACE
Agio II
↳ ↑aldosterone

Urine → urea, water, ions
↳ do not want bacteria + proteins

Nephron

The nephron is the functional unit of the kidney; each microscopic tubule is divided into five segments: Bowman's capsule, the proximal convoluted tubule, the loop of Henle, the distal convoluted tubule, and the collecting duct.

3 functions of the nephron: (1) Filtration; (2) Reabsorption; (3) Secretion

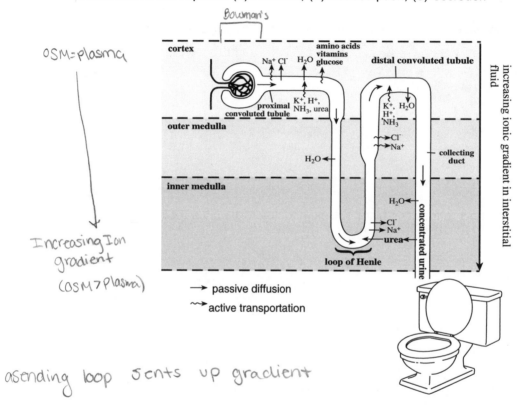

OSM = plasma

Increasing Ion gradient

(OSM > Plasma)

ascending loop Jents up gradient

Critical Thinking Exercise

If the fluid in the nephron is isotonic to the renal interstitium, then it has the same osmolarity at the proximal and distal convoluted tubules. What, then, is accomplished as the filtrate passes from the proximal convoluted tubule, through the loop of Henle, and through the distal convoluted tubule? *Concentrated w/ different contents (waste vs. Ions)*

Directed Practice

- *Topical Tests*: Digestive and Excretory Systems Test 1 (Passage I)
- *Biological Sciences Review Notes*: Biology Ch. 10

Critical Thinking Exercise

What do you think will happen in a patient that has damaged glomerular capillaries that become so permeable they allow plasma proteins to enter into the renal tubule ?

loose protein = loose water = adema

Diuretics, such as caffeine, cause a decrease in water reabsorption resulting in an increase in urine volume. Design an experiment to determine if caffeine blocks ADH receptors or prevents ADH release. Your experiment can only involve measurements of urine volume and administration of ADH and/or caffeine.

Thermoregulation

Metabolic rate

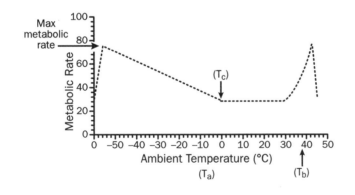

Vasoconstriction/vasodilation → vessels constricts (volume ↓)
→ vessels expands (volume ↑)

Sweating/shivering

Directed Practice

- *Topical Tests*: Endocrine System Test 1 (Passage II)
- *Biological Sciences Review Notes*: Biology Ch. 11

ENDOCRINE SYSTEM: CHEMICAL COMMUNICATION

Endocrine glands

Hypothalamus - produce : ADH + oxitocin (contraction during preg.)
- homeostasis (temp. , hunger)
— CGNH

Anterior pituitary - secretes hormones F   M

indirect (others)   FLAT   PEG   FSH - folical stim. vs. sperm production
                                       LH - ovulation & CL vs. testosterone
              ⤷tropic   direct   ACTH - adrenal cortex; glucolo aicoids
?rolactin-milk production   TSH - causes thyroid to pick up T₃ ↑ release T₄
Endorphins - pain (not feel)
GH - bone + muscle growth (too little = dwoarphism)

Pancreas
    ⤷ secretes insulin (cells take up glucose)

Thyroid
    ⤷ Thyroxine (T₄) , T₃ , calcetone (↓ calcium level)
        ⤷ alters metabolic rate

Parathyroids
    ⤷ PTH = ↑ Calcium

Adrenal glands
    ⤷ mineral quordoguids - change salt + water
    ⤷ regulate glucose
        ⤷ epenefrin - fright / flight

Testes → tetosterone (dureloment male pa

Ovaries - estergin (durelop reproductive

progesterin (maintains lining for infertalization

Glucose regulation

_____↑_____ [glucose] blood → ___↑___ [insulin] → glucose uptake by tissues → _____↓_____ [glucose] blood

_____↓_____ [glucose] blood → _____↑_____ [glucagon] → breakdown of glycogen → _____↑_____ [glucose] blood

diabetes 1 → insulin

diabetes 2 → not sensative

Menstrual cycle

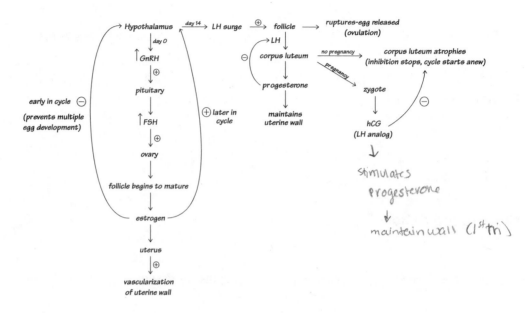

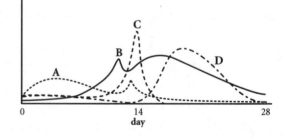

stimulates
progesterone
↓
maintain wall (1ˢᵗ tri)

Critical Thinking Exercise

1. Which of the following graphs represents the levels of luteinizing hormone during the menstrual cycle?

   A. A – FSH
   B. B – estrogen
   C. C
   D. D – progesterone

HCG doubles approximately every three days, and is the primary cause of "morning sickness." Why does "morning sickness" disappear at the end of the first trimester?

Directed Practice

- *Topical Tests*: Endocrine System Test 1 (Passage I), Reproductive System Test 1 (Passage II)
- *Biological Sciences Review Notes*: Biology Ch. 11

Mechanisms of hormone action

• directly through all to nucleus   *• protein*
                                       • use receptor

	Steroid	Peptide/Amino Acid
Precursor	Cholesteral	Amino Acids
Permeability	Yes	No
Transportation	specific carrier	albumin
Receptors	Intracellular	extracellular
Action	genes on/off	2nd messanger Turn proteins on/off
Onset	long	short
Duration	long	short
Examples	Testosteron Estrogen Aldosterone	Insulin

Critical Thinking Exercise

Individuals with the disease testicular feminization (XY genotype but female phenotype) secrete testosterone from their testes and adrenal cortices but lack functional testosterone receptors in target cells. As a result, during puberty, these individuals develop female secondary sex characteristics and have an elevated estrogen level. How is this possible?

GnRH , LH, + estrogen ↑

Directed Practice

- *Topical Tests*: Molecular Genetics Test 1 (Passage III)
- *Biological Sciences Review Notes*: Biology Ch. 11

Passage I (Questions 2–5)

Excessive accumulation of interstitial (extravascular) fluid in tissues is known as edema. Although edema can be caused by a wide variety of disorders, its character and location varies with the particular illness, which makes it a valuable diagnostic indicator. Abnormal capillary dynamics may result in edema via one of four general mechanisms, which are described below.

Mechanism I

The most frequent cause of edema is high capillary blood pressure, which results in excessive movement of fluid into tissue spaces. Continuous overexpansion of extracellular tissue space gradually compromises its elastic network and eventually forms large fluid reservoirs. Elevated capillary blood pressure can also cause fluid to leak into various natural body cavities, such as the peritoneal cavity.

Mechanism II

Another common cause of edema is a decrease in plasma protein concentration, especially that of albumin. Plasma proteins are produced by the liver and then released into the blood. A decrease in plasma protein concentration causes a decrease in plasma osmotic pressure, which leads to a loss of fluid retention in the capillaries.

Mechanism III

The most severe type of edema results from lymphatic obstruction, which can seriously impede the drainage of proteins from extracellular spaces. The two common causes of lymphatic obstruction are surgical removal of regional lymph nodes (which routinely accompanies excision of a malignant tumor) and infection of the lymph nodes with the larvae of certain tropical parasites (which produces inflammatory lesions and eventually results in permanent scarring).

Mechanism IV

Edema can also arise from abnormally high capillary porosity, which leads to leakage of proteins and excess fluid out of the capillary lumen. For instance, certain vasoactive substances, such as histamine, can make capillaries leaky by acting directly on specific endothelial receptors.

Scratch Paper

Unit 3

Scratch Paper

2. In addition to causing edema, which of the four mechanisms would most likely decrease the body's resistance to local infection?

   A. Mechanism I
   B. Mechanism II
   C. Mechanism III
   D. Mechanism IV

3. Based on information in the passage, which of the following conditions would NOT be expected to cause edema?

   A. Decreased fluid reabsorption by kidneys
   B. Decreased lymphatic fluid flow
   C. Increased protein excretion in urine
   D. Increased permeability of capillary endothelium

Scratch Paper

4. Based on the fact that Mechanism II and Mechanism IV both cause edema by way of decreased plasma protein concentration, it could be concluded that:

   A. capillaries are always fully permeable to albumin.
   B. interstitial fluid albumin concentration is normally greater than plasma albumin concentration.
   C. interstitial fluid albumin concentration is normally less than plasma albumin concentration.
   D. histamine decreases blood vessel permeability.

5. Cortisol, a steroid hormone, has been shown to enhance the activity of liver enzymes required for protein synthesis. Based on this information, would cortisol administration be an effective treatment for a patient suffering from edema?

   A. Yes, because cortisol would increase the concentration of plasma proteins and thus enhance fluid retention in the capillaries.
   B. Yes, because cortisol would decrease capillary blood pressure.
   C. No, because cortisol would decrease the concentration of plasma proteins by increasing metabolic rate.
   D. No, because cortisol would increase the risk of lymph node infection.

Unit 3

MOLECULAR GENETICS: DNA → RNA → PROTEIN

DNA

-O—P—O—5 O—N-base (with positions 1,2,3,4 labeled, H (OH = RNA))

5' 3' (helix drawing)

Watson-Crick model

DNA is a double-stranded alpha helix with a sugar-phosphate backbone surrounding nitrogenous bases.

Base-pairs Purines → A G

Pyrimidines → Cytosine
Thymate
Uracil (RNA = the T)

bonds
A = T
C ≡ G

DNA replication

5' to 3'

leading → helicase unwinds

Newly Synthesized DNA Strand

Okazaki Fragments

Direction of Replication Fork Movement

laging

Okazaki Fragments

Mutations — change in DNA

Critical Thinking Exercise

Which daughter strand is more likely to have a mutation?   — Lagging

Protein synthesis

Transcription → DNA to RNA

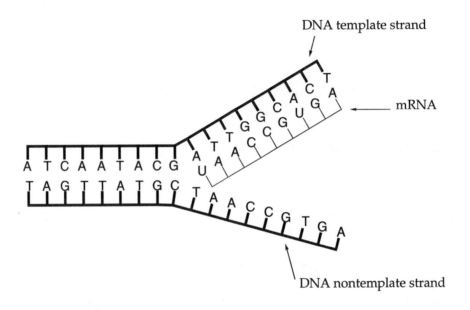

DNA template strand

mRNA

DNA nontemplate strand

Translation → RNA to Protein

Directed Practice

- *Topical Tests*: Molecular Biology Test 1, Molecular Genetics Test 1 (Passage II)
- *Biological Sciences Review Notes*: Biology Ch. 14

RNA

mRNA is messenger RNA. rRNA is ribosomal RNA. tRNA is transfer RNA; tRNA brings amino acids to the ribosomes.

Mutations

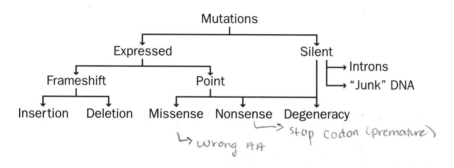

Missense → *wrong AA*

Nonsense → *stop codon (premature)*

Critical Thinking Exercise

→ GC

You have two fragments of DNA: Fragment A melts (comes apart) at 97°C and fragment B melts at 65°C. What can you conclude about the two fragments with respect to their nucleotide composition? *↓ more AT*

Scratch Paper

6. A segment of a DNA strand has the base sequence: 5'—GTTCATTG—3'. What would be the base sequence of the mRNA strand transcribed from this DNA?

   A. 5'—CAATGAAC—3'
   B. 5'—GTTCATTG—3'
   C. 5'—CAAUGAAC—3'
   D. 5'—CAAGUAAC—3'

Directed Practice

- *Biological Sciences Review Notes*: Biology Ch. 14

EVOLUTION

Natural selection

Charles Darwin proposed a mechanism for evolution called **natural selection.**

Hardy-Weinberg

If the following five conditions exist, gene frequencies in a population remain constant and the Hardy-Weinberg law can be applied to predict the frequency of alleles and phenotypes:

1. Random mating

2. No natural selection

3. No migration or emigration

4. Large population

5. No mutations

Equations

$(p + q)^n = 1$
$p + q = 1; p^2 + 2pq + q^2 = 1$

$p^2 = RR$
$2pq = Rr$
$q^2 = rr$

Critical Thinking Exercise

If 84% of the population has rh$^+$ blood, then what is the frequency of the recessive allele?

$100\% \text{ pop.} = q^2 + 84\%$

$q^2 = 16\% \Rightarrow q = 4$

Directed Practice

- *Biological Sciences Review Notes*: Biology Ch. 15

Kaplan's Pacing Strategy—Sciences

13 discrete questions in 13 minutes

7 Passages in 57 minutes

Minutes per **passage pair:** _____

Passage 1

Passage 2

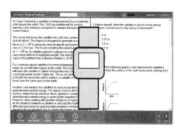

Passage 3

Passage 4

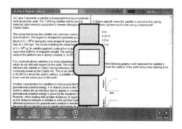

Passage 5

Passage 6

Passage 7

DO NOT TURN THIS PAGE UNTIL YOU ARE INSTRUCTED TO DO SO

Biology
Mini MCAT

Time: 19 minutes
Questions: 1–11

Passage I (Questions 1–4)

Proper functioning of the respiratory system relies on the integrity of mechanical and chemical mechanisms that allow for the efficient exchange of oxygen and carbon dioxide. The lungs themselves are individually enclosed in fluid filled sacs, which join the lungs to the chest wall. Upon inhalation, the lungs, composed of alveoli, fill with oxygen-rich air, allowing oxygen to diffuse from the alveoli into the blood. However, the alveoli are prone to collapse due to surface tension from the air-liquid interface. This collapse, due to the hydrophilic pull of surface-lining water molecules toward each other, is prevented by the body's use of a special detergent called a surfactant, composed of lipids and proteins. This surfactant, produced by type II alveolar cells, interrupts the attractive bonds between water, reducing hydrophilic interactions and lowering surface tension. The presence of surfactant also decreases pulmonary edema, or excess fluid in the lungs. Normally, when an alveolus shrinks due to surface tension, the volume of the interstitial space between the alveolus and capillary increases, leading to a decrease in pressure in the interstitial space, resulting fluid movement into the space and lung.

In respiratory distress syndrome of the newborn, premature babies are born without the ability to manufacture surfactant. These babies often exhibit collapsed alveoli. The collapse of alveoli results in an increase in the energy required to breathe and a decrease in the surface area through which gases can diffuse. Treatment of these babies often includes administering enough surfactant to prevent alveolar collapse. To determine how much supplemental surfactant these babies require, a scientist conducts an experiment to discover the dependence of alveolar surface area on surface tension within that alveolus. Three samples of lung tissue are placed into three separate dishes. In the first dish, pure water is injected into the lung tissue; the tissue is filled with oxygen gas, then deflated in order to calculate surface tension at different lung volumes. In the second dish, the exact same procedure is replicated, but Detergent A is added in addition to water. Finally, in the third dish, the same procedure is repeated, but surfactant, instead of Detergent A, is injected into the lung tissue in addition to the water. A force transducer is used to measure surface tension. The results are summarized in Figure 1.

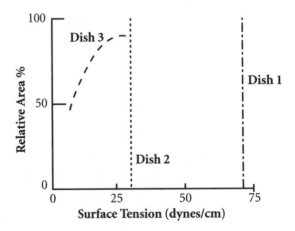

Figure 1

Unit 3

1. A premature baby is born without the ability to manufacture sufficient quantities of surfactant, which results in:

   A. increased pH in muscles of respiration.
   B. lactic acid buildup in muscles of respiration.
   C. increased pH in blood leaving the lungs.
   D. increased oxygen pressure in blood leaving the lungs.

2. Suppose a fourth dish of lung extract is prepared, but oxygen gas is not used to fill and expand the lung. If the scientist wishes to decrease the surface tension in the lung to a minimum value, oxygen should be replaced with:

   A. nitrogen gas.
   B. carbon dioxide gas.
   C. sodium chloride solution.
   D. water containing dissolved oxygen gas.

   b/c between air-gas
   (pick liquid)

3. Which of the following explains the biologist's findings regarding the dependence of surface tension on surface area in dishes 2 and 3?

   A. Upon deflation of the lung, the number of Detergent A molecules on the surface of alveolar cells increases.
   B. As the surface area of an alveolar cell decreases, surfactant moves from the surface of the cell to the center.
   C. Detergent A is hydrophobic and loses its ability to interrupt water's attractive forces as the surface area decreases in the alveolar cell.
   D. The ratio of water to surfactant molecules on the surface of an alveolar cell decreases as the surface area of the cell decreases.

4. Fluid buildup in the lungs may impede blood flow, resulting in an immediate increase in blood pressure in the:

   A. pulmonary veins.
   B. pulmonary arteries.
   C. aorta.
   D. right atrium.

Unit 3

Passage II (Questions 5–8)

Hemoglobin is the protein within erythrocytes that transports oxygen to body tissues. In adults, hemoglobin molecules are composed of two α chains and two β chains ($\alpha_2\beta_2$). Thalassemias are a class of inherited diseases caused by impaired synthesis of hemoglobin subunits. There are two types of thalassemia: thalassemia minor and thalassemia major. Thalassemia minor is found in heterozygotes, who are generally asymptomatic or have mild anemia, and also possess a resistance to malaria. Thalassemia major is found in homozygotes and causes serious symptoms.

α-Thalassemias are caused by deletions of one or more of the α-globin genes in an α-gene cluster. In the most severe form, where the patient is left without any α chains, fetal γ hemoglobin chains and adult β hemoglobin chains form homotetramers (γ_4 or β_4). These abnormal hemoglobin molecules cannot release oxygen under physiological conditions.

Heterozygotes with β-thalassemia are asymptomatic, while homozygotes have severe anemia. When levels of fetal hemoglobin drop, patients often require frequent blood transfusions. Anemia in these patients is due not only to the lack of β-chains, but also to the surplus of α-chains, which precipitate and damage erythrocyte membranes.

β-thalassemias are generally caused by a diverse set of point mutations that alter β-chain levels. For example, mutations in the β chain promoter region, nonsense mutations, frameshift mutations, mutations that alter sequences at the intron/exon boundary, and mutations that alter the AAUAAA cleavage signal at the mRNA 3' end all cause β-thalassemia.

1) B

2)

3) C

4) A

9)

106
14
√84

24   34
24   36
196   216
480   980
574   1196

5. A man with thalassemia major marries a woman with thalassemia minor. If they have three children, what is the probability that all three children will have thalassemia major?

   A. 12.5%
   B. 25%
   C. 50%
   D. 100%

6. A point mutation in the promoter region of β-genes promoter region would have what effect?

   A. Translational repression
   B. Transcriptional repression
   C. Neither type of repression would result
   D. Both types of repression would result

7. In a certain population, 16% of the individuals have thalassemia major. What percentage of this population is heterozygous for the thalassemia gene?

   A. 4%
   B. 24%
   C. 36%
   D. 48%

   $p^2 = 0.16$
   $p = 0.04$
   $p + q = 1 \rightarrow q = 0.6$
   $2pq = 2(0.4)(0.6)$

8. Transcriptional repression occurs in what region within the cell?

   A. Cytoplasm
   B. Ribosomes
   C. Rough endoplasmic reticulum
   D. Nucleus

Questions 9 through 11 are NOT based on a descriptive passage.

9. Wilson's disease is an autosomal recessive trait that results in cirrhosis of the liver and neurological problems. In the Phillips family, 4 out of 100 people have Wilson's disease. Using the Hardy-Weinberg equation, what percentage of this family would you expect to have the heterozygous genotype?

   A. 4%
   B. 32%
   C. 64%
   D. 96%

   $q^2 = 0.04 \rightarrow q = 0.20$
   $p = 0.8$
   $2(0.8)(0.2) = 32$

10. Which of the following is a characteristic of the hormone vasopressin?

    A. It increases water reabsorption in the kidneys.
    B. It increases sodium reabsorption in the kidneys.
    C. Its secretion is regulated by the hormone ACTH.
    D. Its secretion is regulated by the enzyme renin.

11. Retroviruses are a group of RNA viruses that:

    A. transcribe RNA from RNA.
    B. transcribe proteins from RNA.
    C. synthesize DNA from RNA.
    D. immediately lyse their host cells.

Unit 3

HOMEWORK

Review for Biology 3

Topical Tests

- ❑ Digestive and Excretory Systems Test 1
- ❑ Endocrine System Test 1
- ❑ Molecular Biology Test 1
- ❑ Molecular Genetics Test 1
- ❑ Respiratory and Skin Systems Test 1
- ❑ Biology Discretes Test 1
- ❑ Biology Discretes Test 2
- ❑ Biology Strategic Supplemental (MM3228)

Section Tests

- ❑ Biological Sciences Test 1
- ❑ Biological Sciences Test 2
- ❑ Biological Sciences Test 5

Preview for MSCT 3

- ❑ Bring to class your essays and scratch paper from Full-Length 2

Unit 3

MCAT Strategy & Critical Thinking 3

- Your Last Test
- Full-Length 2 Test Review
- A Plan for Test Day

YOUR LAST FULL-LENGTH

Finishing Sections

Triaging Passages

Passage Mapping

Question Strategy

Essay Strategy

Focusing Strategy

Unit 3

WRONG ANSWER PATHOLOGIES REVISITED (SCIENCES)

Type	Why It's Seductive
Faulty Use of Detail	
Opposite	
Distortion	
Miscalculation	
Out of Scope	

Full-Length 2 Biological Sciences Passage V (Questions 30–35)

Radioimmunoassay (RIA) is a technique used for measuring hormone concentrations in blood serum based on highly specific antigen-antibody interactions. To carry out an RIA for a particular human hormone, an antibody to that hormone is prepared by immunizing mice or rabbits with an extract from the human endocrine gland that produces the hormone. A measured quantity of this antibody is then mixed with a known concentration of isotopically-labeled hormone and the blood sample to be assayed, which contains an unknown concentration of unlabeled hormone. RIA is based on the principle that as long as there is too little antibody to bind both the labeled hormone and unlabeled hormone completely, then the unlabeled and the labeled hormone will compete for antibody-binding sites. Thus, as the concentration of unlabeled hormone in the sample increases, the percentage of antibody-bound radiolabeled hormone decreases.

Hormone concentrations can be calculated by comparing the radioactivity counts obtained from the original RIA to a standard curve, such as the one shown in Figure 1. To generate a standard curve for a particular hormone, RIAs are performed on a series of solutions containing different known concentrations of unlabeled hormone. After the radioactivity of each solution is measured, these concentrations are then plotted against the percentage of antibody-bound radiolabeled hormone.

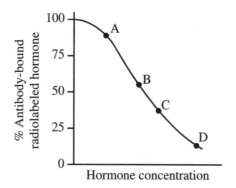

Figure 1

For most hormones, the form that circulates in the blood (the active form) is different from that extracted from the tissues and used to prepare the antibodies and standard curve used for RIAs (the precursor form), though typically, the two forms are very similar in structure and chemistry.

30. According to the passage, an antibody to a particular human hormone is prepared by immunizing laboratory animals with an extract of the human hormone. Which of the following best explains why this technique works?

    A. The lab animal's immune system recognizes the human hormone as "foreign," or antigenic, and produces antibodies in response to its presence.

    B. Human gland cells must first be injected into a host organism, such as a mouse or rabbit, before they can produce the antibodies.

    C. Human hormones will elicit antibody production in mice and rabbits, but not in other animals, such as rats and chimpanzees.

    D. Immunization with human hormone, prior to actual exposure to the hormone, protects the lab animal from infection upon second exposure to the hormone.

31. An RIA for antidiuretic hormone (ADH) performed on a healthy person yielded a concentration of 3 pg/mL. If an RIA were performed on a patient suffering from severe blood loss, which of the following ADH concentrations would the RIA most likely yield?

    A. 0.5 pg/mL
    B. 2 pg/mL
    C. 3 pg/mL
    D. 5 pg/mL

32. If Figure 1 were the standard curve for FSH, which point on the graph would most likely represent FSH concentration in a woman before pregnancy and in her 16th week of pregnancy, respectively?

    A. Point A and Point D
    B. Point B and Point D
    C. Point C and Point D
    D. Point B and Point A

Unit 3

33. RIA is based on the principle that radiolabeled and unlabeled hormone will compete for binding sites on the antibody. Which of the following conditions would NOT compromise the validity of an RIA?

    A. The antibody binds the radiolabeled hormone with a greater affinity than the unlabeled hormone.

    B. The antibody binds the radiolabeled hormone and the unlabeled hormone with equal affinity.

    C. There is enough antibody in the solution to completely bind with the radiolabeled and the unlabeled hormone.

    D. The radiolabeled hormone binds to a site on the antibody other than the antigen-binding site, inducing a conformational change that inhibits the binding of unlabeled hormone.

34. If Figure 1 were the standard curve for insulin, which points on the graph would most likely represent the serum insulin concentration calculated from the RIA performed before and 1 hour after glucose infusion, respectively?

    A. Point B and Point A
    B. Point B and Point D
    C. Point C and Point C
    D. Point C and Point A

35. Suppose that a researcher who wanted to measure the concentration of a particular *active* hormone unwittingly used its structurally similar *precursor* form to develop the antibodies and generate the standard curve used for the RIA. If the researcher then performed an RIA on a sample of unlabeled active hormone contaminated with unlabeled precursor hormone, how would this affect the RIA?

    A. The standard curve generated for the precursor form would be inaccurate and therefore could not be used to calculate unknown concentrations of that form.

    B. The percentage of antibody-bound radiolabeled hormone would be greater than normal, because there would be twice as much unlabeled hormone for the radiolabeled hormone to compete with.

    C. The calculated concentration of the active hormone would be greater than its actual concentration, because the antibody would bind to both the active hormone and its precursor form.

    D. The calculated concentration of the active hormone would be less than its actual concentration, because the antibody would bind to both the active hormone and its precursor form.

Full-Length 2 Biological Sciences Discretes (Questions 11, 14, 26–29, 48–50, 52)

11. Which of the following strands of DNA, when paired with its complementary strand, would have the lowest melting point?
    A. ACTACTA
    B. TCGATAG
    C. CATGTAG
    D. GACGACT

14. Myoglobin, which is an oxygen-carrying protein found in muscle tissue, consists of a single polypeptide chain with an attached heme group. In contrast, hemoglobin consists of four heme-carrying polypeptide subunits. Which of the following best accounts for the difference in shape between the hemoglobin and myoglobin oxygen-dissociation curves?

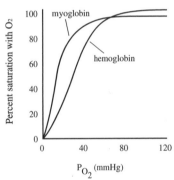

    A. Bohr effect
    B. Cooperative binding of oxygen to myoglobin
    C. Difference in P_{O_2} between blood and muscle
    D. Cooperative binding of oxygen to hemoglobin

Unit 3

26. The hormone calcitonin acts as a regulator of serum Ca^{2+} levels by promoting the incorporation of Ca^{2+} into bone. Which of the following hormones is antagonistic to calcitonin?

    A. Parathyroid hormone
    B. Prolactin
    C. ACTH
    D. Thyroxine

27. In a healthy individual, which of the following blood vessels has the highest partial pressure of carbon dioxide?

    A. Pulmonary arteries
    B. Pulmonary veins
    C. Aorta
    D. Coronary arteries

28. Which of the following structures is NOT derived from embryonic ectoderm?

    A. Eye lens
    B. Pituitary gland
    C. Digestive tract
    D. Adrenal medulla

29. The graph below plots the transmembrane diffusion rates for Compound A and Compound B as a function of their extracellular concentrations. Given that both compounds are approximately the same size, and there are no facilitated diffusion sites, it can most likely be inferred that:

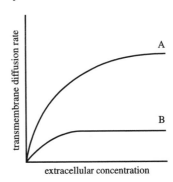

A. Compound A is polar and Compound B is nonpolar.
B. Compound A is nonpolar and Compound B is polar.
C. Compound A is polar and Compound B is polar.
D. Compound A is nonpolar and Compound B is nonpolar.

48. An amino acid is subjected to electrophoresis at pH 8.5 and is observed to migrate to the anode. The isoelectric point of this amino acid:

A. is less than 8.5. – ‾
B. is more than 8.5. ++
C. is equal to 8.5. – +
D. cannot be determined without more information.

When migrate = negatively charged

Unit 3

49. It is hypothesized that the binding of testosterone to corticosteroid receptors in the hypothalamus of a developing male fetus accounts for the sexual differentiation of the human brain. This binding causes the hypothalamus to switch from cyclic production of gonadotropin-releasing factors (which is characteristic of females) to acyclic production. This switch, therefore, is likely to affect the release patterns of:

    A. LH.
    B. FSH.
    C. both LH and FSH.
    D. neither LH nor FSH.

50. Which of the following would form the most stable carbocation?

    A. $(CH_3)_2CHBr$ dissolved in toluene
    B. $(CH_3CH_2)_3COH$ dissolved in acetone
    C. $(CH_3)_3COH$ dissolved in H_2SO_4
    D. CH_3CH_2I dissolved in diethyl ether

52. Mammalian fetal circulation is similar to amphibian adult circulation in that:

    A. gas exchange occurs only in the lungs.
    B. gas exchange occurs only in the placenta.
    C. the heart has only three chambers prior to birth.
    D. there is a mixing of oxygenated and deoxygenated blood within the heart.

Unit 3

**The Lesson Continues
on the Next Page**

Full-Length 2 Verbal Reasoning Passage II (Questions 8–12)

All combinations and associations, under whatever plausible character, with the real design to direct, control, counteract, or awe the regular deliberation and action of the established government, serve to organize faction, to give it an artificial and extraordinary force; to put, in the place of the delegated will of the nation, the will of a party. I have already intimated to you the danger of political parties, with particular reference to the founding of them on geographical discriminations. Let me now take a more comprehensive view, and warn you in the most solemn manner against the baneful effects of the spirit of party, generally. The spirit of party, unfortunately, is inseparable from our nature, having its root in the strongest passions of the human mind. It exists under different shapes in all governments, more or less stifled, controlled, or repressed; but, in those of the popular form, it is seen in its greatest rankness, and is truly their worst enemy.

The alternate domination of one party over another, sharpened by the spirit of revenge, natural to political dissension, which in different ages and countries has perpetrated the most horrid enormities, is itself a frightful despotism. But this leads at length to a more formal and permanent despotism. The disorders and miseries which result gradually incline the minds of men to seek security and repose in the absolute power of an individual; and sooner or later the chief of some prevailing party, more able or more fortunate than his competitors, turns this disposition to the purposes of his own elevation, on the ruins of Public Liberty.

Without looking forward to an extremity of this kind (which nevertheless ought not to be entirely out of sight), the common and continual mischiefs of the spirit of party are sufficient to make it the interest and duty of a wise people to discourage and restrain it. It serves always to distract the Public Councils, and enfeeble the Public Administration. It agitates the Community with ill-founded jealousies and false alarms, kindles the animosity of one part against another, and occasionally foments riot and insurrection. It opens the door to foreign influence and corruption, which find a facilitated access to the government itself through the channels of party passions. Thus the policy and the will of one country are subjected to the policy and will of another.

There is an opinion that parties are useful checks upon the administration of Government and serve to keep alive the spirit of Liberty. This within certain limits is probably true; and in Governments of a Monarchical cast, Patriotism may look with indulgence, if not with favor, upon the spirit of party. But in those of the popular character, in Governments purely elective, it is a spirit not to be encouraged. From their natural tendency, it is certain there will always be enough of that spirit for every salutary purpose. And, there being constant danger of excess, the effort ought to be, by force of public opinion, to mitigate and assuage it. A fire not to be quenched, this spirit demands a uniform vigilance to prevent its bursting into a flame, lest, instead of warming, it should consume.

8. As it is used in the passage as a whole, the phrase "spirit of party" refers to:

    A. the part of a human being associated with the mind, will, and feelings.

    B. a strong inclination to act to further the political goals of a particular organization.

    C. the tendency of conflicting views within a nation to result in concentration of individuals around two different positions.

    D. the animating force or principle of an organization.

9. The metaphor used in the last sentence of the passage reflects most directly the author's view of how the "spirit of party" must be managed in the case of:

    A. monarchies.

    B. patriotic movements.

    C. dictatorships.

    D. democracies.

10. As it is used in the last sentence of the first paragraph, the word "popular" most probably means a government that:

    A. is widely liked or appreciated by the people at large.

    B. encourages maximal participation of the people at large in its functions.

    C. reflects the basic preferences of the people at large.

    D. has been authorized by the people at large.

Unit 3

11. Assume that a group feels that an action being considered by a popular government is wrong. It can be inferred that the author would be LEAST likely to encourage the public to respond to this group by:

    A. supporting the legitimacy of the government's authority to take the action in question.

    B. rebutting in the public forum any statements made by the dissenters criticizing the government's actions.

    C. discouraging those who dissent from organizing around the issue.

    D. discouraging dissenters from making statements calculated to engage the strong feelings of those who share their views.

12. It can be inferred from the passage that all of the following are fundamental to the "spirit of party" EXCEPT:

    A. human nature.

    B. faction.

    C. organization.

    D. elective government.

Unit 3

The Lesson Continues
on the Next Page

MAKE A CALENDAR

Calendar Tips

- Build in your obligations

- Time for family/friends

- One day off a week

- Study time
  - How long?
  - How often?
  - Where?
  - When?
  - Breaks

WHAT TO DO...

... until a week before the Test

- Focus on weak areas.

- Read, Read, Read!

- Diagnose with your Kaplan Score Reports.

- Review your "Why I Missed It" sheets.

- Address any fatigue or focus issues.

- Practice at the computer.

- Create test-friendly habits.

Unit 3

WHAT TO DO...

... exactly one week before Test Day

- Get up at the same time you would on Test Day.

- Visit the test site.

- Start going to bed at an appropriate time.

... during the week of Test Day

- Focus on your strengths.

- Take mini-vacations.

- Eat good meals at regular times.

- Continue your sleep/wake-up schedule all week long.

- Practice in a test-like environment.

Unit 3

THE RULES FOR THE DAY BEFORE THE MCAT

Rule # 1

You do not talk about MCAT.

Rule # 2

You do not talk about MCAT!

Rule # 3

There are no exceptions to Rules 1 and 2.

Rule # 4

You must plan your day.

Rule # 5

Think about your post-MCAT activities.

Rule # 6

Do something you enjoy.

Rule # 7

Carbo-load.

Rule # 8

Gather your test materials.

Rule # 9

Lather, rinse, repeat.

Rule # 10

Unit 3

CHECKLIST FOR MCAT TEST DAY

- Printout of your confirmation email

- Personal Identification (2)

- Snacks / Sports drink

- Kaplan Flashcards / QuickSheets

- Extra jacket or sweatshirt

- Tissues

- Cough drops

- Analgesics

- Antacid

Unit 3

WHAT TO DO...

... on Test Day

- Wake up on time.

- Eat your normal breakfast.

- Warm up physically and mentally.

- Wear comfortable clothing and dress in layers.

- Bring high-energy foods for snacks.

- Arrive at the test site with time to spare.

- Bring all your testing materials.

WHAT TO DO...

... during the MCAT

- Do the tutorial.

- Get comfortable with the computer.

- Do the discrete questions first.

- Triage each section.

- Check your timing every two passages.

- Triage difficult questions for later.

- Answer every question.

- Reset your mind during breaks.

- Focus on what is in front of you.

- Don't discuss the test during breaks or after the exam.

IF I WANT TO VOID MY SCORE

Yes, if you...

- left a large number of questions blank.
- got physically ill during the test.
- had extreme test administration problems.
- shouldn't have been there in the first place.

No, if you...

- felt the test was hard.
- felt like you strategically guessed too many questions.
- didn't finish *every* passage.

WHAT TO DO NOW

- Fill in your calendar with study time and leisurely activities.

- Contact teachers if questions still remain.

- Focus on building stamina and endurance by completing Full-Length Exams and Section Tests.

- Focus on success!

The Lesson Continues
on the Next Page

HOMEWORK

Review for MSCT 3

Section Tests

- ❏ Biological Sciences Test 6
- ❏ Biological Sciences Test 7

Unit 3

Appendix

STUDY CENTER MENU

ONLINE SUBJECT TESTS

These Kaplan tests contain non-MCAT style multiple-choice questions that test your basic science knowledge. They are helpful in reinforcing your science foundation before you integrate it with the crtitical thinking skills necessary for success on MCAT-style passages. If you are weak in a particular field (Physics, Organic Chemistry, etc.), consider taking these tests before attempting the Topical Tests.

You can get your score report through your online syllabus (kaptest.com).

ONLINE SUBJECT TESTS

Biology
❑   SUBJECT TEST 1
❑   SUBJECT TEST 2
❑   SUBJECT TEST 3
❑   SUBJECT TEST 4
❑   SUBJECT TEST 5

Physics
❑   SUBJECT TEST 1
❑   SUBJECT TEST 2
❑   SUBJECT TEST 3
❑   SUBJECT TEST 4
❑   SUBJECT TEST 5

General Chemistry
❑   SUBJECT TEST 1
❑   SUBJECT TEST 2
❑   SUBJECT TEST 3
❑   SUBJECT TEST 4
❑   SUBJECT TEST 5

Organic Chemistry
❑   SUBJECT TEST 1
❑   SUBJECT TEST 2
❑   SUBJECT TEST 3
❑   SUBJECT TEST 4
❑   SUBJECT TEST 5

ONLINE TOPICAL TESTS

These Kaplan tests, available from your online syllabus at kaptest.com, feature passages and questions in MCAT format. The **Topical Tests** are short, focused tests covering those science topics outlined in the *AAMC MCAT Interpretive Manual.* All of these tests train you in test-taking strategies and working under timed conditions. When you take these tests, don't forget to review the explanations!

You can get your score report through your online syllabus (kaptest.com).

ONLINE TOPICAL SCIENCE TESTS

Biology
❑   GENERAL EUKARYOTIC CELL TEST 1
❑   MOLECULAR BIOLOGY TEST 1
❑   MOLECULAR GENETICS TEST 1
❑   ENDOCRINE SYSTEM TEST 1
❑   MICROBIOLOGY TEST 1
❑   RESPIRATORY AND SKIN SYSTEMS TEST 1
❑   DIGESTIVE AND EXCRETORY SYSTEMS TEST 1
❑   REPRODUCTIVE SYSTEM AND DEVELOPMENT TEST 1
❑   CIRCULATORY AND LYMPHATIC SYSTEMS TEST 1
❑   BIOLOGY DISCRETES TEST 1
❑   BIOLOGY DISCRETES TEST 2
❑   BIOLOGY STRATEGIC SUPPLEMENTAL

ONLINE TOPICAL TESTS
(cont.)

Physics
- ❑ TRANSLATIONAL MOTION TEST 1
- ❑ WAVE CHARACTERISTICS AND PERIODIC MOTION TEST 1
- ❑ ELECTROSTATICS AND ELECTROMAGNETISM TEST 1
- ❑ FORCE, MOTION, GRAVITATION AND EQUILIBRIUM TEST 1
- ❑ FLUIDS AND SOLIDS TEST 1
- ❑ SOUND TEST 1
- ❑ WORK, ENERGY AND MOMENTUM TEST 1
- ❑ LIGHT AND GEOMETRICAL OPTICS TEST 1
- ❑ ELECTRIC CIRCUITS TEST 1
- ❑ ATOMIC AND NUCLEAR STRUCTURE TEST 1
- ❑ PHYSICS DISCRETES TEST 1
- ❑ PHYSICS DISCRETES TEST 2
- ❑ PHYSICS STRATEGIC SUPPLEMENTAL

General Chemistry
- ❑ BONDING TEST 1
- ❑ STOICHIOMETRY TEST 1
- ❑ ELECTRONIC STRUCTURE AND THE PERIODIC TABLE TEST 1
- ❑ ACIDS AND BASES TEST 1
- ❑ KINETICS AND EQUILIBRIUM TEST 1
- ❑ ELECTROCHEMISTRY TEST 1
- ❑ THERMODYNAMICS AND THERMOCHEMISTRY TEST 1
- ❑ GENERAL CHEMISTRY DISCRETES TEST 1
- ❑ GENERAL CHEMISTRY DISCRETES TEST 2
- ❑ GENERAL CHEMISTRY STRATEGIC SUPPLEMENTAL

Organic Chemistry
- ❑ SEPARATIONS AND PURIFICATIONS TEST 1
- ❑ OXYGEN-CONTAINING COMPOUNDS TEST 1
- ❑ MOLECULAR SPECTROSCOPY TEST 1
- ❑ HYDROCARBONS TEST 1
- ❑ BIOLOGICAL MOLECULES TEST 1
- ❑ MOLECULAR STRUCTURE OF ORGANIC COMPOUND TEST 1
- ❑ ORGANIC CHEMISTRY DISCRETES TEST 1
- ❑ ORGANIC CHEMISTRY DISCRETES TEST 2
- ❑ AMINES TEST 1
- ❑ ORGANIC CHEMISTRY STRATEGIC SUPPLEMENTAL

ONLINE SECTION TESTS
These Kaplan tests are designed to challenge your MCAT knowledge while building your test-taking endurance.

BIOLOGICAL SCIENCES
- ❑ BIOSCI TEST 1
- ❑ BIOSCI TEST 2
- ❑ BIOSCI TEST 3
- ❑ BIOSCI TEST 4
- ❑ BIOSCI TEST 5
- ❑ BIOSCI TEST 6
- ❑ BIOSCI TEST 7

ONLINE SECTION TESTS
(cont.)

PHYSICAL SCIENCES
- ❏ PHYSCI TEST 1
- ❏ PHYSCI TEST 2
- ❏ PHYSCI TEST 3
- ❏ PHYSCI TEST 4
- ❏ PHYSCI TEST 5
- ❏ PHYSCI TEST 6
- ❏ PHYSCI TEST 7

VERBAL REASONING
- ❏ VR TEST 1
- ❏ VR TEST 2
- ❏ VR TEST 3
- ❏ VR TEST 4
- ❏ VR TEST 5
- ❏ VR TEST 6*
- ❏ VR TEST 7*
- ❏ VR TEST 8*
- ❏ VR TEST 9*
- ❏ VR TEST 10*
- ❏ VR TEST 11*
- ❏ VR TEST 12*
- ❏ VR TEST 13*

* Available both online and in Verbal Reasoning Strategy and Practice Book

WRITING SAMPLE
- ❏ WS TEST 1
- ❏ WS Explanation Booklet
- ❏ Writing Sample Examples Booklet MM3233

ONLINE FULL-LENGTH EXAMS

Kaplan offers you an unparalleled arsenal of full-length practice tests, which are listed to the right. Check with your Center regarding administration of simulated exams.

Kaplan Full-Length Tests
- ❏ Full-Length MCAT #1
- ❏ Full-Length MCAT #2
- ❏ Full-Length MCAT #3
- ❏ Full-Length MCAT #4
- ❏ Full-Length MCAT #5
- ❏ Full-Length MCAT #6
- ❏ Full-Length MCAT #7
- ❏ Full-Length MCAT #8
- ❏ Full-Length MCAT #9
- ❏ Full-Length MCAT #10
- ❏ Full-Length MCAT #11

AAMC Practice Tests
- ❏ Practice Test 3
- ❏ Practice Test 4
- ❏ Practice Test 5
- ❏ Practice Test 6
- ❏ Practice Test 7
- ❏ Practice Test 8
- ❏ Practice Test 9
- ❏ Practice Test 10

FOUNDATION REVIEW COMPANION BOOKLETS
Explanations to Foundation Review Units assigned as Homework.

- ❑ ORGANIC CHEMISTRY FOUNDATION REVIEW MM3257A
- ❑ GENERAL CHEMISTRY FOUNDATION REVIEW...................................MM3258A
- ❑ PHYSICS FOUNDATION REVIEW..MM3259A
- ❑ BIOLOGY FOUNDATION REVIEW MM3260A
- ❑ VERBAL REASONING FOUNDATION REVIEW MM3261A

ONLINE WORKSHOPS
The Online Workshops, available through your online syllabus at kaptest.com, help you prepare for the MCAT at your leisure.

- ❑ MCAT Orientation
- ❑ VERBAL REASONING: Critical Reading Skills
- ❑ VERBAL REASONING: Critical Reading Basics
- ❑ VERBAL REASONING: Critical Reading Challenge
- ❑ VERBAL REASONING: Diagnosing Questions
- ❑ VERBAL REASONING: Argument Dissection Basics
- ❑ VERBAL REASONING: Argument Dissection Challenge
- ❑ WRITING SAMPLE Skills: Writing
- ❑ WRITING SAMPLE Skills: Grammar and Usage
- ❑ WRITING SAMPLE: Advanced
- ❑ MCAT Stress Management
- ❑ PHYSICS: Units and Kinematics
- ❑ PHYSICS: Thermodynamics
- ❑ PHYSICS: DC and AC Circuits
- ❑ PHYSICS: Magnetism
- ❑ PHYSICS: Atomic and Nuclear Phenomena
- ❑ GENERAL CHEMISTRY: Quantum Numbers and Electron Configuration
- ❑ GENERAL CHEMISTRY: Reaction Types
- ❑ GENERAL CHEMISTRY: Chemical Kinetics
- ❑ GENERAL CHEMISTRY: Properties of Solutions
- ❑ ORGANIC CHEMISTRY: Nomenclature and Functional Groups
- ❑ ORGANIC CHEMISTRY: Addition and Elimination Reactions
- ❑ ORGANIC CHEMISTRY: Spectroscopy
- ❑ BIOLOGY: Generalized Eukaryotic Cell
- ❑ BIOLOGY: Microbiology
- ❑ BIOLOGY: Molecular Genetics
- ❑ BIOLOGY: The Skeletal System and the Immune System
- ❑ BIOLOGY: The Lymphatic System and the Respiratory System

BUILDING DATABASES

Choose a topic.	
Why did it happen?	
Exactly what happened?	
Who was involved?	
What were the results?	
Why was it important?	

BUILDING DATABASES

Choose a topic.	
Why did it happen?	
Exactly what happened?	
Who was involved?	
What were the results?	
Why was it important?	

BUILDING DATABASES

Choose a topic.	
Why did it happen?	
Exactly what happened?	
Who was involved?	
What were the results?	
Why was it important?	

BUILDING DATABASES

Choose a topic.	
Why did it happen?	
Exactly what happened?	
Who was involved?	
What were the results?	
Why was it important?	

BUILDING DATABASES

Choose a topic.	
Why did it happen?	
Exactly what happened?	
Who was involved?	
What were the results?	
Why was it important?	

BUILDING DATABASES

Choose a topic.	
Why did it happen?	
Exactly what happened?	
Who was involved?	
What were the results?	
Why was it important?	

Submit your medical school applications with confidence.

After serving in the admissions offices of many top schools, including Harvard, UCLA, and UNC-Chapel Hill, our Medical School Admissions Consultants know what the admissions committees look for in an applicant—and how to communicate it in your application. Whether developing your **personal statement**, completing your **AMCAS**, or preparing you for the **interview** process, our consulting team can advise you every step of the way.

MARC, KAPLAN PRE-HEALTH CONSULTANT
UCLA Admissions experience

"With so many well-qualified students applying to medical schools, a well-constructed personal statement is essential. Medical school admissions committee members are looking for those few candidates whom they could trust with their own health. GPA and MCAT* scores, while very important, do not reflect this personal quality."

"Yama was wonderful. I would be completely lost without his assistance. He helped me select schools, proofread essays, and prepared me for an interview. I think his honesty helped transform me into a better prepared applicant."

—**KAPLAN CLIENT, FALL 2005**

Call at 1-800-KAP-TEST today!

*MCAT is a registered trademark of the Association of American Medical Colleges.